FIRE

IN THE FIREPLACE

Charismatic
Renewal
in the
Nineties

CHARLES E. HUMMEL

INTERVARSITY PRESS
DOWNERS GROVE, ILLINOIS 60515

Second edition © 1993 by Charles E. Hummel
First edition © 1978 by Inter-Varsity Christian Fellowship of the U.S.A.

InterVarsity Press® is the book-publishing division of InterVarsity Christian Fellowship®, a student movement active on campus at hundreds of universities, colleges and schools of nursing in the United States of America, and a member movement of the International Fellowship of Evangelical Students. For information about local and regional activities, write Public Relations Dept., InterVarsity Christian Fellowship, 6400 Schroeder Rd., P.O. Box 7895, Madison, WI 53707-7895.

All Scripture quotations, unless otherwise indicated, are taken from the HOLY BIBLE, NEW INTERNATIONAL VERSION®. NIV®. Copyright © 1973, 1978, 1984 by the International Bible Society. Used by permission of Zondervan Publishing House. All rights reserved.

Cover photograph: Michael Goss

ISBN 0-8308-1663-1

Printed in the United States of America ∞

Library of Congress Cataloging-in-Publication Data

Hummel, Charles E.
    Fire in the fireplace: Charismatic renewal in the 90's / Charles
E. Hummel.
        p.   cm.
    Includes bibliographical references and index.
    ISBN 0-8308-1663-1
    1. Pentecostalism.   2. Pentecostalism—United States.
3. Pentecostal churches—United States.   4. United States—Church
history—20th century.   I. Title.
BR1644.H85   1993
270.8'2—dc20   93-38974
                                                  CIP

| 17 | 16 | 15 | 14 | 13 | 12 | 11 | 10 | 9 | 8 | 7 | 6 | 5 | 4 | 3 | 2 | 1 |
| 07 | 06 | 05 | 04 | 03 | 02 | 01 | 00 | 99 | 98 | 97 | 96 | 95 | 94 | 93 |

2936/224

To Anne
and our children
Lisa, Chuck, Dick and Betsy,
Jim and Wendy

Preface

The charismatic renewal within mainline denominations is now well into its fourth decade. Since it hit the headlines in 1960, this movement has permeated major Protestant denominations, prompted the development of many independent fellowships and influenced the Roman Catholic Church.

Early in the renewal I encountered several vital charismatic fellowships that challenged my traditional evangelical view of spiritual gifts. I witnessed healing, prophecy and speaking in tongues—gifts that I had believed were intended only for the early church. This experience started a spiritual pilgrimage that continued with a fresh study of New Testament teaching and practice. Before I could participate in the charismatic renewal, I needed to work out a biblical theology of spiritual gifts.

The results of that pilgrimage led to the publication in 1978 of *Fire in the Fireplace: Contemporary Charismatic Renewal*. In that book I set forth a biblical basis for expecting the full range of spiritual gifts in every generation. This "third dimension" of the Holy Spirit's activity graciously empowers the church for its worship, witness and service.

Since that time, ministries of inner healing and spiritual warfare have become prominent. John Wimber's Vineyard Fellowship and Kenneth Hagin's prosperity gospel have attracted many followers. Scholarly reflection on baptism in the Spirit has produced a variety of theological insights. These developments have called for a revised and updated version of *Fire in the Fireplace*.

To make way for an assessment of the current scene, this new book has condensed the original exposition of the Holy Spirit's activity in Luke/Acts and 1 Corinthians. But it reaffirms a central conclusion: spiritual gifts are intended primarily for strengthening the body of Christ. *More important than its recovery of certain long-neglected gifts, the charismatic renewal has refocused our understanding of all charisms within the context of ecclesiology—the doctrine of the church.*

I am grateful to many friends who took time to critique chapters in the areas of their professional competence, minimizing errors and suggesting improvements.

Again, I have written for two main groups. First, for those who are attracted to the charismatic renewal but whose doubts about its biblical basis put roadblocks across their path to participation. And second, for those already involved who need biblical guidelines for the proper use of spiritual gifts to build up the body of Christ.

Today many Christians are preoccupied with the question "What is *my* gift and how can *I* use it?" But a different question is more crucial: How can these gifts empower the church to demonstrate and proclaim the love of our Lord Jesus Christ to a needy world? I hope to provide an answer in this revised edition of *Fire in the Fireplace*.

I
The Spreading Flame

1 *The Fireplace & the Fire*

*N*ear the center of Providence, perched on its own promontory, the Rhode
Island statehouse enjoys a commanding view of the city. A short distance to
the west stands the Church of the Holy Ghost. In 1969 it became host to a
unique venture, the newly formed Word of God charismatic community,
which soon began to surprise the entire state.

Several years earlier my family had moved to Rhode Island so that I could
assume the presidency of Barrington, a small Christian liberal arts college. We
were aware that renewal had begun in the Catholic Church; now there were
reports of its presence a few miles away from our home.

One Thursday evening my wife, Anne, and I drove to the church. Though
we arrived early, we had difficulty finding a place to park. We made our way
to the large basement, where about four hundred chairs were arranged in
concentric circles. Although it was not yet eight o'clock, most of the seats were
already filled. We managed to secure chairs in the outside circle near the door
(I thought it was a good idea to sit in the back anyway, just in case we wanted
to make a speedy exit).

Looking around at the crowd, we were struck by its remarkable diversity: old women with shawls and young men in leather jackets; priests and nuns; professional people in dark suits alongside tradesmen in coveralls; blacks and whites and Hispanics; faculty men wearing sport jackets, students in jeans, countercultural young people in garb defying description. What a cross section of society! Never before had we seen such a variety of people together in one room for a religious service.

Yet *shouldn't* such diversity be seen in a Christian congregation? Our Lord moved decisively across the social, economic, racial and religious barriers of his time. The apostle Paul declared: "There is neither Jew nor Greek, slave nor free, male nor female, for you are all one in Christ Jesus" (Gal 3:28). But I had always assumed that he meant the universal church, since such diversity was so rare in a local congregation.

My reflection was interrupted by the voice of a young priest sitting near the center of the circle. Father John Randall welcomed all present, especially first-time visitors. "Some of you may not understand what is going on, but please hold your questions until later. This is not a time for discussion. For the next two hours we will worship and witness as the risen Lord directs the meeting through the Holy Spirit, who will freely manifest spiritual gifts according to his sovereign will. Afterwards there will be several optional groups, one of which will explain to newcomers the nature of this fellowship." He then sat down.

After a few minutes of silence, two guitarists began a hymn new to our ears: "We see the Lord. He is high and lifted up, and his train fills the temple. The angels cry 'Holy.' The angels cry 'Holy is the Lord.' " Most of the people seemed to know this chorus, and they sang with joy and enthusiasm. Several other songs followed—mostly words of Scripture set to music.

One by one, individuals read from the Bible, suggested a song or prayed. Others witnessed to conversion, victory over sin, special healing, wisdom in a difficult situation, new love for neighbors or increased joy in the Lord. Occasionally the guitarists picked up a theme and led in the singing of an appropriate chorus.

Once during the meeting there was a message in tongues that seemed quite in order. Soon afterward, someone gave an interpretation that sounded like a message from the Old Testament—a reassuring word of God's love and his promise to guide our service for him. The message was in keeping with the overall theme of the meeting and was an encouragement to me personally.

The meeting proceeded at a steady, unhurried pace, unplanned in advance and evidently led by the Holy Spirit. There was a dynamic sense of movement. I had come into the Word of God community that night with curiosity about its activity and concern over my own problems. Both gave way to worship and praise as I was lifted out of my self-absorption to rejoice in God my Savior. The time passed so quickly that I was surprised when a glance at my watch showed ten o'clock.

Father Randall concluded with a few announcements. Visitors who wanted to learn more about the Word of God community were invited to meet in a side room. Participants in a six-week "Life in the Spirit" study would assemble in the kitchen. Those desiring special prayer for healing could go upstairs to the sanctuary. A book table was available in the foyer.

As people moved in several directions according to their interest, we headed for our car with gratitude and amazement.

During the autumn we returned several times for fellowship and a better understanding of the Word of God community. Father Randall described how his own life and work as a seminary chaplain had been transformed through the charismatic renewal that had recently begun in the Roman Catholic Church. Two years after the launching of that renewal, about fifteen people who had been meeting weekly for prayer felt a strong desire to form a Christian community. They were invited to serve in, of all places, the Holy Ghost parish, where they soon started the Thursday-evening prayer and praise service.[1]

By 1971 five hundred people were attending the meetings. The leaders became convinced that the ultimate test of charismatic renewal would be its ability to empower an ordinary city parish to meet a variety of human needs. The Word of God community moved across town to St. Patrick's to work in the decaying inner-city Smith Hill area. The community's first goal was to become an integral part of the existing parish.

Soon they renovated and reopened a school which had been closed for two years. Here children could be introduced to Jesus as Lord from their earliest years. Several families sold their suburban homes to buy "three-deckers" (apartment buildings) and form households to welcome individuals coming off drugs and alcohol. Nearby Chalkstone Presbyterian Church cooperated to meet a variety of human needs. The Shepherd's Staff supported two full-time social workers, assisted by volunteers. A cooperative store, Our Daily Bread, sold food at low prices. Eventually there were twenty ministries, from prayer, teaching and hospitality to child care and social action. A renewed parish was having a remarkable impact on an entire city.

Encounters with Renewal

My first experience with charismatic renewal had occurred a few years earlier, on a visit to Yale. As field director of InterVarsity Christian Fellowship, I was asked to confirm reports of charismatic renewal on that campus. I arrived in New Haven with a mixture of anticipation and old memories. During my undergraduate years I had helped start the Yale Christian Fellowship with meetings for Bible study and prayer. But as later student generations came and went, the YCF had fallen upon lean times.

Now, apparently, there was a renewal that featured healing, prophecy and speaking in tongues—spiritual gifts that I had been taught were given only in the first century to establish the early church. My theological belief was now challenged by unexpected events, and the result in me was tension: I wanted to be open to perceive a new work of God, yet I was determined to guard against unfounded enthusiasm.

As I conversed with the Yale students, it became clear that their discovery and practice of Paul's teaching in 1 Corinthians 12 was creating a greater sense of unity, more effective prayer and bolder evangelism among their classmates. Both their use of spiritual gifts and the results appeared thoroughly biblical, although contrary to my own theological tradition.

I discovered that the renewal had come as a complete surprise, unplanned by the student leaders. During the preceding summer three of them had unexpectedly encountered charismatic fellowships in distant parts of the country in the context of Episcopal and Lutheran congregations. Upon their return to campus, they met a newly arrived graduate student who had been active in a charismatic fellowship at Princeton Seminary. From the start, their gatherings on campus were not an official part of the YCF program; rather, they constituted an informal fellowship that was attended by several YCF leaders and members as well as other students, including two Roman Catholics.

The university chaplain spoke appreciatively of the charismatic fellowship, whose around-the-clock prayer vigil, he believed, had been instrumental in his own sudden healing and release from the hospital. These students were active in their own denominational groups and campus organizations. Three had been elected to Phi Beta Kappa. For me it was encouraging to see that charismatic renewal at Yale had been neither divisive nor spiritually exclusive.

The Spirit of God moved in similar fashion in other InterVarsity chapters across the country. But on some campuses the movement was followed by division between ardent advocates and vigorous opponents as enthusiasm for "extraordinary" gifts at times went to an extreme. InterVarsity staff opinion was divided on how to handle the problem.

IVCF general director Charles Troutman wisely followed the advice of the distinguished rabbi Gamaliel to fellow Pharisees who wanted to stamp out the new Christian church: "Leave these men alone! Let them go! For if their purpose or activity is of human origin, it will fail. But if it is from God, you will not be able to stop these men; you will only find yourselves fighting against God" (Acts 5:38-39). Troutman issued a memorandum spelling out this principle for InterVarsity chapters and giving practical suggestions for the field staff.[2]

My early encounters with the Yale renewal eventually led to a profound change in my understanding of the Spirit's activity in the life of the church today. Events I never expected to witness opened new windows into Scripture. Study of crucial New Testament passages gave me a new understanding of the nature and purpose of spiritual gifts in the body of Christ. It was disconcerting to discover that over the years I had not studied the Bible as objectively as

I had thought. Like others, I had viewed its teaching through a lens colored by an inherited theological system, mid-twentieth-century American culture and my limited personal experience.

I came to appreciate the significance of our Lord's criticism of the Sadducees: "You are in error because you do not know the Scriptures or the power of God" (Mt 22:29). The Bible's teaching directs our actions and helps us interpret our experiences. In the process, God's power in our lives opens new windows of understanding his Word. This dynamic interaction deepens our relationship with God, who teaches us through the Scriptures we read *and* the power we experience.

For example, the book of Job gives clues to the meaning of suffering. But we do not really understand this message—in fact, we hardly take it seriously—until we suffer. This principle shaped my understanding of the charismatic renewal through a pilgrimage of many years.

Recognizing that no one is completely neutral, I have tried to be objective in the sense of openness to the subject, willingness to accept new evidence even when it challenged long-cherished beliefs. I have wanted to emulate the Bereans' response to the startling message brought by the apostle Paul on his first missionary journey. Luke reports, "Now the Bereans were of more noble character than the Thessalonians, for they received the message with great eagerness and examined the Scriptures every day to see if what Paul said was true" (Acts 17:11). They did not say, in effect, "Don't confuse us with the facts, our minds are already made up." Nor did they uncritically accept the apostle's teaching. Rather, they gave him a fair hearing, then checked for themselves to see if his message was in harmony with Old Testament writings.

My main concern was for evangelicals like myself who thought that the charismatic renewal emphasized "experience" at the expense of "doctrine." Not that evangelicals have a record of aversion to spiritual experience. For example, we firmly believe that it is not enough to know *about* God; we need to know him personally—like Brother Lawrence, "practicing the presence of God" in daily activities. It is not enough to master principles of prayer; we must learn to pray and experience the difference made by the power of God in our lives. It is not enough to serve our Lord in what seems to be a suitable career; we should receive the Holy Spirit's guidance in vocational choices. Genuine Christian experience is not only based on biblical doctrines; it fulfills the purpose for which they have been given. So it was essential for me to work out a thoroughly biblical theology of spiritual gifts—the enabling power of the Holy Spirit for the life and ministry of the church.

Like many other renewals in the church's history, the charismatic renewal has been as controversial as it is powerful. Since its beginning in the early 1960s it has brought bane as well as blessing. Reports of division and separatism accompany accounts of church growth and effective evangelism. No wonder that some interested observers are repelled while others are attracted.

Organization and Life

The dynamics of church renewal are illustrated in comments by the Reverend Samuel Shoemaker when he was rector of Calvary Episcopal Church in Pittsburgh. Following World War II, he had a remarkable ministry among college students. Many whom I met as I traveled for InterVarsity Christian Fellowship in the Northeast had been changed by God through his influence.

In 1952 Shoemaker was the main speaker for Religion-in-Life Week at the University of Pittsburgh. Representatives from a wide variety of denominations—from Baptist and Episcopal to Roman Catholic and Greek Orthodox—and parachurch organizations were invited to share their faith. Serving as an InterVarsity representative, I had excellent opportunities to present the claims of Jesus Christ in classes, lounges and personal conversations. Student response was surprisingly good for what had cynically become known as "Nod-to-God Week."

During his address at the closing dinner for speakers and student leaders, Shoemaker surprised us by remarking, "Some have likened the Episcopal Church to the fireplace and the Methodist Church to the fire." After pausing for laughter at his denomination's expense, he continued, "But you'll have to admit that the best place for a fire is in the fireplace, not out in the middle of the floor!" He didn't talk then about denominational differences, but dealt with a problem that has plagued all churches: the relationship between organization and the life it is supposed to nurture.

Every organism requires some degree of organization to channel its energy and fulfill its mission. So it is natural for the church to develop confessions of faith, services of worship and programs of activity. Imperceptibly, however, the inner life tends to wane even though the outward form persists. Throughout church history the flame in many organizational fireplaces has flickered and died. Though the fireplace was designed initially to foster a blaze, accumulations of soot eventually clogged the flue and smothered the fire.

The history of human organizations—social, economic and political as well as religious—reveals this sequence: *movement, method, monument.* A dynamic leader rises to meet the needs of the hour. Committed disciples develop a movement with distinctive programs. A second generation of leadership emerges to perpetuate its methods. Eventually these methods are set in concrete, as the movement begins to become a monument. The fireplace may be magnificent, but of the original flames only smoldering embers remain.

Eventually, another generation, feeling the cold, tries to rekindle the fire. Unfortunately, they discover that it does not burn well; the flue is clogged with tradition so that the hearth no longer fosters the expected blaze. Yet the custodians of the fireplace often resist the cleaning and remodeling that are needed. They have grown comfortable in customs and secure in traditions that have gradually assumed divine authority. Change, with its discomfort and risk, is resisted.

So the rekindlers of the flame are tempted—or sometimes forced—to move their fire out into the middle of the floor. At that point one of two things is likely to happen to it: either the fire rages out of control or its isolated coals die down for lack of a proper hearth. Samuel Shoemaker was right: the best place for a fire is in the fireplace, even when it calls for cleaning and remodeling.

Nevertheless, there is another side of the coin. The custodians of the fireplace have a responsibility to preserve lessons of the past—traditions of biblical principles and practice that have stood the test of time. The late professor

George Santayana of Harvard observed that those who do not learn from the past are doomed to repeat its errors. In Old Testament times Aaron's sons were punished for offering "unauthorized fire before the LORD, contrary to his command" (Lev 10:1). The early church was commanded to test the messages of teachers and prophets in the light of Scripture to determine if they were valid.

In recent decades the Lord of the church has fanned smoldering embers and lighted new fires in many fireplaces. Spiritual renewal has appeared in a variety of forms. The most significant movement for its size, its crossing of denominational boundaries and its continuing growth is the Pentecostal/charismatic renewal. David Barrett reports that in 1992 there were 207 million professing charismatic Christians and 204 million denominational Pentecostals; together they make up 24 percent of Christians worldwide[3] (see appendix H).

Like earlier movements, charismatic renewal has produced its share of erroneous teachings and practices that have aroused opposition. A book by evangelical pastor John F. MacArthur Jr. expresses alarm over what he considers heretical elements in this renewal. *Charismatic Chaos* deals with a variety of controversial questions: What is the baptism of the Holy Spirit? Is experience a valid test for truth? What are spiritual gifts? Does God still give revelation? How should we interpret the Bible? Does God still heal and do miracles today? What are we to think of the prosperity gospel and the "signs and wonders" movement?[4]

In the chapters that follow I evaluate charismatic renewal on the basis of participation as well as study. From its beginning, Christian communication has essentially been personal witness to the truth (Acts 10:36-43; 1 Jn 1:1). Like a road sign that does not call attention to itself, a witness points to a way of travel. It is my hope that this book will remove roadblocks that lie across the path of those who desire to understand and participate in the charismatic renewal.

Let's begin by looking at the renewal's historical background and present extent to provide a context for our discussion of the issues it raises for the church today.

2 *A Surprising Renewal*

*O*nce upon a time, three blind men wandered far from their town into the surrounding forest. There they unexpectedly encountered an elephant. All three reached out to feel the strange animal so they could bring a report to the people of their town. But upon their return, they gave contradictory descriptions that perplexed the townspeople. One of the blind men, who had felt a tusk, declared that the elephant was hard and smooth. The second disagreed; he had touched the side and insisted that it was rough and leathery. The third, who had felt the tail, argued that the animal was long and round like a rope. Understandably, the good citizens dismissed those contradictory reports until such time as they might encounter the strange creature for themselves.

The charismatic renewal is much like Aesop's elephant. Reports can be widely different, depending on where the renewal is observed and what the viewer is looking for. The reason for this diversity is the fact that the movement is not defined by the teachings of one leader such as Francis of Assisi, Martin Luther or John Wesley. Unlike most movements, it is not the "length-

ened shadow" of a founder or even a particular group that develops its own
principles, policies and practices. Nor is it like the early-twentieth-century
ecumenical movement, which was initiated at the top by theological scholars
and church leaders to effect organizational unity among major Protestant
denominations.

Rather, widespread charismatic renewal started in the 1960s at the grassroots level as a pattern of events in the lives of a variety of Christians largely
unknown to each other. It sprang up spontaneously over a few years across
the full spectrum of churches—from Protestant to Roman Catholic to Orthodox—in widely diverse forms. Central in this diversity of ecclesiastical and
cultural expressions is the New Testament doctrine and practice of the full
range of spiritual gifts ("charisms") to empower the body of Christ in its
worship, witness and service.

This renewal in the mainline churches, however, was preceded and influenced by the Pentecostal movement, which flourished during the first half of
the century.

The overall Pentecostal-charismatic movement has been marked by a series
of surprises. In the church's history, the content, place, persons and timing of
each sovereign outpouring of divine blessing have had an element of surprise.
A hymn reminds us that "God moves in a mysterious way, his wonders to
perform." Theologian Peter Hocken notes that surprises result from a dispar-
ity between the limitations of human understanding and the greatness of a
divine work that doesn't conform to our expectations or fit into our categories. "Attention to the surprises is important because they show where we need
to revise our thinking, and expand our thoughts to the scope of God's acts."[1]

God's sovereign actions in the world and the church embody his wisdom.
Thus we need to reflect on that wisdom as it is manifested in the origins of
the Pentecostal-charismatic movement. They are important because the origins of any renewal movement most clearly reveal the purpose of the Lord—
his wisdom, love and mercy. That historical perspective helps us to understand
the Holy Spirit's present activity in the church as he illuminates the Scriptures
and manifests his power.

So before we consider the meaning of Pentecost and the role of spiritual gifts in the church today, we will overview four major "surprises of the Spirit" in our century:

☐ Pentecostalism
☐ charismatic renewal in mainline Protestant churches
☐ charismatic renewal in the Roman Catholic Church
☐ charismatic renewal in independent churches

Classical Pentecostalism

In 1992 David Barrett estimated denominational Pentecostal membership in North America to be 22 million—and around the world, 204 million out of 1.8 billion Christians.[2] The Assemblies of God, with 2.2 million in the United States and 22 million worldwide, is by far the largest and best known group. Its history is in large part the story of the entire Pentecostal movement.[3] From the beginning the Assemblies of God missions program has pursued the goal of self-governing, self-supporting fields free from dependence on the American church.

Leading the world in size for a single church is the Yoido Full Gospel Church in Seoul, South Korea, whose pastor is David Yonggi Cho. By 1993 its membership had grown to about 625,000 members. Growth has also been phenomenal in Latin America, where three out of five evangelicals are Pentecostal. Traveling almost anywhere in the world, one is likely to see Assemblies of God congregations; they can be found in the smallest villages as well as the largest cities.

When, where and how did the worldwide Pentecostal movement begin? Many regard the events at Charles Parham's Bethel Bible College in Topeka, Kansas, in 1901 as the seedbed of the Pentecostal movement. It is true that Parham was the first to formulate its doctrinal distinctive of "initial evidence"—speaking in tongues as a confirmation of the spiritual event of baptism in the Spirit. But there was no immediate outpouring of the Spirit in Topeka, and until 1906 Parham's ministry focused on divine healing.

Historical research locates the primary catalyst of Pentecostalism at Azusa

Street in Los Angeles, California. There an astonishing mix of people with different cultural, racial, economic and educational backgrounds participated together in worship, prayer and witness. For three years thousands of visitors came from both the historic denominations and the fringes of society, from all over the United States and various parts of the world. People spoke in unknown tongues, prophesied and raised their hands and voices in praise, and some were healed.

The Azusa Street meetings were led by William J. Seymour, a thirty-four-year-old black Holiness preacher who had studied briefly at a Bible school Parham founded in Houston, Texas. In April 1906 Seymour had come to Los Angeles to serve as pastor to a small black congregation. When the members discovered that he believed in baptism with the Spirit and speaking in tongues, they asked him to resign. Undeterred, he continued to hold meetings in a rented facility on Bonnie Brae Street and then moved to a former livery stable at 312 Azusa Street.

Many of those who visited the Azusa Street fellowship were convinced of the genuineness of its teaching and practices; Seymour encouraged them to share these experiences with others. (In that respect the gathering was similar to the Holy Spirit's descent at Pentecost, when Jerusalem was thronged with pilgrims from all over the Roman world; upon their return home the new converts spread the Christian message.) The new movement spread throughout North America and overseas to Europe and Asia, especially India and China. Except for Chile, its influence in Latin America came later.[4]

Although people had spoken in tongues prior to 1906, the Azusa Street revival gave impetus to modern Pentecostalism, which views that gift as the initial outward evidence of baptism in the Spirit. Those meetings presented a teaching and experience that attracted many who thirsted for spiritual life and power in the midst of a barren theological liberalism and spiritual stagnation that plagued much of American mainline Protestantism after the Civil War.[5]

This worldwide explosion of renewing grace was a complete surprise in significant respects. Led by a young black pastor without theological credentials, it started in an old barn with interracial, international gatherings of people from all walks of life. It was evidence of the apostle Paul's declaration of God's wisdom: "God chose the weak things of the world to shame the strong . . . so that no one may boast before him" (1 Cor 1:27, 29).

Some visitors scoffed at the meetings and rejected the Pentecostal doctrine of a baptism in the Spirit evidenced by speaking in tongues. For various reasons the historic churches were not ready to recognize the presence of the Holy Spirit in such phenomena. Many of the Holiness churches dissociated themselves completely from the Pentecostal movement. Mainline churches in North America had become suspicious of frontier revivalism. Leading evangelicals like R. A. Torrey emphatically declared that the movement was not of God, since spiritual gifts of healing, prophecy and tongues had ended with the first century. In general Pentecostals were dismissed as fanatical "holy rollers," another cultic wave not to be taken seriously by mainline Christians.

Some early Pentecostals were persecuted and excommunicated from their churches; in turn, they often harshly judged Christians who rejected their teaching. Pentecostalism further isolated itself by its hostility toward higher education and formally educated ministers. Turned out of the traditional fireplaces, Pentecostals started fires on their own and eventually built different theological hearths. While the resulting independence produced some aberrations of doctrine and practice, it also provided freedom to develop the full range of spiritual gifts in new denominations unfettered by tradition in this area.

By 1940 a dozen major Pentecostal denominations had formed, including the Assemblies of God, Churches of God, Church of God in Christ, International Church of the Foursquare Gospel and Pentecostal Holiness Church. During the first half of the century Pentecostalism's influence on mainline American church life was negligible. In 1943, however, Pentecostal churches cooperated with evangelical groups to form the National Association of Evangelicals. (Although at the outset Pentecostals were a minority, by 1992 they made up about 60 percent of the five million NAE membership.)

In 1948 fourteen Pentecostal groups formed the Pentecostal Fellowship of

North America. That year an international gathering of Pentecostals convened to provide a worldwide perspective on what God was doing through their renewal. Later called the Pentecostal World Conference, this association continued to meet triennially; it implemented relief efforts in postwar Europe and coordinated evangelistic activities throughout the world.[6]

In 1951 the Full Gospel Business Men's Fellowship International was founded by Demos Shakarian in southern California. It was designed to be an interdenominational organization of charismatic laypeople for evangelism and spreading the message of baptism with the Spirit. FGBMFI started with breakfast meetings and soon began to hold an annual convention. By the mid-1960s it had three hundred chapters and a membership of 100,000, which tripled during the following decade. By 1992 there were about three thousand local chapters in ninety countries.

As we will see later, FGBMFI had an important influence on the fledgling charismatic renewal in the mainline Protestant and Roman Catholic churches during the 1960s.

Protestant Charismatic Renewal

A second major surprise of the Spirit appeared within the historic Protestant churches in the early 1960s. This movement developed in a pattern that was radically different from the beginning of Pentecostalism. There was no equivalent to Azusa Street, one place where it all happened. Nor can it be traced to a few founding figures. In fact, it is difficult to determine precisely when and where the movement began. During the 1950s the varied ministries of Episcopalian Agnes Sanford, Mennonite Gerald Derstine, Methodist Tommy Tyson, Pentecostal Oral Roberts and Presbyterian Jim Brown, in different parts of the country, helped prepare the soil and climate for seeds of charismatic renewal to germinate.

A sudden sprouting began with a dramatic event that eventually made headlines across the nation. On April 3, 1960, rector Dennis Bennett of St. Mark's Episcopal Church in Van Nuys, California, shocked his parish. He stood in his pulpit and reported that in one of the church's home fellowship groups he had experienced a new work of the Holy Spirit in his life, including speaking in tongues. He then offered to resign; the majority of parishioners reacted with antagonism, and the resignation was accepted. The bishop sent the parish a new rector and circulated a pastoral letter banning any further speaking in tongues under church auspices.[7]

Several months later *Time* and *Newsweek* gave national publicity to this event, overnight making Bennett a controversial figure. The *Saturday Evening Post* reported, "The name glossolalia sounds as strange as the act itself. But this practice of praying in 'unknown tongues' spreads, and brings prophecies of still stranger things to come." This eruption of a "neo-Pentecostalism" in the mainline Protestant churches was profoundly disturbing to many of their leaders and members.

Bennett was invited by Bishop Lewis of the Olympia diocese to serve as pastor of St. Luke's, a run-down urban parish near Seattle that was on the verge of closing. Soon St. Luke's became the largest Episcopal church in the Northwest and a center of charismatic renewal for other denominations. Bennett was invited to speak in other parts of the country, and in the historic churches he discovered many fellowship groups which in their Bible study and prayer had begun to manifest spiritual gifts of healing, prophecy and speaking in tongues. His example and writing encouraged hundreds of other clergy in mainline Protestant denominations, as well as small charismatic fellowships that had quietly formed, to "go public" with their new biblical teaching and experience of spiritual gifts. Clearly, Dennis Bennett was not a founder of this charismatic renewal, but a catalyst through which it surfaced and grew.

The glare of sudden publicity on this renewal was detrimental in several respects. It made participants self-conscious and, as a result, defensive. Christians newly involved in these events, without time to reflect on their significance, were forced to defend their experience in the public arena. Some became aggressive and self-righteous, while others withdrew into small groups. But hostility was not all on one side. Many church leaders and congregations harassed the "charismatic" Christians. Some ministers were forced to resign their pulpits.

In the early years participants found little if any teaching by their own churches on the nature and use of spiritual gifts. Many received encouragement and instruction only from Full Gospel Business Men's Fellowship groups, which provided the classical Pentecostal interpretation of baptism in the Spirit.

Data concerning the influence of Pentecostals on charismatic origins show two facts: (1) they were often God's instruments for bringing baptism in the Spirit to other Christians, and (2) they were far from being the only instruments. Although the renewal was indebted to Pentecostalism, it was not simply an offshoot. Yet without the prior rise of the Pentecostal movement, the charismatic renewal with its focus on baptism in the Spirit could not have happened the way it did.

The term *charismatic* was first used around 1963 to distinguish the renewal within historic Protestant churches from the Pentecostal movement. The explosion of nondenominational churches and ministries after 1965 led to the use of *charismatic movement* as an umbrella term for all "Spirit-filled" bodies and people outside classical Pentecostalism. By 1988, North American participants in Protestant renewal numbered 2.2 million. Of these, about 86 percent were in mainline churches and the rest were in nondenominational or independent churches.[8]

During the 1970s and 1980s, first-rate biblical scholarship produced a sound theological basis for the manifestation of all spiritual gifts to empower the church's worship, witness and service. As this doctrine was integrated into their historic theologies, several churches developed interpretations of "baptism in the Spirit" different from that of Pentecostalism. (These are presented in appendix B.)

The spread of charismatic renewal among mainline Protestants was entirely unexpected on both sides of the Pentecostal fence. Pentecostals regarded the historic churches to be dead and beyond resuscitation; that was why the Holy Spirit had passed the baton to them. Yet Pentecostal leader David du Plessis played an important role in helping his church overcome suspicion of the charismatic renewal.

On the other side of the fence, this development did not correspond at all to what any Protestant churches expected or where they looked for renewal. (For example, Lutheran and Southern Baptist theologians had different attitudes regarding the need for renewal in the first place.) None of the mainline church establishments expected anything worthwhile from the Pentecostals, whom they perceived as fanatical, uneducated and overly emotional.

The pattern of this second surprise showed the wisdom of God in several ways. The renewal's slow, unnoticed growth affected people in virtually all the Protestant denominations. Many were unexpectedly blessed through Christians in traditions other than their own. The simultaneous work of the Holy Spirit in different churches showed clearly that the renewal did not belong to any one constituency. Since it was so gradual, it did not threaten the churches or repeat the earlier pattern of large-scale rejection experienced by Pentecostalism.

Furthermore, since charismatic renewal has not been a typical centralized movement with a single program of action, it has been adaptable to the wide variety of ecclesiastical structures. It is significant that although the empowerment of the Holy Spirit is the same for all, it has been manifested uniquely in each structure. Even though many participants have left their churches—for various reasons—the renewal is not essentially separatist or schismatic; for most participants it is a means of becoming more effective within their own churches.

Roman Catholic Charismatic Renewal

In the autumn of 1966 several laymen on the faculty of Duquesne University of the Holy Spirit in Pittsburgh began to seek greater power to proclaim the gospel. Even though their lives were centered in Jesus Christ, they sensed a lack of dynamism in their witness. So they gave themselves to prayer that the Holy Spirit would renew them with the powerful life of the risen Lord. They began to study the New Testament, particularly parts dealing with life in the early church, and looked for the Spirit to come upon them in the same way. That expectation was heightened by reading David Wilkerson's *The Cross and the Switchblade.*

In mid-February 1967 about thirty students and faculty drove out of the city for a weekend spiritual retreat at an inn called The Ark and the Dove. They had been asked to read Wilkerson's book as well as the first four chapters of Acts. Only the professors had been in Pentecostal meetings before this weekend; the students had just a hazy notion of the purpose of the retreat.

Saturday evening had been set aside for relaxation and a birthday party. Yet one student felt drawn to the chapel and was followed by others in ones and twos. As they prayed, the Holy Spirit was poured out on them. There was no human direction or urging; individuals simply responded to the Spirit's leading. Some praised God in new languages, others quietly wept for joy. They continued from ten in the evening until five in the morning. Not everyone was touched immediately, but throughout the night God dealt with each person in an unexpected way. This "Duquesne Weekend," one of the most remarkable events in the charismatic renewal, marked the beginning of its rapid growth within the Catholic Church.[9]

During the following weeks God worked through this group in the lives of many others. Some turned from sinful habits and others from intellectual doubts. Throughout the remainder of the spring semester at Duquesne, the external gifts and the internal fruit of the Holy Spirit continued to flourish in this community. They spread the joy of Christ's love to many Catholics in the university area. As in the mainline Protestant churches, this experience of long-neglected gifts was guided by biblical teaching—the doctrine and practice of the early church.

About this time Ralph Keifer visited South Bend, Indiana, on business. He spent a weekend with Kevin Ranaghan, a doctoral candidate at Notre Dame, and his wife Dorothy. For two days they talked about Pentecostalism and raised every intellectual, aesthetic and psychological objection they could.[10]

On Saturday evening, March 4, about thirty friends and students met at the Ranaghans' home for fellowship. Ralph Keifer reported on the Duquesne weekend and shared his own experience. The next night nine met again to read Scripture, pray and discuss the events at Duquesne. They asked to be prayed for that they might be filled with the Holy Spirit and that through his gifts and fruit their lives might be more fully Christian. There was no prophecy or speaking in tongues, but many experienced a new dimension of prayer that marked the beginning of a deeper life of faith.

Realizing that spiritual gifts are designed to build up the body of Christ, they formed a small community. Students and faculty shared each other's concerns and rejoiced together in victories. The focus of their witness was not spiritual gifts but the Lord Jesus Christ and the power of his saving love to transform relationships.

The general public remained unaware of these events until early April, when about forty-five visitors from Michigan State University joined forty from Notre Dame in a weekend retreat held on campus. Present were several members of nearby Pentecostal churches. News of these events stirred criticism and controversy as curious visitors jammed the next Friday-evening prayer meeting. (That weekend was later referred to as the first "national conference.")

From the beginning of the renewal its leaders stressed the need to integrate the experience of baptism in the Spirit into a community where members would receive support and draw others into this life of joy and service. Ralph Martin and Stephen Clark, leaders in the Cursillo movement, moved to the University of Michigan in Ann Arbor, where they helped organize the Word of God Community. This ecumenical group soon grew to one thousand members. It became a creative center of renewal that also involved Pentecostals and charismatic Protestants. Songs were composed and published. A new periodical, *Pastoral Newsletter,* was distributed. In July 1971 it became *New Covenant,* a monthly magazine with Martin as editor and with seventy thousand subscribers.

In April 1967 there was a second national Catholic charismatic conference on the Notre Dame campus with eighty-five participants. Attendance at the annual conference grew to thirty thousand in 1976, when it convened in the football stadium. The following year the conference met with Protestant denominations in Kansas City, where Catholics made up half of the fifty-two thousand participants. The same year, thirty-five thousand gathered for a charismatic conference in Atlantic City. By then about 700,000 Catholics were involved in the renewal. After that, the huge national conferences gave way to regional gatherings.

The Committee on Doctrine of the National Conference of Catholic Bishops reported on the charismatic renewal in November 1969. They recognized its strong biblical basis. Noting the abuse of certain charisms, the report stated that the cure is not to deny their validity but to ensure their proper use. The committee concluded that the renewal should not be inhibited but should be allowed to develop. Bishops were encouraged to exercise their pastoral responsibility to oversee and guide it. In 1974 six of the seven cardinals in the United States responded in a positive way.

Like all movements, the Catholic charismatic renewal has experienced growing pains of internal disagreement and consolidation. After the brushfire growth of the late 1960s and 1970s, enthusiasm in some places began to wane. In 1990 the Ann Arbor Word of God Community split over leadership differences and lost two-thirds of its members.

Nevertheless, in the early 1990s weekly prayer groups in the United States numbered about five thousand, with an average membership of thirty. "Life in the Spirit" seminars on spiritual gifts continue to enroll many each year. Active participants number about 2.5 million in North America and 81 million worldwide.[11] In June 1992 seventeen thousand charismatic Roman Catholics returned to the birthplace of their movement to celebrate its twenty-fifth anniversary. Leaders emphasized that the conference was not a nostalgia trip but an expression of desire to reenergize the renewal.

The spread of charismatic renewal to the Roman Catholic Church was a double surprise. Peter Hocken notes that in the 1960s "the gulf between Rome and the Reform was such that neither side expected spiritual renewal to spring up on the far bank let alone cross this historic divide."[12] It was particularly shocking for Pentecostals, who were still coming to terms with baptized-in-the-Spirit Christians in mainline Protestant churches. For them and for many charismatic evangelicals, revival of the Church of Rome was impossible; the idea of "Catholic charismatics" was acceptable only if the Catholics left their apostate church.

"Catholic Pentecostalism" was also unexpected on the other side of the gulf. In the late 1960s, following the Second Vatican Council, renewal had been high on the church's agenda. But attention was focused on liturgical reform, biblical studies, promoting lay participation and the like. No one dreamed that renewal of Catholic life would come through restoration of New Testament spiritual gifts.

Although the charismatic renewal among Catholics has much in common with that of mainline Protestants, its origin had several distinctives that gave it a unique shape. First, in a church seemingly dominated by elderly clergy, the renewal surprisingly started with young laypeople in a university setting. Second, the renewal began in a public manner that attracted immediate attention and fostered its spread. Such a beginning in any major Protestant church would probably have caused major problems.

Third, a network of friendship and cooperation among many in the original groups at Duquesne, Michigan State and Notre Dame was already in place. The previous experience of leaders in Catholic renewal groups like Cursillo provided a sense of strategy that gave the charismatic renewal an initial coherence and identity not known among Protestants. Fourth, influential church leaders gave the renewal early support, providing doctrinal and pastoral guidance. Although later on the scene, Catholic theologians soon began to produce excellent scholarly writing to ground this new charismatic experience on a biblical basis within their ecclesiastical framework.

Fifth, and basic, the renewal pioneers had a high degree of commitment and sense of mission to their church that Protestant groups had not yet developed. From the outset there was a grasp of charismatic renewal that went beyond individual experience and saw spiritual gifts primarily as a *corporate* function of the body of Christ. None of the Catholics baptized in the Spirit in those early 1967 meetings believed that the Lord was calling them out of their church. Rather, they were convinced that the charismatic renewal was a fulfillment of the vision of Pope John XXIII as he convened Vatican II in 1961 and asked all Catholics to "pray for a new Pentecost in our day and a renewal of faith, with signs and wonders."

Other Renewal Movements

Further illustrating the diversity of charismatic renewal are three other significant streams with varying kinds and degrees of surprise.

Orthodox Renewal. In 1965 the Orthodox Church in America was formed as a self-governing entity with the blessing of the Russian bishops. It claims about five million people, mostly in Greek, Russian, Antiochian and Ukrainian churches, of whom about one million are English-speaking members.

Orthodoxy has always claimed to be charismatic in its worship and spirituality. It has never taught the cessation of certain spiritual gifts. Signs and wonders—including healing, prophecy and miracles—have been accepted as part of the church's heritage. Yet no major Christian body has been less affected by the charismatic renewal of recent decades.

In 1977 the Service Committee for Orthodox Renewal sought to bring together charismatic leaders from a variety of jurisdictions to help facilitate the movement and sponsor renewal conferences. Its president was Boris Zabrodsky, a Ukrainian Orthodox priest. Charismatic renewal among Orthodox Christians in the United States has grown to involve twelve thousand participants, but in recent years has become somewhat fragmented.[13]

Independent Renewal. The last twenty years have witnessed the phenomenal rise of charismatic churches and ministries not related to any denomination—Pentecostal or mainline. Coalitions of nondenominational groups have become a major force in the overall renewal picture. Their current North American membership of fourteen million is more than twice that of charismatic participants in the mainline churches.

The wide variety of assemblies, associations and ministries can be viewed in three major categories. The first emphasizes the power of the Holy Spirit to build the body of Christ. Many use the concepts of *covenant* and *restoration* in what is seen as raising up anew the New Testament church to free churches and their members from the bondage of denominationalism. A second category produces nondenominational ministries. For example, the Oral Roberts Evangelistic Association draws support from the entire spectrum of the Pentecostal/charismatic movement, not just from nondenominational sources; Youth With A Mission performs a service and training role for existing mainline and independent churches. A third category includes groups attached to a specific doctrine, practice or teacher. An example is the prosperity gospel teaching of Kenneth Hagin. John Wimber's original ministry of signs and wonders also belongs here, but the growing network of Vineyard Fellowships has moved toward the first category. These two movements are considered in chapters twelve and thirteen.

Messianic Judaism. For the first time since the early centuries of the church, a distinctively Jewish form of Christianity has emerged. Pentecostals and most evangelicals were already convinced on the basis of Romans 11:25-26 that in the end times Israel would accept Jesus as its Messiah. But they were expecting only Jewish conversions to Gentile Christianity in larger numbers; the emergence of a truly Jewish Christianity has been a complete surprise.

Through sovereign acts of God's grace, increasing numbers of Jews have accepted Jesus (Yeshua) as the Messiah, affirming their ongoing Jewish identity as "completed Jews." In their own synagogues they celebrate Jewish feasts and use distinctive patterns of worship, including music and dance. Charismatic Messianic Jews have now become the main evangelists of their fellow Jews.[14]

Charismatic Tension

Church history shows that renewal movements consistently arise on the fringes of church life, the periphery of its central leadership. They are turbulent, not tidy. Inevitably there is tension between the creativity of new life and attempts to domesticate it—between kindling the fire and adjusting the fireplace to keep it burning. So it has been with charismatic renewal. We have seen how its various forms sprang up in unexpected places through unlikely people. Unfortunately, for many churches and their members, these surprises have represented more threat than promise.

Renewals tend to make a division between first- and second-class citizens, generating friction between those who respond and those who do not. Often this difficulty is exacerbated by misuse of labels. In this respect the charismatic renewal is no exception. Friend and foe alike widely use the word *charismatics* as a noun for a special class or category of Christians. But according to the New Testament, *all* believers, not just a special group, are "charismatic"—that is, empowered by the Holy Spirit in their worship and service.

Although a church may have special prayer or Bible study groups, we do not call their members the "prayers" or the "Bible students," as if other members did not pray or study the Bible. Likewise *we should scrupulously avoid using* charismatic *as a noun connoting a special theological category of Christian.* It is appropriate, however, to use *charismatic* as an adjective, as in "charismatic renewal" or "a charismatic meeting," to denote an affirmation and expectancy today of the full range of spiritual gifts taught and practiced in the early church.

We now turn to the New Testament to discover the significance of Pentecost and baptism in the Spirit, about which interpretations differ and debate continues. As we do so, we should remember that whenever a river flows swiftly it throws debris onto its banks. Let us not become so preoccupied with the debris that we fail to see the power of the stream itself and to rejoice that the riverbed is no longer dry.

II
The Holy Spirit in the New Testament

3 The Promise of Pentecost

*W*e all look back and wonder about beginnings. *Children are fascinated* with stories of their childhood; families trace their genealogies. Nations produce histories of their origin. Knowledge of our heritage contributes to our sense of identity; we look back to learn more of who we are. Pressures of the present and hopes for the future take on new meaning when we know more about how it all began.

Our survey of the Pentecostal/charismatic renewal has sketched out a complex movement that is far more difficult to describe than Aesop's elephant. It has also given us a frame of reference for looking at the biblical doctrine and practice of the charismatic dimension of the Holy Spirit's activity. In this chapter we consider the beginning of the church's empowerment by the Holy Spirit for its mission in the world.

For this survey we turn to the writing of Luke in his Gospel and the Acts of the Apostles, which highlights the role of the Holy Spirit in the coming of the messianic age. After four hundred years of prophetic silence, the Spirit inspires visions and prophecies that herald the long-awaited Savior of Israel. Baptized at the Jordan River, Jesus of Nazareth becomes the unique Bearer of the Spirit who initiates a new era in the history of salvation.[1] He returns to Galilee "in the power of the Spirit," teaching and healing in the synagogues (Lk 4:14). Yet soon the work of the Spirit in the One will include the many. According to John the Baptist, the Bearer of the Spirit will also baptize with the Spirit, who is to be poured out on the disciples.

The Father's Promise

After his resurrection Jesus appears in a room where the disciples are gathered and opens their minds to understand the Scriptures. He declares that repentance and forgiveness of sins will be preached in his name to all nations, beginning in Jerusalem. "You are witnesses of these things. I am going to send you what my Father has promised; but stay in the city until you have been clothed with power from on high" (Lk 24:48-49).

At the beginning of Acts, which picks up the story, Jesus continues to teach "through the Holy Spirit." He repeats his earlier instructions: "Do not leave Jerusalem, but wait for the gift my Father promised, which you have heard me speak about. For John baptized with water, but in a few days you will be baptized with the Holy Spirit" (Acts 1:2, 4-5).[2] Still the disciples do not grasp the meaning of their ministry; their old way of thinking misses the main point. "Lord, are you at this time going to restore the kingdom to Israel?" they ask (1:6). They still think of the kingdom as a geopolitical conquest within the present age. Jesus replies that it is not for them to know the Father's times or dates. He then repeats his commission and promise: "But you will receive power when the Holy Spirit comes upon you; and you will be my witnesses in Jerusalem, and in all Judea and Samaria, and to the ends of the earth" (1:7-8).

Jesus then ascends out of their sight into a cloud. The disciples "worshiped him and returned to Jerusalem with great joy. And they stayed continually at the temple, praising God" (Lk 24:52-53). Soon the Bearer of the Spirit will become the Giver of the Spirit.[3]

Filled with the Spirit

Fifty days after Passover, the celebration of Israel's deliverance from Egypt, comes the Feast of Pentecost. Marking the end of the spring harvest, its ceremony offers to the Lord the first two loaves of new grain. Pentecost is one of the three great pilgrimage festivals that require Israel's attendance at the sanctuary (Deut 16:16). At this time Jerusalem is thronged with pilgrims from all over the Roman Empire. Many Jews from distant countries have saved for years to cover the travel expense.[4]

Amid the festivities a dramatic event suddenly takes place among Jesus' disciples.

When the day of Pentecost came, they were all together in one place. Suddenly a sound like the blowing of a violent wind came from heaven and filled the whole house where they were sitting. They saw what seemed to be tongues of fire that separated and came to rest on each of them. All of them were filled with the Holy Spirit and began to speak in other tongues as the Spirit enabled them. (Acts 2:1-4)

Luke records several significant aspects of this surprising event. First is its *timing*. The disciples have obeyed their Lord day after day, waiting in Jerusalem for the fulfillment of his promise. Yet the descent of the Spirit is linked not to their spiritual readiness but to the sovereign action of God in history. Pentecost permits the greatest possible impact, for the pilgrims who are swelling Jerusalem's population will soon return home with the new message. They will be the firstfruits of a worldwide spiritual harvest.

A second element in this event is its *origin*. It is not produced by human endeavor; the gift comes unexpectedly from heaven. The downward movement from God to humanity continues to demonstrate the divine initiative. Luke pictures the disciples gathered together, available but not active. They are sitting, not kneeling or standing in the usual Jewish postures of prayer.

Third, Luke reports two *signs* to describe the Spirit's activity: wind and fire. The Greek word here translated "wind" occurs only one other time in the New Testament: later, at Athens, Paul declares that God gives to all life and "breath" (Acts 17:25). The word *wind* echoes Jesus' words to Nicodemus about the wind (Spirit) blowing wherever it pleases (Jn 3:8). Psalm 104:4 declares of God, "He makes winds his messengers, flames of fire his servants." Just as wind represents the Spirit, so fire connotes God's purification of his people.

A fourth element has to do with the *recipients*. The tongues like fire rest on "each" of the disciples, and "all" are filled with the Holy Spirit. Probably the whole body of 120 involved in choosing a successor to Judas in the preceding chapter (Acts 1:15) are present, not just the Twelve. The main point, however, is that here, as elsewhere in Acts, *the Spirit does not come on only a select part of a group; all the disciples are filled with the Spirit* sent by the ascended Christ.

A fifth element is the immediate *result* of the Spirit's coming. Those present hear a specific sound—not just the inarticulate rushing of the wind, but words in other languages. Luke lists more than a dozen different countries and districts represented by these pilgrims. "Utterly amazed, they asked: 'Are not all these men who are speaking Galileans? Then how is it that each of us hears them in his own native language? . . . What does this mean?' " While some are perplexed, others make fun of the disciples with a ready answer: "They have had too much wine" (2:7-8, 12-13).

Today we face the same question: What *was* this strange phenomenon of "other tongues"? Now as then, conflicting explanations are offered. Some scholars note that since the returning Jews would have known the two languages spoken in Palestine—Aramaic and Greek—the disciples were simply speaking in an unusually clear manner. But this interpretation contradicts the narrative, which reports that the pilgrims were bewildered, utterly amazed, perplexed. Why? Luke states the answer three times: because each one heard the disciples "in his own native language" (2:8; see also 2:6, 11).

Another view rejects any miraculous element because it seems not to have served a practical purpose at the time. But is that a valid criterion for accepting or rejecting a possible miracle? Surely interpretation of biblical events should not rest on the shifting sands of our subjective evaluation regarding their practicality or purpose.

Some scholars assert that the miracle consisted not in the disciples' *speaking* but the visitors' *hearing*. This view is based on the unwarranted assumption that speaking in tongues here is necessarily the same as at Corinth (1 Cor 14:22-25), where they are not known foreign languages. This interpretation also contradicts what Luke explicitly states: The Spirit's activity is related to the *speaking* of a message that the pilgrims heard in their own many languages (Acts 2:4, 6).

The most straightforward interpretation is that the disciples were speaking the languages of the countries and districts represented. Luke reports that they spoke in "other" (or "different") tongues.[5] Only at Pentecost does Luke report a variety of linguistic groups hearing a message in tongues in their own language. The visitors certainly did not require this phenomenon, since they understood Aramaic and Greek.

What, then, was the purpose of this miraculous event? In the circumstances it served two purposes, one practical and the other symbolic. This speaking in other tongues attracted the attention of visitors from other countries. It succeeded in bringing together a crowd perplexed and curious to know more about this extraordinary event.

The disciples' speaking in foreign languages was also a sign of the Lord's compassion and purpose to proclaim the good news not just in Jerusalem and Judea but indeed "to the ends of the earth" (1:8). In the providence of God, the world's nations were represented in the God-fearing Jews gathered in Jerusalem. Soon a message of the great deeds of God would spread through missionaries to the distant countries from which the pilgrims came. The miracle of tongues at Pentecost captured at one place and time a preview of the church's mission over the miles and through the years.

Peter's Sermon

When Peter stands up with the other eleven disciples to address the crowd, he first sets the record straight on the charge of drunkenness. Though wine flows freely at festivals, Peter declares that the disciples are not drunk. It is only nine o'clock in the morning, hardly the time for a binge! Rather, this is a fulfillment of Joel's prophecy (see Joel 2:28-29):

In the last days, God says,

I will pour out my Spirit on all people.

Your sons and daughters will prophesy,

your young men will see visions,

your old men will dream dreams.

Even on my servants, both men and women,

I will pour out my Spirit in those days,

and they will prophesy. (Acts 2:17-18)

What did Joel proclaim about the future coming of the Spirit, and how does Peter apply this prophecy? First, the coming of the Spirit is *eschatological*—that is, for the last days. Peter equates this predicted outpouring of the Holy Spirit with the experience that he and the other disciples have just had. It is evidence that the messianic age foretold by the prophets has arrived.

Second, the nature of this gift is *prophetic*. The words "and they will prophesy" at the end of Acts 2:18 do not occur in Joel's prediction. Their addition here in Peter's otherwise direct quotation shows his concern to emphasize the prophetic nature of speaking in tongues. In this instance it takes the form of praise in "declaring the wonders of God" (2:11).

Third, this giving of the Spirit is *universal*. He is poured out on all people, not on just a few select prophets or disciples. It is for men and women, young and old, slave and free; all will prophesy, without distinction of gender, age or social position.

Peter ends the quotation with Joel's universal offer: "Everyone who calls on the name of the Lord will be saved" (2:21). The apostle then reminds the crowd that God accredited Jesus of Nazareth by miracles, wonders and signs, as they well knew. Peter then accuses his hearers of nailing Jesus to the cross. Nevertheless, God has raised him from the dead (2:22-24).

Peter then cites two Old Testament passages (Ps 16:8-11; 110:1) whose fulfillment in Jesus prove him to be the Messiah. The apostle again witnesses to Jesus' resurrection and then links him with the Spirit: "Exalted to the right hand of God, he has received from the Father the promised Holy Spirit and has poured out what you now see and hear. . . . Therefore let all Israel be assured of this: God has made this Jesus, whom you crucified, both Lord and Christ" (2:33, 36).

These words cut the hearers to the heart; they give their own "altar call," asking the apostles, "What shall we do?" Peter answers, "Repent and be baptized, every one of you, in the name of Jesus Christ for the forgiveness of your sins. And you will receive the gift of the Holy Spirit" (2:38).

Peter's command echoes the message of John the Baptist, but now baptism is in the name of Jesus Christ. Like Joel's prophecy, Peter's preaching ends with a promise of salvation, universal in time ("for your children") and in distance ("for all who are far off"). "Those who accepted his message were baptized, and about three thousand were added to their number that day" (2:39, 41).

The Meaning of Pentecost

What is the significance of this particular day of Pentecost? Conflicting insights and answers have consistently made Acts 2 a theological battleground. Admittedly, this is a complex event: foretold by Joel, promised by John the Baptist, explained by Jesus before his ascension, described as it happened by Luke and afterward interpreted by Peter. The debate is usually complicated at the outset by a common failure to define the crucial terms. When that happens, arguments are like ships passing in the night, their shapes visible but making no contact, or like two locomotives headed toward each other on a collision course.

Conclusions about the meaning of Pentecost need to be based on two basic, but often ignored, principles of literary interpretation. First, a word or term can have more than one meaning. In that event, the correct meaning in a specific situation is determined by its context and usage—the subject at hand and how the word is used. For example, the word *bar* can mean an oblong piece of metal, a measure of music, an underwater stretch of sand, the legal profession or a place that serves alcoholic beverages. If a sailor is briefing the crew about the danger of a bar, we do not infer that the discussion concerns possible trouble with a court case or alcohol.[6]

But too often in interpreting a biblical passage we assume that a significant word or phrase has only one meaning. This is especially serious when we derive the definition from a different context and usage by another author, then import it into the text at hand. That procedure opens the door to getting from Scripture whatever we desire to find or prove, rather than helping us discover the author's meaning.

Second, an *event* can have several different meanings, depending on the person or group that is involved. Yet many commentaries on Acts 2 address the significance of Pentecost without first asking, "For whom?" They tacitly assume that the events of Pentecost had the same meaning for Jesus' disciples as it did for the new converts, even though the two groups brought radically different experiences to this festive day. Here we will identify three different meanings of the Pentecost events—for Jesus, his disciples and the new converts.

1. For Jesus, this day has a twofold meaning. First, it marks a significantly different relationship to the Holy Spirit. At the outset of his earthly ministry Jesus was anointed by the Spirit, who continued to empower and direct his preaching, teaching and healing (Lk 3:21-22; 4:1, 4-19). Now, exalted at the right hand of God, he pours out the Spirit on his disciples to empower *their* mission. On Pentecost Jesus baptizes them in the Holy Spirit as John the Baptist had foretold. The Bearer of the Spirit in the Gospels now becomes the Giver of the Spirit to build his church.

For Jesus, Pentecost also marks a public vindication of his ministry that had ended ignominiously on a Roman cross after he was betrayed, denied and deserted by his followers. As far as the Romans are concerned, one more potential revolt by a controversial Jewish leader had been effectively snuffed out. Although troubling to Pilate at the time, in retrospect the event seems to have been little more than a tempest in a Galilean teapot. The Jewish leaders are also glad to be rid of the troublesome young rabbi with his disturbing teaching and blasphemous claims. Even though he said he would rise from the dead, nothing has since been heard from him.

Suddenly, however, one of Jesus' disciples fearlessly proclaims to the Jerusalem crowds that Jesus of Nazareth is the long-awaited Messiah; though rejected and crucified, he has been raised from the dead and exalted as both Lord and Christ. He is now honored in this first public witness, which gathers three thousand converts into his church.

2. For Jesus' disciples, the meaning of the Holy Spirit's coming at Pentecost is described before, during and after the event in a variety of phrases. At the beginning of the chapter we noted the three occasions on which Jesus foretold what his disciples would experience: "I am going to send you what my Father has promised, . . . power from on high." "You will be baptized with the Holy Spirit." "You will receive power when the Holy Spirit comes on you."

Luke describes what happened at Pentecost: all the disciples were "filled with the Holy Spirit and began to speak in other tongues as the Spirit enabled them" (Acts 2:4). With one exception (Eph 5:18), "filled with the Spirit" is used in the New Testament only by Luke. This metaphor is a picturesque way of reporting the power of the Spirit for prophetic ministry. The Spirit's power is not static like a full bucket, but dynamic like water coursing through a pipe to thirsty people (see Jn 7:37-39). Both individuals˙and groups are filled with the Spirit, as the occasion requires. This experience is not once for all; it can be repeated,[7] as in the case of Peter (4:8) and the community (4:31). Throughout Luke-Acts, filling with the Spirit results in prophetic speaking, in its broadest sense, whether in worship or witness or judgment.

Afterward Peter explains the disciples' experience to the astonished crowd in somewhat different words. He first declares it to be the fulfillment of Joel's prophecy: "I will pour out my Spirit on all people. Your sons and daughters will prophesy" (Acts 2:17). Later in his sermon Peter connects this activity with the exalted Christ, who "has poured out what you now see and hear" (2:33). Again the prophetic dimension of the Spirit's activity is emphasized.

To summarize, Jesus foretold that as promised by the Father, the Holy Spirit would come upon the disciples, clothing them with power from on high, baptizing them with the Spirit to empower their witness. Luke describes the experience as being "filled with the Spirit," and Peter uses Joel's phrase "pour out my Spirit." These terms are different facets, each throwing its light on the dramatic Pentecost event. But what is the nature of the gem?

The answer lies in the often-overlooked fact that Luke is not simply a historian, a reporter of events; he is also a theologian who reveals a doctrine of the Holy Spirit in his Gospel and the Acts. Luke alone records the events of Pentecost. Their meaning for Jesus' disciples is to be found in the author's own words and the way he uses them, not definitions of other New Testament writers imposed on the text. The context of these facet-phrases clearly indicates that the gem is an empowering activity of the Holy Spirit for the church, enabling it to fulfill its worldwide mission of proclaiming the gospel of the risen Lord.

Jesus' disciples had been demoralized and scattered by the trial and crucifixion. On the day of his resurrection they were huddled in fear behind locked doors, through which he came to greet them. The ensuing appearances of their Lord before his ascension were also private, unknown to the authorities. Now the disciples stand fearlessly in Jerusalem, under the noses of the Jewish and Roman leaders, to proclaim Jesus of Nazareth as Messiah and Lord. What has made the difference? According to Luke, it is the coming of the Spirit that empowers them to "take the church public."

3. The three thousand who respond to Peter's sermon have an experience very different from the disciples' in terms of personal need, required response and result. Unlike the disciples, they are not already followers of Jesus who have been commissioned for service and are waiting for the Spirit to empower their witness. Rather, these residents and visitors in Jerusalem are hearing the gospel of Christ for the first time. A response of repentance is required from them before they can participate in the messianic age. As a result they receive the gift of the indwelling Spirit to begin their Christian life.

As we have seen in Acts 2:38, Luke records three central and related elements of becoming a Christian. Peter's three verbs are *repent, baptize* and *receive.* Two are commands and one is a promise. Repentance is the sinner's active response to the gospel; water baptism is performed by the Christian community; the gift of the Holy Spirit is received from God.

In the following chapters Luke does not present these elements as a standard formula for conversion; he varies the sequence and sometimes omits one of the three elements. His purpose is not to report stages of the disciples' inner spiritual lives, but rather the prophetic activity of the Spirit to empower their witness and service in the growth of the church.

Baptized in the Spirit

Of the several phrases used to describe the disciples' experience at Pentecost, *baptized in the Spirit* has proved most controversial. Unfortunately, most of the argument fails to recognize that the phrase has two significantly different meanings.

The phrase is first used by John the Baptist for Jesus' mission: "He will baptize you with the Holy Spirit" (Mk 1:8; cf. Mt 3:11; Lk 3:16; Jn 1:33). The meaning of this experience is explained by the risen Lord before his ascension: "In a few days you will be baptized with the Holy Spirit. . . . You will receive power when the Holy Spirit comes on you" (Acts 1:5, 8). Another occurrence comes in Peter's report that the experience of the Roman officer Cornelius and his household was the same as that of the disciples at Pentecost (Acts 11:16).

The only other occurrence of this phrase is in Paul's first letter to the church in Corinth: "For we were all baptized by [with/in] one Spirit into one body" (1 Cor 12:13). Here the use of the term is distinctly different; the context is incorporation into the body of Christ, not empowerment for witness and mission.

(The Greek preposition *en* can be translated "by" or "with" or "in." Although the NIV chooses the first for 1 Corinthians 12:13, it should be either the second or third, in line with the other six occurrences, where Spirit baptism is clearly the distinctive work of Jesus. The NRSV, for example, states, "For in the one Spirit we were all baptized into one body." Although the translation "with" is used for the promise of John the Baptist, the alternative "in" has become common in the charismatic renewal and is used throughout this book.)

A full treatment of differing interpretations of Spirit baptism appears in appendix B. Following is a brief comment on three major views.

1. Standard evangelical. This interpretation holds that the disciples' experience, like that of the three thousand, was the beginning of their Christian life as they were "baptized in one Spirit into one body [of Christ]." Theirs was a once-for-all experience of the Spirit in conversion. Pentecost is considered to be the "birthday" of the church.

This interpretation, however, has several flaws. First, it fails to recognize that the term "baptized in the Spirit" can (and does) have more than one meaning, as determined by context and usage. For example, the word *baptism* doesn't always connote initiation; it can also mean "immerse" or "wash," as in Mark 7:4, which refers to a ceremonial "washing of cups, pitchers and kettles." In Acts 2, however, "baptized in the Spirit" is clearly one of several terms for empowerment.

Second, the standard evangelical interpretation imposes on Scripture an arbitrary distinction between so-called *didactic* (used or intended for instruction) and *descriptive* (narrative) passages; only the former qualify as a basis for "doctrine." In other words, theology must be grounded in explicit teaching, not implicit examples. That is why Paul's single use of *baptize in the Spirit* is given the honor of defining the same phrase's usage in Acts: Paul is a theologian, while Luke is only a historian! This view denies the fact that Luke uses the medium of church history to teach his own theology of the Holy Spirit's empowerment.

The assumed dichotomy between didactic and descriptive also contradicts Paul's explicit teaching in 2 Timothy 3:16: "All Scripture is God-breathed and is useful for teaching [*didaskalia,* the root of the word *didactic*]." Every kind of biblical writing—psalm, poetry, history and parable as well as proverb and prose—is didactic. In fact, the Bible's teaching is often more descriptive than prescriptive. For example, after recounting certain experiences of Israel in 1 Corinthians 10:1-6, Paul comments, "Now these things occurred as examples to keep us from setting our hearts on evil things as they did" (v. 6).[8]

Third, the assumption that the Spirit was first imparted to the disciples at Pentecost forces an unwarranted interpretation of John 20:22. There Jesus breathed on his disciples and said, "Receive the Holy Spirit." The verb is in the present tense, as in his statement, "Peace be with you! . . . I am sending you." Jesus' words are not simply a promise for the future: "You *will receive* the Holy Spirit [at Pentecost]." Actually, the metaphor of Pentecost as the church's birthday lends itself to viewing this prior impartation of the Spirit in the upper room as its conception. (See appendix C, "The Impartation of the Spirit in the Gospel of John.")

2. Pentecostal. This view recognizes in Acts 2 the Holy Spirit's empowerment for prophetic ministry foretold by Joel, promised by Jesus and explained by Peter. But it goes a step further in making Spirit baptism a definitive second experience distinct from and subsequent to conversion—a model for all believers. While the Holy Spirit baptizes a person into Christ at conversion (1 Cor 12:13), Christ later baptizes the believer into the Spirit. In Pentecostal theology, speaking in tongues is required as the initial physical evidence of this second experience.[9]

This interpretation also has several weaknesses. First, although baptism in the Spirit at Pentecost is a pouring out, filling, clothing with power, there is no ground for interpreting that experience as a definitive second stage in the disciples' spiritual pilgrimage. Luke is not writing spiritual biographies of early Christian leaders; his theme is the church's empowerment to fulfill its worldwide mission. The disciples are repeatedly "filled with the Spirit" as occasion requires (as in Acts 4:8, 31). Both the standard evangelical and Pentecostal views make the mistake of importing into Acts 2 an argument foreign to the intent of the author. Luke does not relate the Pentecostal experience to a stage of *salvation,* whether first or second, but to *service,* prophetic witness to the risen Lord.

Second, speaking in tongues was not an evidence of the disciples' individual spiritual maturity, but a means of communicating in the pilgrims' own languages the good news of Jesus Christ. The Spirit's timetable was not personal but historical—the full arrival of the messianic age. Furthermore, the apostle Paul's teaching on tongues (1 Cor 14) does not link this gift to the Christian's inner experience but to the needs of the body of Christ.

Third, Jesus' first disciples cannot serve in every respect as models for subsequent believers. Born and raised under the Old Covenant, they grew in knowledge and faith during the three years of their Lord's public ministry. Only after his resurrection did they understand the meaning of his death, and not until Pentecost did they publicly proclaim the New Covenant. Yet in one respect the disciples present a model for today: *Repeated filling with the Holy Spirit to empower witness and service should be normative for all Christians.*

3. Charismatic. At first, renewal groups within the mainline denominations received most of their encouragement from Pentecostals, especially the Full Gospel Business Men's Fellowship International. So naturally they adopted the Pentecostal interpretation of baptism in the Spirit. Soon, however, theologians in both the Protestant and Roman Catholic churches began to reinterpret this experience within their own theological structures. Most of them accepted a manifestation of the full range of spiritual gifts, but not the Pentecostal doctrine of a second experience evidenced by speaking in tongues.

There has been widespread recognition that *baptism* is a flexible metaphor, not a technical term. "So long as we recognize conversion as truly a baptism in the Spirit, there is no reason why we cannot use 'baptism' to refer to subsequent fillings of the Spirit as well."[10] (See appendix B.)

A model of Spirit baptism that seems most fruitful sees it as "the charismatic dimension of normal Christian life."[11] It is an *experiential faith* element of all forms of vital Christianity that expresses itself in worship, prayer, meditation on Scripture, fellowship, witness, acts of compassion and the like. It includes the whole range of spiritual gifts as well as special ministries mentioned in the New Testament. *In this sense every Christian is, and should be increasingly, charismatic as the church strives toward expressing the full life in the Spirit.*

Christian Community

This model is evident in Luke's first picture of the church in Acts 2:42-47. Here we see the essential characteristics and activities of the early Christian community.

One feature is clear. There were no "lone ranger" Christians; people didn't just drift into this community and show up at services as long as they "felt their needs were being met." Individual repentance and faith were accompanied by baptism, a visible initiation into the community for Christian life and service.

These Christians "devoted themselves to the apostles' teaching and to the fellowship, to the breaking of bread and to prayer" (2:42). Members recognized the authority of the apostles. They had much to learn from these men who had lived and worked with Jesus for three years, and who would be further taught by the Spirit as he had promised (Jn 14:26). The believers were also devoted to each other in a close fellowship *(koinōnia)*. Their worship found expression in the Lord's Supper and the prayers (Acts 3:1).

The community also had a deep social concern. "All the believers were together and had everything in common. Selling their possessions and goods, they gave to anyone as he had need" (2:44-45). Pooling of property demonstrated their concern for physical need, following the example of their Lord, who not only preached but also healed, who provided bread for a hungry crowd and wine for a wedding feast.

As devout Jews, the believers followed their familiar forms of worship. "Every day they continued to meet together in the temple courts" (2:46). They also enjoyed each other's company in a context larger than their "religious" activities: "They broke bread in their homes and ate together with glad and sincere hearts, praising God and enjoying the favor of all the people. And the Lord added to their number daily those who were being saved" (2:46-47). Such was the character and activity of the first Christian community, guided and empowered by the Holy Spirit.

A Growing Church

Before his ascension Jesus promised the disciples an empowerment by the Holy Spirit to be his witnesses "in Jerusalem, and in all Judea and Samaria, and to the ends of the earth" (Acts 1:8). Luke highlights major geographical and ethnic breakthroughs with an account of the Spirit's activity as he *came on* believers to empower prophetic ministry.

1. Judea and Samaria. Soon a great persecution forced many believers to flee throughout Judea and even to much-despised Samaria, where the people's Jewish ancestors had intermarried with Gentiles. (The Jews looked down on the Samaritans, whom they considered schismatics.) Philip became a pioneer evangelist to a city in Samaria where crowds received his ministry with joy. Many believed his message of "the kingdom of God and the name of Jesus Christ" and were baptized (Acts 8:12).

When the apostles in Jerusalem heard that Samaritans had accepted the word of God, they sent Peter and John to investigate. Upon their arrival these apostles prayed that the believers "might receive the Holy Spirit, because the Holy Spirit had not yet come upon any of them. . . . Peter and John placed their hands on them, and they received the Holy Spirit" (8:15-17). Although speaking in tongues is not explicitly mentioned, the result must have been remarkable, since Simon the sorcerer sought to buy this power for his own use (8:18-24).

The fact that the Spirit came upon the Samaritans through this laying on of hands had a double significance for the church's expansion. First, the Samaritans acknowledged the authority of the Jerusalem church. Second, this event provided evidence to Peter and John that the Samaritans were not second-class citizens in the church; like the Christians in Jerusalem, they were empowered as partners in the mission of the church task. The visit by Peter and John helped prevent the formation of two independent churches on opposite sides of a "Samaritan Curtain."

2. The Gentile world. Soon the time came for the gospel to bridge the gulf between Jews and Gentiles. God had prepared a bridgehead on the other side in the life of a Roman army officer. Cornelius, a centurion in the Italian Regiment, with all his family was devout and God-fearing; he prayed regularly and gave generously to the needy. He sent for Peter, who was also being prepared to overcome his prejudice and was led by the Spirit to the Roman home (10:1-26). There he preached the good news about Jesus Christ, "the Lord of all." His witness had much the same content as at Pentecost: the ministry, death and resurrection of Jesus of Nazareth, whom God anointed with the Holy Spirit and power.

When Peter declared, "Everyone who believes in him receives forgiveness of sins through his name," a dramatic event occurred. "The Holy Spirit came on all who heard the message. The circumcised believers who had come with Peter were astonished that the gift of the Holy Spirit had been poured out even on the Gentiles. For they heard them speaking in tongues and praising God" (10:44-46). On the basis of this evidence Peter immediately baptized the new believers in the name of Jesus Christ. Like the Samaritans, the Gentile believers would be full-fledged citizens of Christ's kingdom.

3. Disciples of John the Baptist. Until now Peter, based in Jerusalem, had led the church's expanding mission. After his conversion, Saul of Tarsus—who became known as Paul—arrived in Antioch to assume missionary leadership. While Jerusalem remained the seat of apostolic authority, Antioch became the primary base of operations for the mission into Europe.

On a visit to the city of Ephesus, Paul encountered twelve disciples of John the Baptist who had not heard about the Holy Spirit. The apostle baptized him in the name of Jesus Christ and placed his hands on them. "The Holy Spirit came upon them, and they spoke in tongues and prophesied" (19:6).

This event marked another decisive moment in missionary history. Ephesus was soon to be a new center of the Gentile mission. Luke's historical perspective draws a parallel between the ministries of Peter and Paul. At Samaria the new Christians were linked to the church in Jerusalem through Peter and John; at Ephesus the Spirit came upon John's disciples through Paul. In this way the last special group to receive the gospel was linked to the apostolic and missionary task of the Christian church.

Although this is the last dramatic outpouring of the Holy Spirit recorded by Luke, he continues to mention the Spirit's activity through the end of Acts. Also called the Spirit of Jesus, the Holy Spirit directs Paul where to preach (16:6-7), appoints overseers of the flock (20:28) and foretells Paul's arrest in Jerusalem and imprisonment by the Gentiles (21:11). From beginning to end, Luke's narrative highlights the Spirit's activities to direct and empower the mission of the church.

Luke: Historian and Theologian

This brief summary shows that the author's narrative is more than descriptive. His purpose is to teach the empowering dimension of the Holy Spirit's activity, beginning at Pentecost in the church's expansion throughout the Roman Empire. Luke says that the Spirit "fell on" (a term used three times), "came upon" (twice) or was "poured out" (twice) on the believers. As a result, they "received" (twice) or were "filled with" (five times) the Spirit. This action produced observable or audible results: speaking in tongues (three times), healing (three times), preaching (twice), witness with power (once). These manifestations stirred praise, strengthened the community and empowered its service.

In Acts the presence of the Spirit is evidenced in a visible, dynamic and often dramatic way. It is "charismatic" in the sense of directly manifesting the Spirit's power. The result is prophetic in the broad sense of praise and worship, witness and preaching. Luke's dynamic terminology demonstrates that when the Spirit is present something happens. People know that God is in their midst.

Luke also describes the Spirit's activity in another way. Four times he speaks of individuals as "full of" the Spirit with no specific action, but with the evidence of a certain quality or characteristic. For example, "Jesus, full of the Holy Spirit, returned from the Jordan and was led by the Spirit in the desert" (Lk 4:1). In the Christian community seven men "full of the Spirit and wisdom" were selected to supervise a controversial food distribution (Acts 6:3). Whether in witness to the world or service to the community, the believers depended on the Spirit for guidance and power.

In Acts the primary significance of the Spirit's activity is historical and prophetic. Initial *and repeated* filling with the Spirit empowers the church's ministry. We now turn to the writing of the apostle Paul for further teaching on the empowering dimension of the Holy Spirit's activity through what he calls spiritual gifts.

4 Gifts of the Spirit

*H*ow recently have you read an article or heard a sermon on "discovering your spiritual gifts"? Do you ever wonder what these gifts really are, how they relate to natural abilities and where they fit into your Christian life? What about present-day manifestations of so-called "supernatural" gifts of healing, prophecy and tongues—ardently advocated and vigorously attacked?

In this chapter we will discover answers to these questions in three basic New Testament passages. In 1 Corinthians 12, Romans 12 and Ephesians 4, Paul spells out and illustrates the nature and purpose of spiritual gifts (charisms). First we will consider their general characteristics and the ways they are listed; we will then consider specific gifts that are frequently misunderstood. Chapter five will review the role of spiritual gifts in church history and their significance today.

What Are Spiritual Gifts?

On his second missionary journey (A.D. 49-52) Paul planted a church in the influential city of Corinth. Three years later he received distressing reports of serious problems in the young church. The apostle then wrote a lengthy letter of encouragement, rebuke and instruction that reveals a paradoxical situation. In Christ the Corinthian Christians have been "enriched in every way. . . . Therefore [they] do not lack any spiritual gift" (1 Cor 1:5, 7). Yet at the same time the church suffers from quarreling and divisions, spiritual pride, unjudged sexual immorality, lawsuits against each other and disorder at the Lord's Supper. After dealing with these sins, Paul gives extended teaching on the purpose and practice of gifts and fruit of the Holy Spirit in chapters 12 to 14.

Chapter 12 has four main divisions: the nature of spiritual gifts, a list of nine charisms, the body and its members, and a list of ministries and gifts. Paul's opening statement declares his purpose: "Now about spiritual gifts, brothers, I do not want you to be ignorant" (v. 1). The Greek word *pneumatikoi* literally means "spirituals" and can be translated either "spiritual gifts" or "those who manifest spiritual gifts." At the outset Paul makes it clear that these are activities initiated by the Holy Spirit, not simply natural talents or abilities.

The apostle Paul begins his discussion of the nature of spiritual gifts by pointing out that they *focus on Christ*. He reminds the Corinthians of their former pagan religion in which they were *forcibly influenced* by demonic powers, in contrast to their new life in Christ in which they are now *led* by the Spirit. Far from violating people (as did the evil spirits in the Gospel records), the Holy Spirit frees them to develop their potential. Also, the Spirit never leads anyone to say "Jesus be cursed." Rather, it is he who enables a person to make the true confession of Christian faith: "Jesus is Lord" (12:3). So spiritual gifts can be properly exercised only as an expression of a personal relationship with the Lord Jesus Christ brought about by the Holy Spirit.

The apostle now explains three fundamental characteristics of spiritual gifts: their unity in diversity, manifestations of the Spirit and their role within the body of Christ.

First, the diverse spiritual gifts have the same source: "There are different kinds of gifts, but the same Spirit. There are different kinds of service, but the same Lord. There are different kinds of working, but the same God works all of them in all" (12:4-6). The terms used by Paul tell us much about the nature and purpose of these gifts. There are "different kinds" *(diaireseis)*, which can also refer to distribution (v. 11). "Spiritual gift" *(charisma)*, also called "charism," is a gift of divine grace. "Service" *(diakonia)* indicates their purpose, for the benefit of the church. "Working" *(energēma)* conveys the idea of power to produce results.

Underlying a remarkable diversity is an essential unity, because the same Spirit, the same Lord and the same God are distributing the different kinds of gifts. The trinitarian model is reflected in the three basic passages. Here they are gifts of the Spirit; in Romans 12:3 they are called gifts from God; in Ephesians 4:1 the giver is Christ.

Second, Paul continues with comments on charisms that shed additional light on their nature, purpose and occurrence. "Now to each one the manifestation of the Spirit is given for the common good. . . . All these are the work of one and the same Spirit, and he gives them to each one, just as he determines" (vv. 7, 11).

The word *phanerōsis* ("manifestation") is especially significant, as it conveys the idea of disclosure or announcement. For example, a ship's manifest is a visible inventory of the unseen cargo deep in the hold. In the only other New Testament occurrence of this term, Paul speaks of commending himself by his "open statement" (2 Cor 4:2 RSV) of the truth. A spiritual gift, then, is a sign of the presence and power of the Holy Spirit that belongs to the new creation.

This manifestation is *given* (literally, "keeps on being given"), not once and for all but repeatedly. Paul urges believers to keep on being filled with the Spirit (Eph 5:18). These gifts are meant for the *common good,* not to promote individual status. And they are for *all;* three times Paul makes it clear that each believer participates (1 Cor 12:6-7, 11). As Joel promised and Peter preached, the Spirit is poured out on young and old, men and women, slave and free. No one has all the gifts, and none are left out. Paul teaches that spiritual gifts are not limited to office or position in the church—a tradition that developed in later centuries and was perpetuated by much of the Reformation.

Finally, while neglecting no one, the Spirit distributes the gifts *as he determines.* It is not for the Christian either to demand or to disparage certain gifts—as is frequently done today—according to what is considered important or unacceptable. The sovereign Lord through the Spirit will equip his church for its worship, service and witness in his own way.

One Body, Many Members

Third, Paul emphasizes the role of spiritual gifts within the congregation. In the remainder of 1 Corinthians 12, Romans 12 and Ephesians 4 he presents the model of the human body to illustrate the *unity* of the Christian community underlying the *diversity* of its members. "For we were all baptized [in] one Spirit into one body—whether Jews or Greeks, slave or free—and we were all given the one Spirit to drink" (1 Cor 12:13).

This is Paul's only use of the phrase "baptize in the Spirit." The Corinthians had been baptized *with/in* the Holy Spirit. In this context the phrase probably has a double connotation of "being initiated into" and "being overwhelmed by."[1] Paul affirms that Christians are in the Spirit and the Spirit is in Christians, parallel to our being in Christ and Christ being in us (2 Cor 5:17; Col 1:27). In both phrases ("baptized in the Spirit" and "given one Spirit to drink") the tense of the verb indicates a single past experience.[2] But whatever the precise meaning of these phrases, Paul's main point is clear: *all* the Corinthian believers, regardless of national or social status, spiritual maturity or diversity of gifts, have been incorporated into the one body of Christ; *there are no first- and second-class Christians.*

With the unity of the body affirmed, Paul makes four observations about its members in 1 Corinthians 12. First, there is variety: "Now the body is not made up of one part but of many" (v. 14). The foot is needed as well as the hand, the ear as well as the eye, if the body is to exercise its several functions.

Second, the design is of God, who "has arranged the parts in the body, every one of them, just as he wanted them to be" (v. 18). Any complaints about the kind and number of members must be taken up with their Creator!

Third, Paul shows how the members are interdependent, not only in their functions but also in their feelings. In verses 15-20 he encourages members with an "inferiority complex"; in verses 21-24 he rebukes those who feel superior. He is concerned that "there should be no division in the body, but that its parts should have equal concern for each other. If one part suffers, every part suffers with it; if one part is honored, every part rejoices with it" (vv. 25-26). For better or worse, all members are bound together.

Drawing an *analogy* between a social structure and the human body was common in the Greek and Roman world. But Paul considers it a *reality.* "Now you *are* the body of Christ, and each one of you *is* a part of it" (v. 27). Each gift must be understood and appreciated in the context of the body. Perhaps the greatest contribution of the charismatic renewal to the church is a rediscovery not simply of certain long-neglected gifts, but of the reality and necessity of their corporate function within the community.

In Romans 12:4-5 Paul reaffirms briefly the model of the body for understanding how spiritual gifts function. "Just as each of us has one body with many members, and these members do not all have the same function, so in Christ we who are many form one body, and each member belongs to all the others." In Ephesians 4:12 the apostle expresses the same truth with a different emphasis in terms of gifted individuals: "[they] prepare God's people for works of service, so that the body of Christ may be built up."

Lists of Spiritual Gifts

All told, the New Testament has nine lists of spiritual gifts. They are incorporated in appendix D, with a detailed analysis of their characteristics. Before considering significant differences among the four major lists, we need to notice four features they have in common.

First, the lists are *representative,* a random sample, rather than exhaustive. Each is different and reflects the concern of the author at that point. For example, since Paul's letter to Corinth deals with problems in that church, his two major lists are oriented in that direction. Appendix D shows that there is considerable overlap among the lists.

Second, attempts to determine the value or rank of spiritual gifts from their *order of appearance* are futile at best, biased at worst. Inferences of relative value are not valid unless it is the author's clear intent to rank the items in order of importance. Sometimes the *last* word in a sentence is the most important. Furthermore, Paul emphasizes that, as with the parts of the body, no one gift is most important for every occasion. Nevertheless, some scholars who disparage speaking in tongues take satisfaction in pointing out that since Paul lists this gift last in 1 Corinthians 12:28, it must be valued least. Ironically, those scholars do not consistently apply their principle to the last gifts in two other major listings: in Romans 12:8, "showing mercy" (a prime characteristic of our God) and in Ephesians 4:11, "teachers" (their own profession). Too often biblical interpretation is influenced by "whose ox is being gored."

Third, Paul doesn't rigorously *classify* these gifts. They sometimes overlap or occur together; for example, a gift of specific faith may involve a healing. Furthermore, the apostle makes no distinction between what we call "natural" and "supernatural."³ Nor does he differentiate between our categories of temporary and permanent, normal and abnormal, which are sometimes imposed on the texts. Paul's one concern is that *every gift should be used as needed* to strengthen and empower the body of Christ in its worship, witness and service.

Fourth, we should recognize that spiritual gifts *are not* themselves *natural abilities.* Nor do all of them depend on such talents for their manifestation, even though some charisms utilize them. Failing to understand this distinction, some translators have gratuitously added to the text words of their own to convey a meaning that Paul did not intend. For example, some translations change Paul's simple "message of wisdom" in 1 Corinthians 12:8 to "the ability to speak with wisdom," as if this gift depended on a person's intellectual capacity. In the following chapter we will consider the relationships among spiritual gifts, abilities and ministries. Next, however, certain charisms in the four major lists need to be highlighted.

1 Corinthians 12:8-10
Paul gives a list of nine charisms as follows.

To one there is given through the Spirit the message of wisdom, to another the message of knowledge by means of the same Spirit, to another faith by the same Spirit, to another gifts of healing[s] by that one Spirit, to another miraculous powers [workings of miracles], to another prophecy, to another distinguishing between spirits, to another speaking in different kinds of tongues, and to still another the interpretation of tongues.

Six of the nine spiritual gifts in this list—prophecy and discernment, tongues and interpretation, healings and miracles—will be examined in chapters six through ten of this book. Here let us briefly consider wisdom, knowledge and faith.

1. Message of wisdom. In 1 Corinthians Paul uses the words *sophia* ("wisdom") and *sophos* ("wise") twenty-eight times, with all but two of the occurrences in the first three chapters. Worldly wisdom depends on human ideas and eloquence (1:17, 20; 2:1, 4). But God's wisdom is revealed in Jesus Christ (1:24, 30). Against the philosophy of this world Paul sets the crucified Christ (1:23); against this world's eloquent words he sets the power of the Spirit (1:24; 2:4).

What, then, is a "message of wisdom"? In general usage today wisdom denotes good judgment based on knowledge, a wise plan or course of action. As a spiritual gift the message would be wise from God's and not just a human perspective. Although the precise content of a "message of wisdom" for the church today is debatable, its essential characteristic as a spiritual gift should be recognized. British theologian James Dunn notes, "The *charisma* of God is the particular word given to a particular instance and is 'mine' only in the act and moment of uttering it."⁴ The gift is in the giving and receiving, as is evident in the following story.

The elders of Grace Presbyterian Church were wrestling with the problem of too little space for a rapidly growing congregation. It did not seem possible to reschedule present services and programs yet again, much less add new ones. Should they add a larger sanctuary to the present building or purchase adjacent property for an entirely new one? Time and again, extended discussion of the pros and cons of each alternative led only to an impasse.

As the session waited on God in prayer for guidance, a younger member unexpectedly spoke up. "I believe God is challenging our assumption that the physical plant should be enlarged to accommodate our growing congregation at this location. So let's rent the high-school auditorium for Sunday services to make room here for the growing church school, and pray about some of our families moving out to start a new church in the developing north side of town." After a few minutes of silence the others nodded in agreement, convinced that this was indeed direction from the Lord through the Holy Spirit.

2. Message of knowledge. Paul's use of *gnōsis* ("knowledge") in this letter is less clear. At times it seems synonymous with wisdom. But it also denotes information or facts: "This is what we speak, not in words taught us by human wisdom but in words taught by the Spirit, expressing spiritual truths in spiritual words" (2:13). Knowledge, acquaintance with the facts, provides a basis for wise judgment or action.

Some Corinthians evidently prided themselves on their gift of knowledge. In a controversy about food consecrated to heathen deities, they claimed special knowledge to justify their behavior (1 Cor 8). But since this gift was exercised without the fruit of the Spirit, Paul reminds them, "Knowledge puffs up, but love builds up" (8:1). At the outset of his letter he deals at length with the consequences of misusing gifts of wisdom and knowledge.

The content of a "message of knowledge" today is also debated. In the charismatic renewal the message or "word" of knowledge is viewed as information, not otherwise available, imparted by the Holy Spirit. The traditional view counters that the information must already be available in Scripture and is simply remembered or applied. This question, related to the gift of prophecy, is considered in chapter six of this book. Meanwhile, here is an example of this gift in the ministry of inner healing.

A pastor had spent many hours with a man in his congregation who had ongoing problems that he was unable to resolve. The usual questions about childhood experiences, his marriage, the situation at work produced nothing significant. As the counseling seemed stalled at a dead end, the pastor unexpectedly had the mental picture of a word that had not occurred to him: *homosexual.* When asked whether he had a problem in this area, the man turned white as a sheet, broke down and poured out the story of his defeat and despair. That opened the door to a path of therapy and recovery.

3. Faith. From Genesis to Revelation the Bible emphasizes the importance of faith. This word, like some others in this list of gifts, has several different meanings. Saving faith is the positive response to God's offer of salvation through which the sinner is justified and receives the Spirit (Rom 5:1; Gal 3:2). Since this faith is the means by which all become Christians, it is not the same as the special gift mentioned here. Nor is this faith the biblical truth Paul refers to in Jude 3: "the faith that was once for all entrusted to the saints." Rather, the gift of faith, exercised by some members of the body, is a conviction that God will act decisively in a specific occasion. The exercise of this faith—the kind that can "move mountains" (1 Cor 13:2)—is sometimes related to other gifts such as knowledge and healing.

A missionary in Vietnam was concerned about the need of young churches in his area for Bibles and other literature to foster their spiritual growth. He talked with a regional customs official who was vigorously enforcing the policy against importing such literature, but it was to no avail. The door was shut and locked. As the missionary was praying that God would change the official's mind, he suddenly became convinced that it would happen. Such conviction was a new experience for him. In faith he made arrangements for overseas funding and for a large quantity of literature to be sent to him, confident that it would not be confiscated. When the shipment arrived in customs, the missionary opened it in the presence of the official, who waved it through without a word.

1 Corinthians 12:28

Paul concludes this chapter with a list of eight gifts.

> And in the church God has appointed first of all apostles, second prophets, third teachers, then [workers of] miracles, also [those having] gifts of heal-ing, [those able to] help others, [those with gifts of] administration, and

[those speaking in] different kinds of tongues.

The words in brackets were gratuitously added to the text by the NIV translators and retained in the 1984 edition. It is indeed clear that the first three are *persons,* or "gifted individuals," like those listed in Ephesians 4:11. But the remaining five are not persons; they are *actions* or *occurrences.* The Greek text simply reads: "then miracles, then gifts of healing, helps, administration, kinds of tongues." This random sample consists of charisms (not people) found earlier in the 12:8-10 list and the one in Romans 12:6-8.

The distinction between gifted individuals and charisms is indicated by Paul's rhetorical questions in the next verse. For the first three he asks, "*Are* all apostles? *Are* all prophets? *Are* all teachers?" For the five charisms, "*Do* all work miracles? *Do* all have gifts of healing? *Do* all speak in tongues? *Do* all interpret?" It is also significant that Paul identifies as "first," "second" and "third" only the three kinds of gifted individuals for their importance in the church; he does not rank the five charisms that follow. *No one spiritual gift is most important for all occasions; its value at a given time is determined by its usefulness to meet a specific need.*

Chapter 12 concludes with two statements in verse 31, one looking back at the teaching about spiritual gifts, the other introducing the way they are to be exercised. Most versions translate the first in the imperative as a command: "Eagerly desire the greater gifts." This interpretation, however, contradicts Paul's teaching that the Corinthians should be content with whatever gifts the Spirit manifests without feeling superior or inferior. Actually, the form of the Greek word *zēloute* ("desire") in this verse can also be translated in the indicative as a description of what is already happening: "You are eagerly desiring [what you consider] the greater gifts." This reading fits the context of what the Corinthians were doing and why they had fallen into difficulties. It has the added grace of leading to Paul's description of the right way to use spiritual gifts.

The second half of verse 31 is commonly mistranslated "And now I will show you the most excellent way," as if love, a fruit of the Spirit, is more important than gifts of the Spirit. A correct translation of *kath' hyperbolēn* is "according to excellence." Chapter 13 teaches that without the excellent way of love all charisms are valueless. The apostle doesn't offer a choice between spiritual gifts and fruit; both are vital to the Christian life.

Romans 12:6-8

In his letter to the church in Rome, written in the spring of A.D. 57, Paul gives another list of spiritual gifts in the context of serving God. The apostle calls for sacrificial living, renewal of the mind and discovery of God's will. He urges the Roman Christians not to think more highly of themselves than they ought, but rather with sober judgment, "in accordance with the measure of faith God has given you (v. 3).

> And having different gifts [charismata] according to the grace [charis] given to us, whether prophecy, according to the proportion of the faith; or serving, in the serving; or the [one] teaching, in the teaching; or the [one] encouraging, in the encouragement; the [one] sharing, with generosity; the [one] leading, in diligence; the [one] showing mercy, in cheerfulness. (my literal translation)

Some modern translations add words to the text to make it more readable in English. For example, verse 6 becomes "If a man's gift is prophesying, let him use it in proportion to his faith" (NIV). Although this motivation is commendable, here it has two unfortunate results. It tends to reaffirm the prevalent view of spiritual gifts as personal possessions. It also unnecessarily reinforces a still-prevalent chauvinism by adding masculine pronouns to the inspired text. (On that score verse 6 could better be translated "If anyone's gift is prophesying, let it be used in proportion to faith.")

As noted above, chapter six of this book takes up the gift of prophecy. The other six charisms here are often mistakenly considered "natural," as opposed to the "supernatural" gifts of prophecy, healing and tongues. So we need to reaffirm that all charisms, regardless of the categories we may impose on them, are specific expressions of grace—"new creation" gifts of God for the church.

Service in the New Testament covers a variety of practical ministrations, such as relief for the poor. Although something so mundane as helping with an inner-city soup kitchen or setting up rooms for Sunday-school classes doesn't produce a bestseller on spiritual gifts, it is no less a manifestation of the Holy Spirit when motivated by the love of Christ for human needs. *Teaching,* in the tradition of the rabbis, explains and applies truths of revelation already given in Scripture. *Encouraging* others in difficulty appeals to both the heart and the will, expressing love and offering hope.

With the last three gifts Paul calls for right attitudes: *sharing* generously, *leading* diligently and *showing mercy* cheerfully. Since some of these charisms overlap, we should resist the temptation to systematize them in separate categories.

None of the nine charisms in 1 Corinthians 12 requires the possession of a specific ability or talent for its manifestation. Some of those listed here, however, such as certain kinds of service, teaching and leadership, can make use of specific abilities or skills.

Immediately following the list, Paul commands: "Love must be sincere. . . . Be devoted to one another in brotherly love. Honor one another above yourselves" (vv. 9-10). Charisms are to be exercised in love; the gifts and fruit of the Spirit always belong together. Use of spiritual gifts without love can be an ego trip; professed love that disparages these gifts fails to strengthen the body of Christ.

Ephesians 4:11-13

For three years Paul had made the influential city of Ephesus (in what is now Turkey) a center for evangelism. His letter was probably written from prison in Rome about A.D. 60. Since it does not have the usual personal greetings and comment on specific issues, Ephesians seems to be a circular letter also intended for other churches.

A list of gifts appears in chapter 4, where the apostle is urging Christians to live a life worthy of their calling. They are to bear with one another in love and keep the unity of the Spirit through the bond of peace (vv. 1-3).

In this passage, unlike those we studied above, Christ is specified as the giver: "But grace *[charis]* was given to each of us according to the measure of Christ's gift *[dōrea]*" (v. 7 RSV). He is pictured as the victorious king of Psalm 68:18 in a triumphal procession. From that supreme position he sends his gifts.

It was he who gave some to be apostles, some to be prophets, some to be evangelists, and some to be pastors and teachers, to prepare God's people for works of service, so that the body of Christ may be built up until we all reach unity in the faith and in the knowledge of the Son of God and become mature, attaining to the whole measure of the fullness of Christ.

This list has two other significant differences from those we have already considered. The word Paul uses is not *charisma* ("spiritual gift") but the more general *dōrea* ("gift, bounty"). Furthermore, in this list the gifts are people—individuals with specific ministries. These differences are often overlooked in a "nose count" of spiritual gifts that lumps all of the lists together.

What is the function of each person? In answering that question we must remain open to the possibility that a term can have more than one meaning or function. The Greek word *apostolos* is also translated "representative" (2 Cor 8:23) and "messenger" (Phil 2:25)—one who speaks with the authority of the sender. The term *apostle* is applied to several different groups in the New Testament.[5]

1. Jesus' twelve disciples are called apostles (Mt 10:2). The Twelve and Paul were "apostles of Christ" in a special sense. Earlier in Ephesians Paul declares that the church is "built on the foundation of the apostles and prophets, with Christ Jesus himself as the chief cornerstone" (2:20; see also 3:5).

2. A wider group, including the Twelve, were those who had seen the risen Lord and so were included in Paul's list of credible witnesses to the gospel message (1 Cor 15:7).

3. In a broader sense some church planters and delegates were called "apostles of the churches" (see 2 Cor 8:23). Among them were Paul's coworkers Barnabas (Acts 14:4) and Epaphroditus (Phil 2:25), and Andronicus and Junias in Rome (Rom 16:7). Another group, including Timothy and Titus, performed these ministries but are not expressly called "apostles."

Are there apostles today? The answer is both no and yes. Since the apostles in the first two categories were witnesses of the resurrection and formed the foundation of the church, their ministry was a first-generation phenomenon that was not repeated. The third category, however, has been needed in every generation—messengers of Christ attested by the Holy Spirit and recognized by the church. (A related question about prophets will be addressed in chapter six.)

An *evangelist* is one who presents the gospel. All Christians are expected to be witnesses, telling the good news of Christ in their lives. But an evangelist is specially used by the Holy Spirit to bring people to faith in Christ as their Lord and Savior.

A *pastor* is a shepherd looking after the sheep. This metaphor is spelled out by Peter to church elders: "Be shepherds of God's flock that is under your care . . . not greedy for money, but eager to serve; not lording it over those entrusted to you, but being examples to the flock" (1 Pet 5:2-3). When the Chief Shepherd appears, they will receive their reward. A *teacher* opens up the Scriptures and applies them to daily life. It has been debated whether these gifts constitute one or two ministries. The grammatical construction indicates that if not combined, they are at least related in the nurture of the church.

The order in which these gifted individuals are listed seems to follow a developmental pattern: apostles and prophets establish the church; evangelists bring in new members; pastors and teachers guide and instruct. Note again that the fact that teachers are last doesn't mean they are of least importance; these ministries mutually support each other.

Some translations erroneously state that these few individuals have a three-fold function on behalf of their congregation: "*for* the equipment of the saints, *for* the work of ministry, *for* building up the body of Christ" (see Eph 4:12). The NIV and NRSV, however, correctly show that the function of these gifted individuals is "to prepare God's people for works of service, so that the body of Christ may be built up." Building takes place not by just a few "ministers" in the church but through all the members as they manifest a variety of spiritual gifts in worship, service and witness.

A current example is evident in the Stephen Ministries program that operates in hundreds of churches across the country. Instead of everyone in the congregation looking to the clergy for counsel, needy members are served by a group of laypeople trained in pastoral care and available to meet with them regularly. As a result, a variety of experiences and backgrounds are matched up with those who most need that kind of counsel. Through these lay pastors the Holy Spirit manifests a variety of spiritual gifts as the need arises.

Paul ends this section stressing the importance of love. "Speaking the truth in love . . . the whole body . . . grows and builds itself up in love, as each part does its work" (vv. 15-16). Truth without love can be brutal; love without truth is sentimental. Genuine love conveys the truth in a sensitive, constructive way. This admonition turns our attention to the fruits of the Spirit, the most important of which is love.

Spiritual Gifts and Church Governance

The New Testament also makes provision for governance of the local congregation. The first deacons, in Acts 6:1-6, were required to be "full of the Spirit and wisdom." In 1 Timothy 3:1-13 and 5:17-20 and Titus 1:5-9 the apostle Paul spells out the qualifications and activities of overseers *(episkopoi)*, elders *(presbuteroi)* and deacons *(diakonoi)*. As noted above, Peter teaches how elders as shepherds and overseers are to serve the flock, "not lording it over" them (1 Pet 5:1-4). Such responsibility for governance is what today we call "office" or "ministry" (with a different meaning from the ministry of spiritual gifts by all members of the congregation).

German theologian Arnold Bittlinger, an early leader in the charismatic renewal, points out two misunderstandings. As time went on, the spiritual gifts were increasingly left to officers in the church. Their manifestation by "non-official" church members receded more and more into the background. (This process will be traced in chapter five.) The charismatic renewal has challenged this unbiblical concept of the ecclesiastical ministry as a position of power. The New Testament model of ministry by all believers has been increasingly recognized and practiced. But in some quarters the pendulum has swung to the other extreme: the ministry of governance is displaced by charisms.

Bittlinger observes that just as a car needs a steering wheel to direct it, the church requires gifted individuals for special ministries. But a car also needs a motor for power; likewise, the church must have the dynamic of the Holy Spirit manifesting diverse spiritual gifts through all the members. A car with a motor but no steering wheel is dangerous, as church history has shown on many occasions when uncontrolled charismata caused havoc. No wonder that the steering wheel has gained such prominence. "To be sure, it is essentially less dangerous for a car to have a steering wheel without a motor. One can steer in utmost peace without causing any kind of havoc—but at the same time the car does not move! Motor and steering wheel belong together."[6]

Filled with the Spirit

We have seen how Luke consistently uses the phrase *filled with the Spirit* for the empowering action of the Holy Spirit in prophecy, preaching and healing. Paul uses it only once:

> Be filled with the Spirit. Speak to one another with psalms, hymns and spiritual songs. Sing and make music in your heart to the Lord, always giving thanks to God the Father for everything, in the name of our Lord Jesus Christ. (Eph 5:18-20)

To what extent do the context and usage of this phrase here indicate the same meaning as Luke's? How does "filled with the Spirit" relate to spiritual gifts?

The form of the verb *be filled* is significant in several respects. First, it is a command; this action for Christians is not optional but imperative for all. Second, it is in the continuous present tense and should be translated as "keep on being filled." Paul has in mind not a once-for-all event but a repeated experience. Third, the verb is passive; while the believer is responsible to be open, it is the Holy Spirit himself who fills and manifests his power.

Fourth, the verb is in the plural, addressed mainly to the Christian fellowship. So it is not surprising that the immediate consequences are corporate: "Speak to one another . . . Sing and make music . . . always giving thanks to God." The meaning of the phrase "speak to one another" is illuminated by the parallel passage in Colossians 3:16: "Let the word of Christ dwell in you richly as you teach and admonish one another with all wisdom, and as you sing psalms, hymns and spiritual songs with gratitude in your hearts to God." One result of being filled with the Spirit is the strengthening of the body of Christ through spiritual gifts such as teaching, wisdom and encouragement.

Another result is singing and making music wholeheartedly to the Lord. The Holy Spirit glorifies the Lord Jesus by inspiring the praise of his people. The verb *psallō* ("making melody") may be taken as singing psalms, its meaning in 1 Corinthians 14:15 and James 5:13. Commenting on Ephesians 5:19-20, Greek scholar F. F. Bruce writes: "If we are to distinguish between the three kinds of musical composition, 'psalms' may refer to the Old Testament Psalter; . . . 'hymns' may denote Christian canticles such as have been recognized in several places in the New Testament (including verse 14 above); 'spiritual songs' may be unpremeditated words singing 'in the Spirit,' voicing praise and holy aspirations."[7] (The last is also mentioned by Paul in 1 Corinthians 14:15.)

Filling with the Spirit also results in giving thanks to God for everything in the name of Christ. To do this in difficult circumstances for which we are not naturally thankful requires the power of the Spirit.

It is evident that Paul here uses Luke's phrase *filled with the Spirit* as empowerment for the manifestation of spiritual gifts. Both authors teach the empowering dimension of the Holy Spirit's activity for the worship, service and witness of the church, but from different perspectives. Luke's purpose as a historian is to emphasize the outward dimension of the Spirit's activity for inauguration of the messianic age and growth of the church. Paul's teaching on spiritual gifts focuses inwardly on the Spirit's empowerment of the church's worship and service.

Gifts and Fruit of the Spirit

A discussion of spiritual gifts is not complete without a consideration of their relationship to the fruit of the Spirit. Sometimes the differences between gifts and fruit are blurred; at other times one is emphasized at the expense of the other. So we need to examine the basic New Testament teaching about the fruit of the Spirit and how it complements the use of spiritual gifts.

In his letter to the Galatians Paul urges that they live by the Spirit so that they will not gratify the desires of their sinful nature. He identifies fifteen of those actions and attitudes, including sexual immorality and debauchery, idolatry and witchcraft, envy and selfish ambition that leads to discord and factions (5:16, 19-21).

The apostle then contrasts those sins with living by the Spirit. "The fruit of the Spirit is love, joy, peace, patience, kindness, goodness, faithfulness, gentleness and self-control" (vv. 22-23). Foremost is love, which also is cited in proximity to the four lists of charisms we have studied. It appears that there are several main distinctions between the fruit and the gifts of the Spirit.

First is the difference between being and doing, attitudes and actions. The list in Galatians 5 sketches character, the kind of person the Christian is expected to *be* (or become): loving, patient, kind, self-controlled. It is the character of Christ in the pressures of ministry and opposition. The gifts of the Spirit, on the other hand, denote some of what the believer *does* as a member of the body of Christ: serving, healing, contributing, prophesying, teaching, encouraging.

Second, *all* the fruit of the Spirit is meant for *all* members of the body of Christ as they mature in the Christian life. No one should say, "Don't expect me to love or be kind; that isn't my fruit." Spiritual gifts are just the opposite; members of the body manifest *different* charisms as the Holy Spirit determines.

Third, the fruit of the Spirit is for all times and places. But his gifts are for specific times and needs—for example, a word of knowledge or wisdom in a perplexing situation; healing for physical or emotional illness; donation for a financial need; or encouragement for someone during a time of trial.

The apostle neither blurs the distinction nor severs the connection between gifts and fruit; love, joy and peace, for example, do not appear in his lists of charisms. Some Christians emphasize gifts with insufficient concern for fruit. Others claim that the real evidence of the Spirit's filling lies in Christian character. But Paul doesn't offer a choice; both are essential to the church's health and effectiveness.

In the last analysis, the value of all we do depends on our character; apart from right attitudes and motives, even the best actions mean nothing. Love is paramount; without it sacrificial service and spiritual gifts mean nothing. Paul reminds the Galatians, "The entire law is summed up in a single command: 'Love your neighbor as yourself' " (5:14).

The apostle's definitive statement on the gifts and fruit of the Spirit, especially love, appears in 1 Corinthians 13.

If I speak in the tongues of men and of angels, but have not love, I am only a resounding gong or a clanging cymbal. If I have the gift of prophecy and can fathom all mysteries and all knowledge, and if I have a faith that can move mountains, but have not love, I am nothing. If I give all I possess to the poor and surrender my body to the flames, but have not love, I gain nothing. . . . And now these three remain: faith, hope and love. But the greatest of these is love. (vv.1-3, 13)

5 *Where Have All the Charisms Gone?*

H *ow relevant today is the apostle Paul's model of a Christian community?* Should we expect the Holy Spirit to manifest the full range of charisms referred to in Paul's letters to Corinth and Rome? The Pentecostal/charismatic renewal answers yes as participants witness to the occurrence of all these gifts for strengthening and encouraging the body of Christ.

On the other hand, many in Western Protestant churches answer with an unequivocal no. They believe that so-called supernatural gifts of prophecy and knowledge authenticated by miracles, healings and tongues were no longer needed once the New Testament revelation was complete and the church was launched. For example, dispensational scholar Merrill Unger states in his commentary on 1 Corinthians 13: "The question of the permanency of certain gifts is the subject of the chapter, not, as popularly supposed, the topic of love. ... [T]he gifts of prophecy, tongues and knowledge would no longer be needed and no longer manifested when the finished written revelation of God has arrived."[1]

Since all biblical interpreters are influenced to a greater or lesser degree by their culture, theological tradition and personal experience, we need to look at the background of this view. Where did it come from, and what shaped its development? After a brief historical sketch we will evaluate this view in light of the exposition of the spiritual gifts and the Holy Spirit's enabling ministry in the preceding chapter. Then we will deal with the principles and current practice of charismatic renewal.

Historical Perspective

Did in fact the manifestation of certain "extraordinary" spiritual gifts die with the last of the apostles and the closing of the canon of Scripture? Recent studies provide ample historical evidence that such was not the case. Pentecostal scholar Ronald A. N. Kydd has examined documents from the first three centuries. The claim that certain gifts were withdrawn is repudiated by the testimony of several influential teachers from those years. For example, the apologist Justin Martyr in Rome (c. A.D. 100-165) wrote, "For one receives the spirit of understanding, another of counsel, another of strength, another of healing, another of foreknowledge, another of teaching, and another of the fear of God."[2] Irenaeus (c. A.D. 130-200), bishop of Lyons, confirmed this report, describing many spiritual gifts in the church of his day, including prophecy, discernment and healing. He wrote, "Some have foreknowledge of things to be, and visions and prophetic speech, and others cure the sick by the laying on of hands and make them whole, even as we have said, the dead have been raised and remained with us for many years."[3]

Drawing from a variety of sources—bishops and heretics, philosophers, poets and theologians—Kydd concludes that throughout the first two centuries a full range of spiritual gifts was important to the church, which was "strongly charismatic up until A.D. 200."[4]

After that things began to change in the West as increasing formalism quenched the use of spiritual gifts. Nevertheless, Christians were still open to unusual manifestations of God's presence. At the beginning of the third century, for example, the brilliant theologian and apologist Tertullian (c. A.D.

160-220) in Carthage reported witnessing extraordinary gifts of the Spirit, including prophecies and visions. "We also regard the rest of the powers of the Holy Spirit as tools of the Church to whom the Spirit was sent, administering all of the outstandingly impressive gifts to everyone just as the Lord distributes to each."[5] Tertullian vigorously maintained that spiritual gifts constitute the full Christian experience.

(This brilliant theologian was won to Montanism, a reform movement that protested against the religious establishment and combined a desire for return to apostolic purity with a revival of spiritual gifts. The movement produced courageous missionary pioneers and martyrs. But their zeal and enthusiasm provoked a strong reaction by church leaders who attributed the "heresy" of Montanus to preoccupation with miraculous gifts. As a result the church became wary of those manifestations of the Spirit. So, ironically, Montanist excesses served to tighten the very ecclesiastical control against which they were protesting.)

Later in the third century, Presbyter Novatian (d. A.D. 257) in Rome wrote concerning the Holy Spirit: "Indeed this is he who appoints prophets in the church, instructs teachers, directs tongues, brings into being powers and conditions of health, carries on extraordinary works, furnishes discernment of spirits . . . brings together and arranges all other gifts there are of the charismata and by reason of this makes the church of God everywhere perfect in everything and completed."[6]

Yet the New Testament model of "ministry as charism" was soon replaced by an organizational model of "ministry as office," with the most important gifts taken over by the clergy. The body of Christ in which all members were to minister changed into an ecclesiastical hierarchy performing religious service for the "laity." This situation was reinforced by the conversion of the Roman emperor Constantine, who officially recognized Christianity in A.D. 313. After that there is little evidence of full charismatic experience. The New Testament model of spiritual gifts was not compatible with a highly organized, socially powerful church whose prestige gave it the feeling and appearance of success. In turn, the church became a bastion of the political status quo.

Nevertheless, in the second half of the fourth century Bishop Hilary (d. A.D. 367) quoted Paul's list of gifts in 1 Corinthians 12 and commented, "Here we have a statement of the purpose and results of the Gift; and I cannot conceive what doubt can remain, after so clear a definition of His origin, His action, and His powers."[7]

The claim that so-called supernatural charisms ceased with the apostolic era is contrary to historical fact. Even though waning, they persisted during the first four centuries as some of the church's ablest leaders affirmed their continuing role to empower the church in its life and mission.

The Cessation Doctrine of Spiritual Gifts

How, then, did this designation of certain gifts as temporary prevail? By the fifth century the Western church generally viewed them as given for the founding of the church and then withdrawn because they were no longer necessary. However, Augustine (A.D. 354-430), influential theologian and bishop of Hippo, reported that these gifts of the Spirit could still occasionally be seen. Nevertheless, he adopted the "temporary purpose" argument to explain their widespread absence.[8]

In reality they waned not in a church that was growing in spiritual power without them, but in a church that was departing from other New Testament principles and practices as well. By the end of the fifth century spiritual gifts had been "desupernaturalized" and "organized" by the clerical hierarchy.

External political and social developments also influenced the church's attitude toward spiritual gifts. After the western part of the Roman Empire fell in the fifth century, the stream of Christian thought and life divided. The Roman or Latin tradition developed a different attitude toward charisms, including speaking in tongues, from that of the Greek or Orthodox tradition.

In the West, civil government disintegrated as a result of barbarian invasions. Amid the ensuing political chaos, the church remained as the only viable organization of civilized life. Forced by necessity to exercise many functions of secular authority, it became very practical and this-worldly. Western Christianity thus developed an authoritarian organizational pattern that stressed the unity of the body at the expense of the diversity of its members. It is not surprising, then, that a spontaneous exercise of spiritual gifts through the laity now held little if any place in the church's life.

The eastern part of the Roman Empire, however, retained a strong central government at Constantinople that until 1451 provided a stable society in which the church could develop. As a result, it was not forced to take over the secular functions assumed by its counterpart in the West. The Eastern Orthodox Church remained more otherworldly and mystical, encouraging introspection and individuality. It allowed for the diversity of the body's members through which gifts of the Spirit could flourish. Theologian Athanasius Emmert observes, "The spiritual gifts of 1 Corinthians 12, with the possible exception of glossolalia, have always been considered normative by nearly all of the Orthodox within the life of the Church."[9]

In the western church the doctrine of withdrawn spiritual gifts was refined in the fire of controversy during the Reformation. The Roman Catholic Church validated its authority on the basis of miracles performed in its midst. Cardinal Bellarmine (1542-1621), the Vatican's theological watchdog, taunted the Protestant Reformers: If they taught the truth, he asked, where were the miracles? Reformer John Calvin (1509-64) countered by reaffirming Augustine's teaching that miraculous gifts no longer occur because they were given to support the early church while it was still young and weak. After the death of the apostles, these gifts, no longer needed, were withdrawn. Calvin wrote, "The gift of healing, like the rest of the miracles, which the Lord willed to be brought forth for a time, has vanished away in order to make the new preaching of the Gospel marvelous forever."[10] This view served Calvin well as an answer to Cardinal Bellarmine.

The Reformers also perpetuated the concept that charisms are limited to appointed offices of minister, deacon and elder—as opposed to the apostle Paul's model of their functioning through all members of the body of Christ. The stature of Augustine and Calvin as biblical scholars and church leaders has continued to give credence to cessationism, the doctrine of "withdrawn" miraculous gifts.

Nevertheless, post-Reformation Protestantism was not unanimous in accepting Calvin's verdict. Methodist leader John Wesley, like some of the early church fathers, observed a correlation between lost gifts and the general state of the church.

The causes of their decline was not as has been vulgarly (commonly) supposed because there was no more need for them. . . . [T]he real cause was: the love of many, almost all Christians so called, was waxed cold. . . . [T]his was the real cause why the extraordinary gifts of the Holy Spirit were no longer to be found in the Christian Church; because the Christians were turned heathen again and had only a dead form left.[11]

Although Wesley did not believe that miraculous activities of the Spirit had ceased, he didn't consider the question to be of great importance to his own ministry.

At the close of the nineteenth century, Augustine's and Calvin's doctrine of temporary miraculous spiritual gifts continued to prevail throughout Western Protestant churches. Presbyterian theologian Charles Hodge succinctly put it this way: "In that [apostolic] age there was a plenitude of spiritual manifestations and endowments demanded for the organization and propagation of the church, which is no longer required. We have no longer prophets, nor workers of miracles, nor gifts of tongues."[12] His 2,250-page, three-volume *Systematic Theology,* an authoritative evangelical text for almost a century, devotes only twelve pages to spiritual gifts, and half of those are historical notes.

By the early 1960s, when charismatic renewal sprang up in the Western churches, the New Testament doctrine of spiritual gifts had been reshaped beyond recognition. They had been *desupernaturalized* through the elimination of anything miraculous. The more important charisms had been *institutionalized* as the prerogatives of ordained clergy. Some were redefined: messages of wisdom, knowledge and prophecy were considered merely aspects of teaching—that is, perceptive interpretation of revelation already given in Scripture. Furthermore, spiritual gifts were *reinterpreted* as sanctified abilities possessed by the Christian.

What gifts does that model leave for the so-called laity? Mainly service, encouragement, financial contributions, leadership and acts of mercy (Rom 12); faith—providing it is not for anything miraculous (1 Cor 12); evangelism (Eph 4); and hospitality (1 Pet 4). No wonder that the subject of spiritual gifts in the first half of our century was low on the totem pole of Western Protestant theology.

An Evaluation of the Cessation View

Two major arguments are used to support the doctrine that certain "miraculous" gifts were meant only for the first-century church. First, they were intended only as "signs" to authenticate genuine revelation given through the New Testament writers. Second, Paul teaches in 1 Corinthians 13 that those gifts lasted only until the canon of Scripture was complete.

1. Sign gifts. Although the biblical worldview opposes a natural-supernatural dichotomy, as we have noted, the Scriptures do distinguish between *recurring,* predictable events and those that are *miraculous.* Both Old and New Testament words for "miracle" connote three elements: power, wonder and sign.[13] A miracle is an extraordinary, powerful event that arouses wonder and serves as a sign or token pointing beyond itself. In the Old Testament miracles served two major purposes. They were acts of mercy or judgment by the Lord of history to reward or punish; they also served to authenticate the message of prophets sent with a "word from the Lord." The first purpose is evident in the deliverance of Israel from Egypt (Ex 1—15). The second appears in Isaiah's promise to King Hezekiah that he would recover from his serious illness and live fifteen more years; as a confirming sign, the shadow on the sundial moved backward ten steps (Is 38:1-8).

In the Gospels most of Jesus' miracles were healings, acts of mercy that were an integral part of his preaching and teaching ministry. (We will study them further in chapter nine, "Healing of Persons.") His miracles, sometimes called "signs," also authenticated his prophetic ministry (Jn 10:37-38) and evidenced the presence of the kingdom (Lk 11:20). According to Paul, "signs, wonders and miracles" were also the "mark [of] an apostle" (2 Cor 12:12).

The cessation view of spiritual gifts affirms that miracles served as signs to authenticate divine revelation through the apostles. That revelation was recorded and preserved in the apostolic writings that became the New Testament canon. Therefore, when the canon was closed there was no further need for miracles, including miraculous spiritual gifts of prophecy, tongues and healing.

This syllogistic form of reasoning—the statement of two premises from which a logical conclusion is drawn—is valid only when both premises are correctly phrased. In this case a fatal flaw is the assumption that the words *apostles, prophets, healing* and *tongues* have *only one* meaning or function. Such reductionism fails to recognize alternative meanings indicated by their context and usage. We have already seen that the New Testament has several distinct groups of apostles, with different functions. In the next chapter we will see that in both Old and New Testaments there are two different kinds of prophecy. (In 1 Corinthians 14, for example, Paul states that the purpose of prophecy and tongues at Corinth is to edify—strengthen, encourage and comfort—the church, not to give new revelation.) As an integral part of Jesus' ministry, miraculous healings also demonstrated his compassion for the sick and desire to make them whole. When we recognize the multiple purposes and meanings of these spiritual gifts, we find no grounds for relegating them to the first-century church.

2. *"The perfection."* In 1 Corinthians 13 the apostle Paul begins, as we have seen, with a declaration that without love even the ultimate in spiritual gifts neither pleases God nor strengthens Christian character. The decisive question is this: Is *love* translated into deed through this charism? The value of spiritual gifts lies in the extent to which they demonstrate the love of Christ.

For Paul love is neither an abstract ideal nor a sentimental feeling. He doesn't define what love *is,* as an end in itself, but describes how it *acts* and *reacts,* what it does and doesn't do in the rough-and-tumble of life (1 Cor 13:4-7). The Christians at Corinth needed to realize that love is *patient* and *kind* with new believers. Love doesn't *envy* the more prominent spiritual gifts of others, nor does it *boast* about miracles and healings. Love is not *proud* of spiritual wisdom and knowledge. Love is not *rude* or *self-seeking* in the exercise of prophecy and speaking in tongues.

Love always protects, trusts, hopes, perseveres. It lies at the most basic level of life—relationships with God and others. It anchors the soul far below the waves of surface activity, even spiritual gifts.

In verses 8-12 Paul demonstrates the permanence of love by contrasting it with the transience of spiritual gifts: "Love never fails. But where there are prophecies, they will cease; where there are tongues, they will be stilled; where there is knowledge, it will pass away. For we know in part and we prophesy in part, but when perfection comes, the imperfect disappears."

A time will come when charisms of prophecy, tongues and knowledge are no longer needed. Paul calls it *to teleios* ("the perfection"). Opposing interpretations of this term lie at the heart of the question about spiritual gifts today. In order to understand its meaning, we must first look at the context.

In 1 Corinthians 13 the exposition of love—the most important fruit of the Spirit—links Paul's teaching about the nature and purpose of spiritual gifts in the preceding chapter and his teaching about their practice in the following chapter. The Corinthians' greatest need, the solution to their many problems, was to understand and practice love as described in this chapter. (On this point, Unger's view that the impermanence of certain gifts is the real theme has the tail wagging the dog; that is simply one illustration of love's permanence.)

What, then, does the apostle say about "the perfection"? Verse 12 contrasts the perfect with the imperfect: Now we see but a poor reflection and know only in part; then we will see face to face and know fully, even as we are fully known. Paul's reference to a poor reflection may be an allusion to the Corinthian mirrors, which were famous for their clarity even though the best of them gave a somewhat distorted image. When would that perfect sight and knowledge take place? At the end of the first century, when "the finished written revelation of God had arrived," as claimed by the cessation doctrine? If so, why did the church widely continue to manifest gifts of prophecy, tongues and knowledge—along with all the others—for several more centuries?

Both a "plain reading" of the text, as Martin Luther called for, and scholarly consensus recognize that clear sight and full knowledge will come only when we see the Lord himself and know as we are fully known. Only then will charisms, given by the Spirit to empower the church in every generation, pass away. Making "the perfection" occur at the end of the first century is an example of proof texting—seeking support for a particular theological view by reaching into a passage, pulling out a term and giving it a meaning unsupported by its context and usage.

Nowhere does the New Testament teach that certain "supernatural" or "extraordinary" spiritual gifts are meant to last for only a few more years. In 1 Corinthians Paul devotes two long chapters to explaining the nature, purpose and practice of charisms. Here, if anywhere, we would expect him to identify any gifts earmarked for early retirement and prepare the believers for their withdrawal. Yet on the contrary, Paul not only emphasizes the value of all gifts but devotes chapter 14 to detailed instruction in the proper use of prophecy and tongues. The cessation view of so-called supernatural gifts lacks both hermeneutical and historical support for relegating gifts of healing, prophecy, knowledge and tongues to the first century.

Charismatic Essentials

We have seen that much opposition to the charismatic renewal has resulted from confusion about the nature and use of spiritual gifts. Now we will apply what we have learned to several significant questions. How does the enabling power of the Holy Spirit relate to his other activity in the Christian life? What is the relationship of natural abilities to charisms and to gifted individuals? What practical guidelines can help the use of spiritual gifts to build up the body of Christ?

1. A third dimension. Both Protestant and Roman Catholic doctrines of the Holy Spirit have dealt with his work in creation, revelation, the Incarnation, regeneration and sanctification, and final redemption. For many centuries they have treated spiritual gifts as an aspect of sanctification (growth in the Christian life), essentially the believer's natural abilities or talents for the service of God. In the Pentecostal/charismatic renewal, however, the resurgence of long-neglected charisms has opened a window into New Testament teaching and practice. It is apparent that some of these gifts are more than, or different from, the use of a person's natural abilities in the process of sanctification.

Early in the charismatic renewal (1967), Reformed theologian Hendrikus Berkhof perceived the Spirit's empowerment as a third dimension of the Spirit's activity, significantly different from justification/regeneration and sanctification. Yet it is not a separate *stage* of spiritual experience; it belongs with the others and forms a unity with them. Being filled with the Spirit, manifesting his gifts, equips the individual repeatedly at every stage of the Christian life to be an instrument of the Spirit in the church and the world. "The filling by the Spirit means that the justified and sanctified are now turned, so to speak, inside out. In Acts they are turned primarily to the world; in Paul to the total body of Christ; but this is merely a difference in situation and emphasis."[14] After centuries of neglect, the significance of this dimension of the Spirit's activity is gradually being recognized.

We need to affirm two essential points. First, charismatic experience is not considered "beyond Christ," as is sometimes charged. Justification is Christ's righteousness *for* us, and sanctification is his life formed *in* us. Spiritual gifts (being filled with the Spirit) are Christ's work *through* us as the Holy Spirit, whom he has sent, empowers members of his body for its worship, witness and service.

Second, although charisms are not primarily for personal use, they evidence the individuality of the Christian as a member of the body. Regeneration (new birth) and sanctification (holy living) have the same characteristics for all. But through the empowerment of the Holy Spirit, members of the body, in unity of love and purpose, function differently.

2. Spiritual gifts and natural abilities. The charismatic renewal has produced widespread interest in spiritual gifts. Books and manuals, workshops and tests now focus on "discovering your gift" as if it were a personal possession. Often it is equated with a natural ability. To clear up the current misunderstanding, let's define the terms and then see how they relate to each other.

A major problem of communication, as we noted in the previous chapter, lies in the fact that the word *gift* has two different meanings. First it connotes "something given to show friendship, affection, support, etc.; a present." It can also mean "a natural ability; talent."[15] The latter, although indeed a gift from the Creator (like other blessings), differs from a *spiritual gift* in several respects.

It is obvious that people differ widely in their natural abilities. Some are outstanding in one area—like music, art or athletics—but lacking in others. An ability or talent is innate—something a person is born with; it can be developed through practice to a high level of proficiency. By the same token, if it is not used this skill can atrophy. It can be used for personal advantage or for the glory of God. But an ability such as musical talent becomes a *spiritual* gift only when it is used to meet a need of the body of Christ.

When Julia was four years old, she began to amuse herself by picking out tunes on the piano. Recognizing an innate ability, her parents provided music lessons through which she became proficient. In high school she learned on her own how to play the guitar. Soon Julia had an occasional opportunity to play it in a new prayer and praise fellowship. Her natural ability then produced a spiritual gift to meet a need of the fellowship. The gift of music was in the giving and receiving, an event guided by the Holy Spirit. Another person with the same ability, not guided by the Holy Spirit, might have played on an ego trip, out of harmony with the flow of the meeting.

We have seen that a spiritual gift is significantly different from a natural ability in several respects. First, it is dynamic—an activity, empowered by the Holy Spirit, which can be seen or heard. It is manifested to meet a specific need of the body of Christ. For example, a message of wisdom or knowledge illuminates a course of action; a healing makes someone well; a prophecy or a message in tongues with interpretation rebukes or encourages the community as the situation requires. Such manifestations are a sign of the presence of the Spirit to empower the church in its worship, service and witness.

Second, a charism does not necessarily make use of a natural ability. For example, none of the nine listed in 1 Corinthians 12 is dependent on a person's talent. A word of knowledge doesn't have to come through someone with a high IQ, nor a prophecy through the most eloquent, nor a healing through the most empathic. Paul expects that a prophecy or message in tongues can potentially come through any member (1 Cor 14). On the other hand, some spiritual gifts do make use of a natural ability. In the Romans 12 list, a teaching or act of leadership or service may well draw upon personal talent and experience guided by the Holy Spirit.

Two extreme views of spiritual gifts should be avoided. As we have seen, they are not simply "natural abilities" sanctified by the Holy Spirit. Nor are they "supernatural powers" imparted to the Christian through baptism in the Spirit, as taught by some in Pentecostal/charismatic circles. Early in the charismatic renewal Arnold Bittlinger defined a spiritual gift as "a gracious manifestation of the Holy Spirit, working in and through but going beyond the believer's natural ability for the common good of the people of God."[16] And, we might add, often apart from the believer's natural ability.

The gifts of Christ to his church in Ephesians 4:11—apostles, prophets, evangelists, pastors and teachers—are "gifted persons" through whom the Holy Spirit frequently and consistently manifests charisms for a specific ministry. In the early church, for example, Philip was an evangelist and Agabus was a prophet. Today individuals like Billy Graham have a lifelong ministry of evangelism. Others like Charles Colson have a prophetic ministry in the biblical sense of calling God's people to repentance and change of lifestyle in a secular, materialistic culture with a veneer of Christianity. Francis and Judith MacNutt engage in an effective ministry of healing in all dimensions of illness. In them and in many other gifted individuals the Holy Spirit works *through, beyond* or sometimes *apart from* their natural abilities.

3. Discovering your gift. Misunderstanding about abilities and spiritual gifts is perpetuated by widely used Fuller Evangelistic Association manuals which employ the terms interchangeably for personal possessions.[17] *Spiritual Gifts and Church Growth, Part One: Bible Study* is helpful in showing the prevalence, variety and effectiveness of spiritual gifts in the New Testament. Its great merit is a break with traditional "cookie-cutter" hermeneutics which imposes on the text shapes of external distinctions such as supernatural-natural, temporary-permanent and abnormal-normal. The manual accepts the full range of spiritual gifts taught and practiced in the New Testament and widely experienced today.

Part Two: Workshop, however, aims to guide a process of "discovering the spiritual gift God has given to each of us and putting this gift or gifts to use for the health and growth of the church." The manual presents "five steps toward discovering your spiritual gift" with the assurance that the process is quick and simple. A questionnaire of 125 questions, similar to a personality test, is scored according to four categories: much, some, little and not at all. The statistical result then indicates the person's gift(s). A "Wagner-Modified Houts Questionnaire" also provides a list of twenty-six gift definitions and Scripture references. Each gift is designated as "the special ability to . . ."

Unfortunately, this definition of spiritual gift as a personal possession discovered through testing reinforces two primary characteristics of American culture: self-preoccupation and confidence in techniques. The person who thinks "I have discovered my gift" focuses mainly on when and where it can be used and how it can be "developed," often with resulting feelings of anxiety, compulsion or guilt depending on whether it is used and the outcome. How much better to become an active member of a Christian fellowship, focused on the Lord in worship and sensitive to the needs of others who are present, responding to the Spirit with whatever gift he may want to manifest to meet a need of the body. "Discovery" of a specific pattern of giftedness will occur in the life of the community, corroborated or corrected through the response of the other members.

We need to recognize that the manifestation of spiritual gifts—like every other activity in the Christian life—is a combination of the divine and human, two sides of the same coin. At the beginning, as the Holy Spirit convicts us of our sin, we repent. Then we are instructed, "Continue to *work out* your salvation . . . for it is God who *works in you* to will and to act according to his good purpose" (Phil 2:12-13). This principle can be a guide and encouragement in the area of spiritual gifts.

The Body of Christ
The most significant contribution of the charismatic renewal is not simply the recovery of certain long-neglected and rejected spiritual gifts, but *a recognition that the primary purpose of all charisms is to empower the Christian community.* When spiritual gifts are considered primarily as an aspect of individual sanctification, the key question is "What is my spiritual gift? How can I discover and use it?" But when charisms are understood primarily as a function of the body of Christ, a much different question emerges: "How does the Spirit desire to manifest his gifts through members of the body to strengthen its life and mission in the world?"

Theologically, charisms are not a subcategory of individual sanctification but an integral element in ecclesiology, the doctrine of the church. All three of Paul's major teachings about spiritual gifts are given in the context of the body of Christ. Their manifestation is not primarily a barometer of maturity in the individual Christian life but a sign of the presence and power of the Holy Spirit to equip the church for its mission.

The model of the body has several important practical implications for the use of charisms. It is evident that no one member is most important at all times. For example, on one's hand the little finger, weak as it is, may be just what is required to retrieve a dropped key from a small aperture. The value of any member depends on its usefulness to meet a specific need.

Suppose you are walking through woods near a lake and suddenly *hear* a cry for help. As you turn toward the water, you *see* that a child has fallen off a dock, whereupon you *run* to the spot and *pull* the youngster out. It is obviously absurd to argue about which member of your body was most important in carrying out the rescue—ears, eyes, feet or hands. Each met a specific need. If any of them had not functioned at the right time, the child would have drowned.

By the same token the importance of a spiritual gift cannot be determined apart from the needs of the community. If the problem is perplexity, a message of wisdom is required; if illness, then healing; if a message from the Lord, then prophecy. If a member is out of work and needs food for the family, then a gift of money and not a message in tongues is called for. When this concept is finally grasped, no member has reason to feel inferior, as Paul teaches in 1 Corinthians, or to complain because he manifests a "lesser" gift; nor can another be proud because hers is a "greater" gift.

This corporate arena for charisms has one additional essential feature: the provision of feedback on results as the church learns to use the gifts. At times the community can offer a corrective for their misuse. It is one thing for someone to give a prophetic message about the healing of a person in a distant city whose situation isn't known and cannot be validated. It is quite another thing for that message to come in the context of a prayer and praise service or home fellowship where the sick person is known and loved, where the one who gives the message is present week by week to share responsibility for its outcome. The charismatic movement has been poorly served by individual "loose cannons" traveling around the country, accountable to no one, firing out their messages and claims and then leaving.

When unexpected events seem to contradict our theology, we Christians face a dilemma. Something has to yield if we are to keep our thinking and living integrated. Either this purported activity by God is spurious or our theology needs to be revised. We must either find good reason for rejecting the witness to unexpected manifestations of the Holy Spirit or accept them as windows for viewing biblical teaching in a new light.

By its very nature, renewal questions long-held traditions and beliefs. Yet every such challenge is not necessarily valid. Embracing new experiences, however vital, without the test of Scripture can lead into a morass of subjectivism and even heresy. On the other hand, if we refuse to accept the possibility that God is indeed acting in unexpected ways, opening the eyes of his people to scriptural truths long overlooked or misunderstood, we run the risk of smothering a fire that is being kindled by the Holy Spirit.

Church history is replete with examples of both responses. They remind us that renewals are times of vigorous action and reaction. Biblical teaching reopened and relived often conflicts with established beliefs and programs. Custodians of the fireplace sometimes resist the painful remodeling necessary to accommodate the new fire. On the other hand, Christians involved in renewal often kindle their blaze out in the middle of the floor.

In the following chapters we will examine the historical evidence for the continuing use of several controversial gifts: prophecy, speaking in tongues and healing. We will also study their biblical basis and some guidelines for their use today.

III
Controversial Gifts

6 *"They Will Prophesy"*

*I*n January 1990 a long-simmering local dispute over the gift of prophecy boiled over into national controversy. Ernest Gruen, pastor of Full Faith Church of Love in a Kansas City suburb, preached a sermon titled "Do We Keep Smiling and Say Nothing?" that indicted the Kansas City Fellowship.[1] He accused this new charismatic church of sending out false prophets, of prophesying that area churches should close down (and join KCF) and of outright lying. KCF leader Mike Bickle was charged with being deceived by Satan. Gruen then duplicated the tape of his sermon and disseminated it across the country; following came a 233-page document of accusations. As national leaders chose opposing camps, the controversy escalated to open conflict.

In that same month, public awareness of KCF ministry had already been heightened. An article in *Charisma* magazine published prophecies for the decade from eleven leaders including KCF ministers Paul Cain, John Paul Jackson and Bob Jones. A conference in Anaheim, California, arranged by

Vineyard leader John Wimber, featured KCF ministers and drew a reported nine thousand participants. Because these ministers had begun to gain national credibility, charges that they were promoting "charismatic heresy" shocked many across the United States.

Ensuing discussion raised basic questions about the prophetic dimension of the charismatic renewal: Are the ministries of apostle and prophet still valid? What is the gift of prophecy, and how should it be used in our churches? Is too much emphasis being placed on futuristic predictions? How can independent charismatic congregations develop a procedure for doctrinal accountability?

Three major groups are concerned about these issues. Many Pentecostal and charismatic Christians consider prophecy a "word from the Lord" that brings to the worshiping fellowship an awareness of God's presence, strengthens the body of Christ and guides specific details of our life. Yet many Reformed and dispensational Christians charge that the use of prophecy today undermines the unique authority of the Bible and gives too much attention to unreliable forms of "subjective" guidance. They hold the cessationist view that prophecy and other miraculous gifts were withdrawn once the New Testament was complete.

In the middle are many Protestant and Catholic Christians who are neither "charismatic" nor "cessationist" but are simply unsure about the gift of prophecy. Even though they don't see it in their own churches and are uneasy over excesses in the charismatic movement, they do not oppose the use of prophecy.

In this chapter we first consider relevant Old Testament texts to discern the nature and purpose of prophecy. Our study of the varied contexts and usage of the term will remain open to the possibility that it has more than one meaning. We will then follow the same procedure to examine prophecy in the New Testament to discover what similarities and differences there may be. We can then consider the role of prophecy today in and through the church.

Israel's Prophets
In ancient Greece it was the philosophers who were honored for their intel-

lectual brilliance and explanations of the world. The thought of Plato (c. 427-347 B.C.) and Aristotle (384-322 B.C.) has profoundly influenced Western philosophy and science down to the present time. Their modern counterparts are the university professors who carry on the tradition of searching for an intellectual framework to give coherence and meaning to life.

In Israel, however, the most influential figure was the prophet—one who spoke for God, revealing his character and purposes for his people and their world. Although the prophet might have a superior intellect and education, like Moses the lawgiver and Daniel the political administrator, that was not the essential qualification. Amos was an obscure shepherd and caretaker of sycamore-fig trees; Deborah was one of Israel's judges in a time of crisis; Anna was an elderly widow who worshiped at the temple when Jesus was born. The one thing they had in common as prophets was a "word from the Lord."

The Old Testament reveals a God who speaks, expressing his character, thoughts, feelings and intentions in words. His words were communicated by the Spirit through the prophets. For example, "Haggai, the LORD's messenger, gave this message of the LORD to the people" (Hag 1:13). In another situation God said to the prophet Jeremiah, "I have put my words in your mouth" (Jer 1:9). As special messengers, the prophets spoke on the authority of the one who sent them, not on their own. In that sense they were like ambassadors who carry messages from the president or prime minister of their country. The apostle Peter explained, "For prophecy never had its origin in the will of man, but men spoke from God as they were carried along by the Holy Spirit" (2 Pet 1:21).

What was the nature and purpose of a prophetic message? The answer may surprise many today who think of prophecy only in terms of foretelling the future. That is only one element, and not always the most important, in biblical prophecy, which has three main purposes.

First, it evaluates the present situation from God's perspective. From time to time the people of Israel turned away from worshiping the true God and obeying his law. As they went after idols, the rulers allowed economic and

social injustice to flourish throughout the land. Then a prophet would bring
a message of judgment on their sin. For example, Jeremiah proclaimed,

> Has a nation ever changed its gods?
>
> (Yet they are not gods at all.)
>
> But my people have exchanged their Glory
>
> for worthless idols. . . .
>
> On your clothes men find
>
> the lifeblood of the innocent poor,
>
> though you did not catch them breaking in. (Jer 2:11, 34)

Second, the prophet calls people to repentance and reform—a return to their
God and obedience to his law in the establishment of justice. Otherwise,
judgment of their sin will come swiftly.

> If you will return, O Israel,
>
> return to me. . . .
>
> Circumcise yourselves to the LORD,
>
> circumcise your hearts,
>
> you men of Judah and people of Jerusalem,
>
> or my wrath will break out and burn like fire
>
> because of the evil you have done—
>
> burn with no one to quench it. (Jer 4:1, 4)

Third, in addition to "forthtelling," Old Testament prophecies sometimes have
a foretelling of future events. For example, Matthew's Gospel has many quotations of Old Testament prophecies fulfilled in Jesus, the long-awaited Messiah. And there is a still-future dimension of biblical prophecy about the end
times, especially in Ezekiel, Daniel and Revelation.

From the second century until the present there have been repeated predictions about political and economic events pointing to the imminent return of
Christ. Despite the fact that Jesus warned against trying to predict such "times
or dates" (Mt 24:36; Acts 1:7), and despite the repeated failures of past attempts, there is always a market for this unwarranted use of biblical prophecy.[2] In times of crisis like the Cold War and the Gulf War, people want the
security of history written in advance. Too often this focus on timetables for

the future offers escape from responsibilities for living in the present.

Two Kinds of Old Testament Prophecy

There is another set of categories that can be used to distinguish kinds of prophecy in the Old Testament. First there is *canonical* prophecy, a message that has been committed to writing and included in the accepted canon (collection) of inspired Scripture. A good example is found in Micah, who prophesied between 750 and 686 B.C. to the people of Judah. His main thrust concerns their evil activities.

> Woe to those who plan iniquity,
>
> to those who plot evil on their beds!
> At morning's light they carry it out
>
> because it is in their power to do it. . . .
> Therefore, the LORD says:
> "I am planning disaster against this people,
>
> from which you cannot save yourselves." (Mic 2:1, 3)

Micah's prophecy also has an element of foretelling.

> In the last days
>
> the mountain of the LORD's temple will be established
>
> as chief among the mountains;
> it will be raised above the hills,
>
> and peoples will stream to it.
>
> Many nations will come and say, . . .
> "He will teach us his ways,
>
> so that we may walk in his paths."
> The law will go out from Zion,
>
> the word of the LORD from Jerusalem. (Mic 4:1-2)

Micah recognized the divine authority of his prophecy: "I am filled with power, with the Spirit of the LORD, and with justice and might" (3:8). He warned against false prophets who would contradict his message and assure the people that all would be well (2:6-7). Moses had recognized the possibility of false prophecy, for which he gave a test and prescribed punishment (Deut 18:20-21).

British scholar Graham Houston has called attention to another function of Old Testament prophecy that has been largely overlooked. "It was regarded differently, not so much as a revelation of God's secrets but as a powerful sign of his presence with his people at crucial times."[3] For example, after Moses appointed seventy elders to help govern the people, the Lord "took of the Spirit that was on him and put the Spirit on the seventy elders. When the Spirit rested on them, they prophesied, but they did not do so again." Shortly afterward, Moses declared, "I wish that all the LORD's people were prophets and that the LORD would put his Spirit on them" (Num 11:25, 29).

Another example of this secondary kind of prophecy occurred when young Saul was anointed Israel's first king. The prophet Samuel told Saul that he would soon meet a procession of prophets and that "the Spirit of the LORD will come upon you in power, and you will prophesy with them." When this occurred, the people were amazed and asked, "Is Saul also among the prophets?" (1 Sam 10:5-11).

In these cases there is no record of what the prophets said under the Spirit's influence, no indication that the prophecies were new revelation that would become Scripture. In that sense the prophecies were not canonical but what we may call *congregational.* In other words, they served as a powerful sign of God's presence among his people without necessarily bringing a specific message that needed to be preserved.

A variation of this prophetic function occurred in the life of David. Immediately after Saul's death in battle, David was anointed king over a country in which many were still loyal to the first king. So David had to struggle to capture Jerusalem and consolidate his authority. Soon a number of valiant warriors from the various tribes came over to his cause. Among them was Amasai, an army commander from the tribe of Benjamin.

Then the Spirit came upon Amasai, chief of the Thirty, and he said:

"We are yours, O David!

  We are with you, O son of Jesse!

Success, success to you, and success to those who help you,

  for your God will help you." (1 Chron 12:18)

This was not a revelation but a pledge of allegiance and a blessing to encourage David at a critical time in his life.

Joel, himself a canonical prophet, looked forward to a day when the Spirit would be poured out on all God's people so that they would prophesy (Joel 2:28-29). We have seen how that prophecy was fulfilled at Pentecost. So the Old Testament clearly recognizes two types or functions of prophecy: *canonical,* in which revelation takes the form of inspired words with absolute authority to become Scripture; and *congregational,* in which people led by the Spirit speak spontaneously and appropriately on particular occasions. The second function is by no means a substitute for Scripture; rather it serves as a supplement, a sign of God's presence among his people.

The Messianic Age
The last Old Testament canonical prophet was Malachi, whose name means "my messenger." He addressed the community of Jewish exiles who had returned from captivity in Persia to rebuild the temple and walls of Jerusalem. After a period of spiritual renewal, the people had again departed from the law of Moses and intermarried with foreigners. Malachi's prophecy (c. 400 B.C.) indicts God's people, calling for repentance—a return to God and obedience to his law. He foretells fiery judgment for the wicked and healing for the righteous. Malachi concludes with a promise for the future: "I will send you the prophet Elijah before that great and dreadful day of the LORD comes. He will turn the hearts of the fathers to their children, and the hearts of the children to their fathers" (Mal 4:5-6).

Throughout the following four centuries of political, social and economic upheaval, the voice of the prophet was stilled. Nevertheless, faithful Jews kept alive the flame of Old Testament promise that the Messiah would come to reestablish the throne of David and usher in a new era of freedom.

One day in the temple at Jerusalem the messianic age suddenly began to dawn. Luke records a resumption of revelation and prophecy in unexpected ways. First the angel Gabriel appeared to Zechariah, a priest standing alone in the Holy Place to offer incense. In their old age he and his wife Elizabeth would finally have a son, "filled with the Holy Spirit even from birth," to be named John. The son would fulfill Malachi's prophecy, for he would preach "in the spirit and power of Elijah" (Lk 1:15, 17). A son was indeed born to Zechariah and Elizabeth, and at the time of the boy's circumcision Zechariah was "filled with the Holy Spirit and prophesied" that John would become a prophet of the Most High, to prepare the way of the Lord to save his people and guide their feet "into the path of peace" (Lk 1:15, 17, 67, 76-79).

Luke reports that Jesus was conceived by the Holy Spirit, baptized by John and anointed by the Spirit at the river Jordan, then empowered by the Spirit for his ministry of preaching, teaching and healing. After the resurrection Jesus promised his disciples that they too would be empowered by the Holy Spirit for their mission to spread the gospel to all nations. In due course that promise was fulfilled in Jerusalem at Pentecost, as they declared the wonders of God in the foreign languages of the Jewish pilgrims. In his Pentecost sermon, as we saw in an earlier chapter, Peter explained the phenomenon as a fulfillment of Joel's prediction that the Spirit would come on all people and "they will prophesy" (Acts 2:18). Luke's narrative in Acts reports other instances of prophecy. And in his letters, the apostle Paul gives extensive instruction on the role of this spiritual gift in the church.

As we consider prophecy in the New Testament, several questions come to mind. What are the content and function of Christian prophecy? Who is eligible to prophesy in the church? Is prophecy just an aspect of preaching and teaching? What is the connection between apostles and prophets in the New Testament?

Our quest for answers to these questions is indebted to the seminal research of evangelical theologian Wayne Grudem in a doctoral thesis submitted to the University of Cambridge. A revised version of his work has been published as *The Gift of Prophecy in the New Testament and Today*. He makes a case for the distinction between canonical and congregational prophecy which we have found in the Old Testament.[4]

Apostles and Prophets

In the Gospels the twelve whom Jesus chose to follow him are called "disciples"—that is, pupils or adherents of a teacher or school of thought.[5] In Acts 1:26, however, they are called "apostles" as Matthias is chosen to replace Judas. In his letters Paul consistently uses that term to connote his authority as a special messenger or ambassador of Christ (for example, see Gal 1:1, 11-12). In that respect the apostles are the New Testament counterpart of the Old Testament prophets; both are empowered to speak and write the very words of God.

We may ask, "Why was this new term chosen?" At that time the Greek word *prophētēs,* in everyday use, could mean "spokesperson" in a general way rather than someone with full divine authority. First-century Jewish literature also had a wide range of meanings for the term we translate "prophet," from Old Testament prophet to someone who had special insight or could predict the future. In Paul's letter to Titus the word means a "proclaimer" or "announcer" (1:12).

Since the word *apostle* was not common, it could be used to designate a limited group without creating a conflict with the Old Testament expectation of widespread prophecies among all the people. In the word's primary sense, noted earlier, the apostles became the counterpart of those Old Testament prophets who declared the authoritative "word of the Lord." In the New Testament, those called prophets served a different purpose not connected with the writing of Scripture. Grudem describes it as "ordinary congregational prophecy" in which Christians did not speak with divine authority but reported something God had laid on their heart or brought to their mind.[6]

In his letter to the Ephesians Paul declares that the church is "built on the foundation of the apostles and prophets" to whom the Holy Spirit has revealed "the mystery of Christ" (2:20; 3:4-5). Grudem considers the four most common interpretations of what the phrase "apostles and prophets" means. He concludes, on the basis of historical facts and the uniqueness of the apostles, that neither the Old Testament prophets nor all the New Testament prophets of local congregations are meant. Rather the two words apply to one group, "apostle-prophets" or "apostles-who-are-also-prophets." To them was given the authoritative revelation that became Scripture.[7]

Prophecy reported in Acts, on the other hand, is not doctrinal but directional, not revelation for all times and places but a message for specific situations. A prophet manifesting this type of gift is Agabus, a Jerusalem prophet who came to Antioch and "through the Spirit predicted that a severe famine would spread over the entire Roman world" (Acts 11:28). In response the disciples decided to send relief to the Christians in Judea.

At the end of his third missionary journey Paul planned to visit Jerusalem. Agabus intercepted him with a prophecy. He took Paul's belt, tied his own hands and feet with it and declared, "The Holy Spirit says, 'In this way the Jews of Jerusalem will bind the owner of this belt and will hand him over to the Gentiles' " (Acts 21:11). As it turned out, two details of this prediction were inaccurate. The Jews did not bind Paul and hand him over to the Romans; rather, the Romans rescued Paul from Jewish violence and then bound him themselves. (Old Testament canonical prophecy did not contain such errors of detail.) It appears that Agabus received a revelation or vision of Paul imprisoned by the Romans and then gave a prophecy that interpreted it in his own words. Still, the prophecy was accurate in a general sense, since it was the Jews' violent rejection of Paul's message that resulted in his arrest by the Romans.

Earlier in his last missionary journey Paul had met some disciples of John the Baptist in Ephesus and baptized them in the name of Christ. "When Paul placed his hands on them, the Holy Spirit came on them, and they spoke in tongues and prophesied" (Acts 19:6). When Paul arrived in Tyre he stayed a week with some disciples. "Through the Spirit they urged Paul not to go on to Jerusalem" (21:4). In Caesarea he stayed at the house of Philip the evangelist, who had four daughters who prophesied (21:8-9); Luke gives no report of the content of their prophecies. There is no indication in any of these references that the persons had apostolic authority and infallibility.

Prophecy at Corinth
We now turn to 1 Corinthians 14, Paul's classic instruction on the use of prophecy and tongues. (Tongues will be considered in chapter seven of this

book.) After Paul's teaching on love, the most important fruit of the Spirit, he returns to the subject of spiritual gifts. "Follow the way of love and eagerly desire spiritual gifts, especially the gift of prophecy" (v. 1). It is significant that the verb *desire* is in the plural form, so this is addressed not to individuals but to the entire congregation.

At the outset Paul defines the purpose of the prophecy he advocates: "strengthening, encouragement and comfort" as it "edifies the church" (vv. 3-4). Congregational prophecy gives all the members an opportunity to participate; in this chapter Paul repeatedly states that potentially everyone could prophesy (vv. 5, 24, 31). (This is not canonical prophecy; there was no apostle in the Corinthian church at that time.) This spiritual gift has always been needed and should continue to be valued for strengthening the body of Christ.

Sometimes prophecy is addressed to the community, at other times to individuals. An example of the latter occurred at a Sunday-evening prayer and praise service at the end of a weekend teaching mission in a Midwestern church.

During the service someone shared a vision of a Tudor-style house, describing it in detail, room by room, on each floor. The person then heard the Lord saying, "I am coming into your house. I want you to open all the doors to me." The mission leader noticed at the back of the church a couple who were sitting with heads bowed, sobbing profusely. Going to them, he asked, "What's wrong?" The man answered, "That's my house, and the Lord is coming into my heart." His wife nodded, "Yes, that's our home, and the Lord is coming into it." Through the earlier meetings the couple had been converted to Christ; now they wholeheartedly committed themselves to his lordship in every area of life. And two years later the couple continue enthusiastically to serve their Lord.

Another benefit of prophecy accrues to non-Christians who may come into the meeting. "He will be convinced by all that he is a sinner and will be judged by all, and the secrets of his heart will be laid bare. So he will fall down and worship God, exclaiming, 'God is really among you!' " (vv. 24-25).

Paul expresses two major concerns about the use of congregational prophecy: there must be order in worship and protection against false prophecies. Toward the end of 1 Corinthians 14 he gives a model for worship in which the body of Christ receives spiritual gifts as the Holy Spirit chooses to manifest them through the members.

> When you come together, everyone has a hymn, or a word of instruction, a revelation, a tongue or an interpretation. All of these must be done for the strengthening of the church. . . . Two or three prophets should speak, and the others should weigh carefully what is said. And if a revelation comes to someone who is sitting down, the first speaker should stop. For you can all prophesy in turn so that everyone may be instructed and encouraged. The spirits of prophets are subject to the control of prophets. For God is not a God of disorder but of peace. (vv. 26-32)

Several terms in this passage call for explanation: "revelation," "the others" and "weigh carefully." The first refers to a specific revelatory activity of the Holy Spirit. But the word *apokalypto* ("to reveal") does not necessarily connote a new message with divine authority. For example, in Philippians 3:15 Paul states that where the readers take a different view from his, "that too will God make clear (reveal) to you."

We may ask, then, what authority does congregational prophecy carry? British writer Donald Bridge observes, "The same authority as that of any other Christian activity in the church, like leadership, counseling, teaching. . . . If it is true, it will prove to be true."[8] Spiritual gifts are not infallible; they need to be tested by Scripture illumined by the Holy Spirit.

Who are "the others" in verse 29 charged with "weighing carefully" the prophecies? Some limit them to the few involved in the prophecies as they also manifest the companion gift of "distinguishing between spirits" (1 Cor 12:10). Yet "the others" can also be the whole church, whose responsibility for such weighing is clearly mandated in 1 Thessalonians 5:21 and 1 John 4:1-6. It is important to recognize that this gift of discernment, like prophecy and other charisms, can potentially be manifested by any member of the body as the Spirit determines. (The role of distinguishing between spirits in spiritual warfare will be considered further in chapter eleven.)

Lecturer David Prior suggests several specific criteria for this testing: "Does it glorify God? Is it in accord with Scripture? Does it build up the church? Is it spoken in love? Does the speaker submit to judgment by others?"[9] Prophecy should speak primarily to the present condition of the church rather than prediction of future events.

In giving this model for congregational prophecy, Paul invokes his canonical authority as an apostle: "If anybody thinks he is a prophet or spiritually gifted, let him acknowledge that what I am writing to you is the Lord's command" (1 Cor 14:37). On that basis he concludes, "Be eager to prophesy, and do not forbid speaking in tongues. But everything should be done in a fitting and orderly way" (vv. 39-40).

Prophets and prophecy in the New Testament are treated as a normal and integral part of church life. The importance of prophecy is evidenced by its inclusion in all nine gift lists (see appendix D). The only mention of prophecy "ceasing" is made in reference to the future perfection of seeing the Lord face to face and knowing him fully as he now knows us (1 Cor 13:8-12).

The New Testament pictures thousands of Christians in churches across the Roman Empire empowered by the Holy Spirit to prophesy, as Joel foresaw, and to realize Paul's goal of "strengthening, encouragement and comfort" for the body of Christ. Prophecy was a sign for unbelievers (1 Cor 14:22). It was an assurance of God's presence, giving his insights and guidance, empowering the church to live out the truths of Scripture in their particular age and location as the Holy Spirit directed.

Congregational Prophecy and Scripture

We have seen how Old Testament canonical and congregational prophecy, serving different functions, have parallels in the New Testament. The apostles spoke the very words of God, words that were entirely trustworthy and authoritative, often to become inspired Scripture. Congregational prophecy, on the other hand, was a revelation—perhaps in the form of a dream, vision, phrase or sudden insight—interpreted and applied in fallible human words that needed to be tested. Scripture has general teachings for the church at all times; congregational prophecy gives a specific message for a certain time, place and situation. Pastor George Mallone observes, "Prophecy today, although it may be very helpful and on occasion overwhelmingly specific, is not in the category of the revelation given to us in Holy Scripture. . . . A person may hear the voice of the Lord and be compelled to speak, but there is no assurance that it is pollutant-free."[10]

Although most charismatic teaching today recognizes this distinction, it is frequently overlooked in practice. Prophecies are often prefaced with the Old Testament phrase "Thus says the Lord," which is not used by any recorded New Testament prophets.

This point was a crucial bone of contention in Kansas City. Mike Bickle, leader of the KCF, believes that prophecy today has three components— revelation, interpretation and application; the last two, he says, may have imperfections or errors. That explanation is rejected by his opponents, who equate prophecy today with that in the Old Testament, where one erroneous statement branded the prophet false. Thus Ernest Gruen charges, "A prophet who admits he is right only 40% of the time is not only a non-prophet, he is dangerous."[11]

The relationship between current prophecy and Scripture can be summed up in two principles. First, the gift of prophecy is not an *addition* to Scripture; no loose-leaf Bibles are needed. Collecting prophecies for future use is misguided. Second, prophecy is not an *alternative* to Scripture; it is not a substitute for consistent biblical exposition. In fact, grounding in the Word of God is the best soil for bearing prophetic fruit.

Prophecy and Teaching

A popular view of prophecy interprets it as essentially a form of teaching, presumably to avoid false prophecies by making this gift simply an exposition of Scripture. This position raises two basic questions: Is it supported by the meanings of the two terms *teaching* and *prophecy,* as defined by their usage and context? To what extent does this view guard against false prophecy?

In Paul's three lists of different kinds of gifts (Rom 12:6; 1 Cor 12:28; Eph

4:11), teaching *(didaskalia* or *didachē)* is separate and distinct from prophecy. Furthermore, teaching is always based directly on Scripture. For example, Paul tells the Romans that Old Testament Scripture "was written to teach us" (Rom 15:4). He instructs Timothy that "all Scripture" is "useful for teaching" (2 Tim 3:16). This kind of teaching was the repetition and explanation of the Old Testament and of authentic apostolic teaching. Timothy was not told to *prophesy* Paul's instructions; he was to *teach* them (2 Tim 2:2). It was not prophecy but apostolic teaching that first provided the doctrinal and ethical norms by which the church was regulated. Elders were exhorted to be "apt" teachers as they labored "in preaching and *teaching*" (1 Tim 3:2; 5:17 RSV).

On the other hand, the thought that occurs to a prophet is pictured as coming spontaneously in a worship service (1 Cor 14:30). This "revelation" comes to "someone who is sitting down," not to a teacher who is standing and expounding Scripture to the congregation. The "revelation" is of divine origin; none of the forty-four occurrences in Paul's writings refers to human teaching. No prophecy is ever said to consist of reflection on a text of Scripture, interpreting and applying it to life.[12]

So prophecy, as described and taught in Scripture, is not simply an enforcement and application of biblical teaching. Nor is teaching or preaching, however effective, what the New Testament writers call prophecy.

Second, making prophecy a category of teaching hardly preserves it from error; the New Testament warns against false *teachers* as well as false *prophets* (for example, Tit 1:11; 2 Pet 2:1). In fact, common criticisms of prophecy can also be leveled at the teaching of Scripture. It is often asked, What good is an imperfect prophecy that may contain some error? We might equally ask, What good is an infallible Scripture with fallible teachers? Ironically, today many preachers who object to the phrase "I say to you" as preface for a prophecy do not hesitate to stand with open Bible and declare "God says to you" as they launch into their own interpretation. The congregation is warned against the dangers of prophecy, but they are expected to accept without question the pastor's teaching. How many preachers today would be open to having their sermons "weighed carefully" by the people (as Paul requires for prophecy) and challenged on their interpretations?

In a fallen world every spiritual gift—teaching and evangelism as well as prophecy and tongues—can be misused. The more accepted the gift, the greater the potential for error. In recent centuries how many erroneous doctrines have attracted a following of "Bible-believing" Christians through false prophecy? and how many through misinterpretation of Scripture? For example, popular teachers like Hal Lindsey misuse the Bible to predict a timetable for Christ's return.[13]

Pastor John MacArthur Jr. vigorously attacks the use of prophecy in the charismatic renewal. His approach (as with healing and tongues) overlooks the mainline Protestant and Catholic renewal as it focuses on the independents. From them he selects bizarre examples of teaching and experience to condemn the entire charismatic movement.[14]

Critics complain that charismatic Christians build their theology on experience rather than on Scripture, which must be the yardstick of all teaching. Yet MacArthur's argument against the current use of prophecy is based on a catalog of bad experiences, not on Scripture. His book *Charismatic Chaos* is woefully deficient in exposition and discussion of the basic New Testament passages dealing with the gift of prophecy (1 Cor 14 and 1 Thess 5:19-20). MacArthur dismisses Grudem's view of congregational prophecy in one footnote that misunderstands and misrepresents Grudem's view of revelation.

Criticism by caricature is neither scholarly nor honest; it clouds the issues and appeals to emotion. Its sword also cuts two ways. MacArthur's method of evaluating charismatic renewal could also be applied to his own dispensational camp, which has its share of bizarre teaching and bad experiences. Predictions of the exact day of the rapture, teaching that only Paul's letters are Scripture and warnings of far-fetched end-time conspiracies could be collected in a book titled *Dispensational Delusions.* But that would hardly contribute to a fair evaluation of all dispensational ministry, including MacArthur's.

Prophecy in Practice

Let's conclude with some practical suggestions for the use of congregational prophecy. Like all teaching of Scripture, prophecy needs to be tested. The apostle Paul warns that "we prophesy in part" (1 Cor 13:9). Our prophecy is imperfect; the "revelation" may be misunderstood or misapplied. Nevertheless, it can be a message from God. Therefore Paul commands, "Do not treat prophecies with contempt. Test everything. Hold on to the good. Avoid every kind of evil" (1 Thess 5:20-22).

The following principles and guidelines can keep the gift of prophecy from straying into the abuses that have brought justifiable criticism on its use.

1. The primary area for prophecy today is the congregation, the body of Christ. The context of 1 Corinthians 14 is corporate worship in which the members share "a hymn, a word of instruction, a revelation, a tongue, or an interpretation . . . for the strengthening of the church" (v. 26). Here also is a careful weighing that perceives error or lack of appropriateness for the occasion.

2. It is better to preface a prophecy with "I believe the Lord is telling me" than with "Thus says the Lord." This careful phrasing will not hurt the prophecy's effectiveness but serve as a reminder that it does not have the authority of Scripture.

3. Predictions of the future—which are not the main purpose of prophecy—should be considered encouragements or warnings, not guarantees. In planning for the future people should not place too much emphasis on a prophecy.

4. The church is to be governed by overseers and deacons, not prophets (1 Tim 3:1-7; 5:17).

5. Although potentially all members of the body can prophesy, the messages may come more frequently and consistently through some for whom this will be a special ministry.

6. Look for confirmations of a prophecy through others who share similar thoughts, perhaps through another prophetic word or Scripture or mental picture.

7. Do not be discouraged by mistakes. Application of long-neglected spiritual gifts such as prophecy must be carried out through a process of trial and error.

Wayne Grudem suggests several steps for leaders to encourage use of this spiritual gift: *Pray* for the Lord's wisdom on how and when to broach the subject. *Teach* on this subject in the church's regular Bible instruction times. *Be patient* and proceed slowly to avoid alienating people. *Recognize* and *encourage* the gift of prophecy where it has already been manifested, although without that label. When it is accepted by the congregation, *make opportunities* for prophecy during the less formal worship services of the church, such as on Sunday evenings and in Wednesday prayer meetings and house groups. Finally, if manifestations of this gift grow, *place even more emphasis on Scripture* as the primary means through which the Holy Spirit daily guides our life and service for the Lord.[15]

Recognizing the value and limitation of congregational prophecy frees this spiritual gift from two errors. It will not be rejected for fear of undermining confidence in the unique revelation of Holy Scripture. Nor will it be accorded the infallibility and authority of canonical prophecy. The charism of congregational prophecy can then fulfill its potential for the church's "strengthening, encouragement and comfort."

7 Speaking in Tongues

*T*he youth committee of a Lutheran church had been considering new ways to reach a wider spectrum of teenagers. After an intensive search they discovered a promising program, only to reach an impasse in their final deliberation. Several members voiced reservations about whether its novel features would really work. Should they run the risk of failure? Others pointed to the disadvantages of staying on the same course.

As debate sharpened division, a sense of heaviness pervaded the meeting. At the outset the members had agreed to seek consensus in major decisions. Up to this point a united committee had worked together enthusiastically. Now it appeared that their project would reach a dead end.

Susan, a younger member of the committee, was depressed over the prospect of another year of losses. Suddenly she had a sense of peace and hope that she wanted to share with the others but couldn't express. Susan found herself giving a message in tongues. An interpretation declared, "The Lord has not given us a spirit of fear but of power. Move forward in faith. Be courageous and see how your much-loved youth will respond." The committee unanimously decided to launch the new program and soon saw that promise fulfilled in the many new young people who became involved.

Speaking in tongues is one of the spiritual gifts that stir most controversy both inside and outside the church. Since its beginning in the early 1960s the charismatic renewal has been dubbed the "tongues movement." Thrust into the limelight, this controversial charism all too often has taken center stage. Although it has a place in the cast of spiritual gifts, speaking in tongues does not deserve the role of hero (or villain) often assigned to it.

The Greek word *glōssa* means "tongue" as both a physical organ of speech and a language or dialect. Most New Testament versions simply translate it "tongue" with the connotation of language. The phrase *glōssais lalein,* meaning "to speak in tongues," is the basis for calling the phenomenon "glossolalia." In 1 Corinthians 12:10 the apostle Paul refers to "different kinds of tongues," indicating that there may be more than one function or purpose. So in each passage where this gift is manifested or discussed, the meaning needs to be determined by context and usage.

In this chapter we will consider the function of speaking in tongues in the New Testament. To what extent is it overemphasized or underappreciated today? After a look at the early church's experiences in Acts, we will turn to the apostle Paul's teaching in 1 Corinthians and consider how tongues relates to prophecy. We will then survey how the two gifts have fared in church history and the issues surrounding speaking in tongues today.

Tongues in Acts

At Pentecost the disciples' speaking in tongues declared the wonders of God in the foreign languages of the pilgrims. There it had the twofold purpose of attracting attention and prefiguring the worldwide scope of the gospel of Christ. This phenomenon is called *xenolalia*—speaking in a recognizable foreign language with which the speaker is not familiar.

Luke records three additional instances of speaking in tongues. After some Samaritans became Christians through Philip's evangelism, Peter and John came from Jerusalem to check out the situation. As the apostles laid hands on the Samaritans, the Holy Spirit came upon them. Although Luke does not explicitly report a speaking in tongues, it is implied by the request of Simon the former sorcerer (Acts 8:14-19).

Peter later went to Caesarea and preached to Roman centurion Cornelius and his household. As the Holy Spirit came upon all the hearers, they began "speaking in tongues and praising God" (Acts 10:46). Peter immediately baptized the new believers in the name of Jesus Christ.

After several years the apostle Paul was preaching in Ephesus, where he encountered twelve disciples of John who had not heard about the Holy Spirit. He baptized them in the name of the Lord Jesus and laid his hands on them, whereupon "the Holy Spirit came on them, and they spoke in tongues and prophesied" (Acts 19:6).

On these three occasions there was no need for speaking in recognizable foreign languages, since in each case the apostles had been communicating in the local vernacular. So the utterance was simply *glossolalia,* a "language" unknown to the speaker. As a form of prophecy, speaking in tongues was an evidence of the Spirit's activity in the messianic age empowering the church for its witness. There is no indication that it was intended to be an evidence of a "baptism in the Spirit" that initiated a second stage in the Christian life. (See chapter three and appendix B.)

Order in Worship

In 1 Corinthians 14 Paul discusses at length the role in public worship of prophecy and speaking in tongues. He gives specific guidelines for the use of these gifts in a productive and orderly way. In this teaching we discover two purposes for speaking in tongues in addition to the one we have seen in Acts.

As the Christians at Corinth were enriched in Christ, they exercised the full range of spiritual gifts (1:4-7). Yet some of these charisms were misunderstood and misused with serious consequences. Words of knowledge and wisdom were generating pride, party spirit and divisions. Prophecy and speaking in tongues were a cause of disorder, a problem the apostle deals with in chapter 14.

Today, assessment of speaking in tongues is complicated by the fact that in 1 Corinthians Paul seems to offer a proof text for every point of view! Some happily quote "Where there are tongues, they will be stilled" (13:8). Others urge, "I would like every one of you to speak in tongues" (14:5). Many in the middle cautiously note the instruction, "Do not forbid speaking in tongues" (14:39). Few biblical subjects have so many theological and cultural preconceptions influencing their interpretation.

Much of the difficulty of understanding 1 Corinthians 14:2-25 lies in Paul's style of argument. He is not writing a theological treatise, but a letter in which he shares elements of his own experience as well as illustrations from life. Seeming contradictions emerge as he alternates between prophecy and speaking in tongues, comparing one with the other. The style is similar to that of Romans 7; these two chapters are among the most difficult of Paul's writings to understand.

The key to unlocking the meaning of this chapter is the central issue of *intelligibility*. Spiritual gifts are designed to empower the body of Christ. If they are to achieve this goal, charisms of inspired speech must be understood and used with discretion. *The problem with speaking in tongues at Corinth was basically a lack of communication; without interpretation it failed to build up the body of Christ, because its message was not understood.*

Building the Body of Christ
Interpretation of Paul's 1 Corinthians 14 teaching about speaking in tongues often overlooks the fact that he criticizes only the *uninterpreted* use of this charism. His first comparison of tongues and prophecy makes this clear: "He who speaks in a tongue edifies himself, but he who prophesies edifies the church. . . . He who prophesies is greater than one who speaks in tongues, *unless he interprets,* so that the church may be edified" (vv. 4-5). In other words, prophecy is more valuable than an uninterpreted message in tongues which cannot be understood. "Unless you speak intelligible words with your tongue, how will anyone know what you are saying? . . . For this reason anyone who speaks in a tongue should pray that he may interpret what he

says" (vv. 9, 13). With interpretation, tongues, like prophecy, edifies (builds up) the body of Christ.

Paul illustrates the need for intelligibility with two familiar examples, musical instruments and foreign languages (vv. 7-8). If a flute or harp does not distinctly sound its notes, no one knows what tune is being played. And if a trumpet doesn't give a clear call, who will prepare for battle? Likewise, if someone speaks a language the hearer doesn't understand, they are foreigners to each other (vv. 10-11). The apostle desires for the Corinthians the recognized tune and clarion call of understandable messages.

Uninterpreted, the charism neither benefits the church nor converts unbelievers who happen to be present. In verses 22-23 Paul writes, "Tongues, then, are a sign, not for believers but for unbelievers. . . . So if the whole church comes together and everyone speaks in tongues [without interpretation], and some who do not understand or some unbelievers come in, will they not say that you are out of your mind?"[1] It was not uncommon in Corinth for unbelievers to visit Christian assemblies as well as synagogues. If the message was in a recognizable foreign language, as at Pentecost, these visitors in a cosmopolitan commercial city would hardly conclude that the Christians were out of their minds. So it is evident that the speaking in tongues here was not xenolalia.

Paul's expressed concern for public speaking in tongues is not for its style but for its content. The word *glōssa* ("tongue" or "language") has no inherent connotation of ecstasy—an overpowering feeling or trance.[2] Unfortunately, *Webster's Dictionary* defines *glossolalia* as "an ecstatic utterance of unintelligible speechlike sounds, regarded as caused by religious ecstasy."[3] This misrepresentation of speaking in tongues is perpetuated by some translations—for example, the New English Bible, which calls it "ecstatic speech," adding an adjective not found in the text.

Commentaries often disparage speaking in tongues as ecstatic and emotional. Nothing so unsettles the rationalistic mind as the specter of emotionalism running rampant in speech that cannot be understood. Some even say it is demonic. The Corinthians may well have exercised this charism, like others such as evangelism and praise, with great emotion. But such enthusiasm is not inherent in the gift itself; the wide variety in current practice is largely due to cultural differences.

The problem of uninterpreted messages in tongues, which Paul is dealing with toward the end of his letter, hardly ranks with practices that earlier receive his severe criticism: party spirit, divisions, sexual immorality, lawsuits and disorder at the Lord's Supper. In fact, the charism of tongues appears to be much less a problem to Paul than it is to some modern interpreters who describe it with a variety of disparaging terms such as "nonethical," "subpersonal," "ostentatious." Again, some modern explanations of spiritual gifts tell more about the interpreter than they do about the text.

We have already noted Paul's model for worship with believers coming together with a hymn, word of instruction, revelation, tongue and interpretation to strengthen the church (v. 26). The picture here resembles the meetings sketched in Ephesians 5:18-20 and Colossians 3:16-17. The members expected an opportunity to participate with a variety of spiritual gifts. While *all* would not necessarily take part in any one meeting, the significant point is that *any one* of them might do so as the Spirit led. Here there is no support for a clergy-laity dichotomy in which the former reserve the right to exercise what they consider the most important gifts.

Paul further states, "If anyone speaks in a tongue, two—or at the most three—should speak, one at a time, and someone must interpret. If there is no interpreter, the speaker should keep quiet in the church and speak to himself and God" (vv. 27-28). Here is a picture just the opposite from the frenzied, irrational practice of glossolalia in pagan religions. The Corinthians were no longer coerced by evil spirits, "influenced and led astray to mute idols" (12:2). They were now led by the Holy Spirit, whose fruit is "love, joy, peace . . . and *self-control*" (Gal 5:22-23). Paul's instructions for the use of this gift assumes that it could and should be controlled by the speaker (1 Cor 14:28). His expressed concern is not the volume or enthusiasm of the messages in tongues but their *intelligibility* through the gift of interpretation, so that the church can be built up.

It is significant that the apostle does not instruct the church to deal with possible misuse of speaking in tongues and prophecy through authoritative control by its leaders. He says nothing about forming a committee to organize and monitor the service. Rather, these gifts have the built-in balance of the two complementary gifts of interpretation and discernment. Paul's confidence lies in control by Christ, the head of the body, through the Holy Spirit as he manifests his power and direction through the individual members.

If speaking in tongues was causing a problem, what was the recommended solution? One quick answer, often used today, might have been to eliminate the practice. Apparently some at Corinth had urged such action, since Paul thought it necessary to command in verse 39, "Stop forbidding speaking in tongues" (literal translation).[4] The divinely inspired solution was to use this charism according to his directions for building up the body of Christ. To achieve that goal, the apostle concludes with the instruction that "everything should be done in a fitting and orderly way" (v. 40).

Private Prayer
Paul also teaches that private speaking in tongues can strengthen the individual: "For anyone who speaks in a tongue does not speak to men but to God. Indeed, [without interpretation] no one understands him; he utters mysteries with his spirit [by the Spirit]. . . . He who speaks in a tongue edifies himself" (vv. 2, 4). This kind of speaking in tongues is a form of prayer. With the spirit (literally, "in spirit") the individual speaks mysteries—that is, divine truths. This function of uninterpreted tongues (not understood by others) has value in building up the individual member of the body. Again, when there is no interpretation, "the speaker should keep quiet in the church and speak to himself and to God" (v. 28).

How does speaking in tongues differ from ordinary prayer? "For this reason anyone who speaks in a tongue should pray that he may interpret what he says. For if I pray in a tongue, my spirit prays, but my mind is unfruitful. So what shall I do? I will pray with my spirit, but I will also pray with my mind; I will sing with my spirit, but I will also sing with my mind" (vv. 13-15).

The first statement follows from the main argument so far: unless the message is interpreted, speaking in tongues cannot build up the church. The speaker does not understand what he is saying; otherwise he would not have to pray for an interpretation.

Verses 14 and 15 give rise to conflicting interpretations. First, what does Paul mean by saying that his spirit prays? Some take it as an expression of emotion. But in this discussion Paul never uses *spirit* for feelings, which play no part in this teaching about tongues. Rather, this praying in tongues is the manifestation of a spiritual gift in which the speaker is responding to the influence of the Holy Spirit. The degree of emotion often varies with the personality and the circumstances.

Second, Paul explains that in this kind of prayer his mind is unfruitful. But what does that mean? Some scholars interpret this unfruitfulness in terms of the *result*—that is, it is of little or no value. If that is so, why does Paul practice this gift? The Greek word *akarpos* can also mean "unproductive" in the sense of "not active."⁵ Here Paul focuses on the *process;* he calls his mind unproductive because it is the Holy Spirit, not his mind, producing what is said. This alternate meaning of the term better fits its context and usage in this passage.

According to Paul, speaking in tongues may occur in public worship providing it is followed by interpretation. If not, the individual is to remain silent and "speak to himself and to God." Private prayer may be in a tongue by the Spirit or in ordinary language produced by one's mind. This understanding of the passage guides the contemporary exercise of tongues in charismatic fellowships. In practice, relatively few members manifest the gifts of tongues and interpretation. Most persons use this means of prayer silently in meetings or in private, finding that it does strengthen their devotional life, as Paul indicates. Some term it their "prayer language."

For example, a few weeks after Frank began attending a weekly charismatic prayer and praise meeting he had an unexpected experience. As the group was standing with raised arms to sing "Alleluia, alleluia, give thanks to the risen Lord," he found himself singing quietly in unfamiliar words. With an unusually strong sense of the Lord's presence, he continued his praise and thanksgiving in this strange "language." Later Frank discovered an explanation of this experience in 1 Corinthians 14:15. He realized how quickly in his daily devotions he ran out of his own words to praise God. Now with prayer in tongues Frank could continue his praise for a much longer period that strengthened his relationship with Christ.

In Acts we discovered two kinds of speaking in tongues. At Pentecost it took the form of *xenolalia* (recognizable foreign languages) to declare the wonders of God to pilgrims from other parts of the Roman Empire. On other occasions Luke reports only that speaking in tongues consisted of praise and prophecy, presumably in the local language.

At Corinth *glossolalia* served two purposes. When manifested in corporate worship, it was an unknown "language" that required interpretation to be understood by the church. It could also be useful without interpretation in private prayer. After giving specific instructions for corporate use of both prophecy and tongues, Paul concludes with encouragement and admonition: "God is not a God of disorder but of peace. . . . Therefore, my brothers, be eager to prophesy, and do not forbid speaking in tongues. But everything should be done in a fitting and orderly way" (vv. 33, 39-40).

Historical Perspective

How did the gifts of prophecy and speaking in tongues fare after the first century? The apostolic fathers, who had direct contact with Paul or a disciple, often combined the two in the single category of prophecy.[6] One reason may have been to avoid giving ammunition to those who were attacking Christians for alleged irrational behavior. Nevertheless, Irenaeus reported contemporary manifestations of both gifts. "In like manner we do hear many brethren in the church, who possess prophetic gifts, and those who through the Spirit speak all kinds of languages, and bring to light for the general benefit the hidden things of men and declare the mysteries of God."[7]

Writing voluminously around A.D. 225, Tertullian commented specifically on speaking in tongues as well as prophecy.[8] As late as the fourth century, Cyril of Jerusalem thought it possible that his candidates for baptism might receive the gift of prophecy.[9] But by that time these gifts were no longer continuously exercised in the church. So an explanation had to be found to account for their general disappearance.

Augustine formulated the doctrine that speaking in tongues had been a special gift for evangelism in the apostolic period, after which it was meant to pass away. Spontaneous prophecy and tongues as a way for the Spirit to speak directly to the Christian community were becoming unwelcome in a church that had adopted more liturgical forms of worship.

A further development inhibited the exercise of tongues in the Western church: it gradually came to be considered an evidence of demon possession. Around the year 1000 a book of public services reflected that view in a section titled "Exorcism of the Possessed": "Signs of possession are the following: ability to speak with some facility in a strange tongue or to understand it when spoken by another; the faculty of divulging future and hidden events; display of powers which are beyond the subject's age and natural condition."[10]

That church policy, which persisted for many centuries, may explain why speaking in tongues was seldom mentioned during those years. Fear of demonic influence masquerading as speaking in tongues continues to be reflected, for example, in the writing of influential twentieth-century theologian Ronald Knox: "To speak with tongues you had never learned was, and is, a recognized symptom in cases of alleged diabolical possession."[11]

Granted that in some cases it can be a demonic counterfeit, the biblical response is not to forbid the practice but to "test the spirits" (1 Jn 4:1).

Nevertheless, charisms of prophecy and speaking in tongues did not disappear entirely. They recurred in certain renewal movements that also included healings and miracles. One was the ascetic movement that swept through Egypt and Asia Minor during the fourth to sixth centuries. Another renewal involving charismatic activity comprised the Cistercian, Franciscan and Dominican movements in France and Italy during the twelfth and thirteenth centuries.[12] Evidence of isolated occurrences of prophecy and tongues in more recent centuries have also been discovered.

Modern Cultural Views

Why do a variety of otherwise competent contemporary scholars approach the subject of speaking in tongues with such negative bias? The answer may not be theological so much as cultural. As we have noted, in each generation Christian attitudes are strongly influenced, and often shaped, by prevailing secular forces.

For the last two centuries in our Western world the Age of Reason has cast a long shadow. The so-called Enlightenment of the eighteenth century exalted reason as the final arbiter of knowledge. Scientific rationalism claims to be the only valid way to explain the universe. A charge of irrationality or emotionalism is the kiss of death to almost anything except love, sports, politics and war. Among the general public, speaking in tongues is widely associated with psychological instability; at the very least it is so foreign as to be completely dismissed. This attitude has been fostered by interpretations based more on modern cultural presuppositions than on biblical and historical evidence.

The comparative-religion school views Christianity as essentially a variant of the common religious experience of humankind. Other religions also feature conversion, sacrifice, rituals, prayer and glossolalia. It is noted that both the ancient world and some cultures today have ecstatic experiences involving a frenzy. Christian glossolalia, therefore, is considered simply one version of this experience and without religious value. "Words and sounds which are without connection and meaning to men are uttered in ecstasy. The phenomenon is well known to students of the psychology of primitive and emotional types of religion. Such outbursts were known in the Hellenistic mystical religions of the time."[13] This view is a classic example of how a presupposition (that all religions are basically the same) can blind an interpreter to the evidence (the radical uniqueness of Christianity).

A second evaluation of speaking in tongues grants the essential difference between Christian and pagan practices but still links the former with abnormal religious emotionalism: "the release of strong emotion which cannot find satisfying expression in more normal ways . . . [is] an innocuous way of letting off superficial spiritual steam."[14] This view ignores abundant evidence that glossolalia, like prayer and preaching, can be either calm or emotional in the experience of many normal individuals who are hardly in need of an emotional safety valve. Most so-called scientific studies of tongues have been based on models that either assume at the outset that such experience is pathological or have been used subjectively without accepted controls. Nevertheless, the charge that speaking in tongues is linked with emotionalism or psychological disorder has forged an iron-bound prejudice in the public mind. To use a baseball metaphor, this spiritual gift has three strikes against it even before getting a chance to bat.

A third view continues to link speaking in tongues with demonic influence, an openness to the intrusion of evil powers. Given the prevalence of the occult in our society, this concern should not be overlooked. Nevertheless, we need to understand how Satan works. Paul warns against "false apostles, deceitful workmen, masquerading as apostles of Christ. And no wonder, for Satan himself masquerades as an angel of light" (2 Cor 11:13-14). The Bible pictures Satan as a clever enemy, a counterfeit—hardly the popular image of a red devil with recognizable horns and hoofs. The danger of a counterfeit lies in its likeness to the real thing. Counterfeiters do not make their one-hundred-dollar bills triangular, printed with red ink and bearing a picture of Mickey Mouse.

We underestimate Satan's ingenuity if we suppose that his greatest deception is likely to come through speaking in tongues, the spiritual gift least acceptable to our rationalistic culture. Isn't it probable that instead he would misuse gifts of knowledge and teaching, which are so highly esteemed and even idolized? Cults and sects have largely thrived under the leadership of persuasive preachers, with open Bible, who cloak false teaching in the garb of biblical authority. No wonder both Peter and Paul warn against false *teachers* (2 Pet 2:1; 2 Tim 4:3-4).

Glossolalia in Practice
According to Paul, speaking in tongues is not *rational*—that is, produced by

the mind as in ordinary language (1 Cor 14:14). But that does not mean it is *irrational* (senseless, unreasonable, absurd). This gift is a *nonrational* (apart from reason) means of speaking or praying with wordless sounds beyond conceptual language.

What, then, is the purpose of such speech which cannot be understood without interpretation? Although a complete answer may not be possible, several points can be made.

Many in the charismatic renewal do not consider this charism to be the Pentecostal initial physical evidence of baptism in the Spirit—a specific second stage of Christian experience. Instead they view it as one of many responses to the Holy Spirit to empower their devotional life or give a message to the community. It provides a means for extended praise, thanksgiving and intercession beyond ordinary expression, when words fail the desire to keep communicating with God—whether in private prayer or in public with interpretation.

This charism is often the gateway to a deeper relationship with the Lord as the Holy Spirit brings a new sense of his presence and power. For some it is a highly emotional experience, perhaps like their conversion; for others it is quiet and calm, like other milestones in their Christian life. Praying in tongues can be started or stopped at will, just like ordinary prayer, and like congregational prophecy, which is "subject to the control of prophets" (1 Cor 14:32). Autobiographical reports reveal a wide variety of initial experiences and meanings.

Another use of tongues involves singing in the Spirit, a spontaneous melodic expression of worship. In private or public, the participants go beyond ordinary speech into a transcendent language of praise as they improvise music to express their joy. Contemporary singing in the Spirit has brought a rediscovery of jubilation, the spontaneous overflowing of joy that was prevalent in the church from the fourth to the ninth centuries.[15] This wordless praying and singing aloud, a vital dimension of Christian worship, was largely lost in the following centuries. Through the charismatic renewal this mode of praise, along with a new hymnody of psalms and songs, is being recaptured.

The question whether speaking in tongues is a real language is frequently debated. Some linguistic analysis has concluded that the sounds do not technically qualify as a language. But that hardly renders them meaningless, as some immediately infer. The scientific method can no more measure the religious value of glossolalia than it can the significance of the bread and wine in Communion or the water in baptism. Scientific analysis is good as far as it can go, but the questions of meaning, value and purpose in human experience go far beyond its competence.

Occasionally, however, speaking in tongues constitutes a recognizable foreign language unfamiliar to the speaker but recognized by someone present. These miraculous experiences of xenolalia—unexpected and unexplained— have been verified by reliable witnesses. The following example recently occurred in New York.

A missionary to Indonesia was on furlough, visiting Episcopal churches to report on his church-planting ministry and gain additional support. At the end of a service several church members came forward for prayer. One woman unexpectedly gave a brief message in tongues. Afterward the missionary asked the rector when she had been in Borneo. The answer was "Never." The missionary was amazed, since she had spoken fluently in the local dialect of his mission. Her message was a word of encouragement from the Lord to continue courageously in his difficult pioneering ministry.

Glossolalia is also a rebuke to our rationalistic culture, whose intellectual pride infects the church. The mind, one of God's great gifts, is often exalted at the expense of other dimensions of human nature. Recovery of speaking in tongues can be a sign that "God's foolishness is wiser than human wisdom" (1 Cor 1:25 NRSV).

A pattern of prophecy, interpreted tongues and singing in the Spirit has come to life in hundreds of charismatic fellowships that expect the Holy Spirit to manifest these charisms and guard against their misuse.[16] Like others in the past, this renewal challenges theological traditions and organizational structures to remodel their fireplace, where necessary, to accommodate this newly kindled fire. Many churches in the renewal are also rediscovering the ministry of healing in its various forms, as we shall see in chapter eight.

8 Biblical Health and Wholeness

*A*t first David Hadley thought his severe stomach pains were due to indigestion. But as they kept recurring, he finally went to see his doctor. The x-rays showed ulcers needing immediate medication and possible surgery.

When the news came to David's friends at church, they had special prayer for him. They asked God to strengthen David's faith, meet his financial needs, comfort his family and give wisdom to the doctors. The situation seemed well covered until someone asked, "Why don't we pray for David's healing?"

Silence prevailed. Then the responses came: "How do we know it is God's will? Maybe God wants to test his faith. Perhaps this is a chance for David to be a good witness through his illness. After all, even the apostle Paul had to bear his thorn in the flesh." And so they left their prayers, hoping for the best.

That night Laura Nelson, who had attended this prayer meeting, was awakened by the cries of her young son. He had gone to bed complaining about how his ear hurt. She immediately phoned the doctor. He prescribed an antibiotic and sedative, which her husband rushed out to get at an all-night drugstore. Soon the medication began its work. It never occurred to the parents to question whether healing was God's will for their son.

A Double Standard

Christians pray confidently for courage, finances, comfort and wisdom. But often we are reluctant to pray for healing. We immediately call the doctor to cure through medicine, yet hesitate to ask God to heal through prayer. This double standard reaches far back into church history. It involves a misunderstanding of sickness that began in the early centuries and still prevails, blinding us to the biblical view of healing.

Today the church has not only a responsibility but also a new opportunity to exercise its God-given healing ministry. Despite the marvels of medical science, our technological approach to illness is not thoroughly successful. Americans now spend more than $900 billion annually on health care. Yet we have some of the highest rates in the world for heart disease, respiratory ailments and cancer.

The large gap between what we pay for health care and what we get is largely due to a modern misunderstanding of sickness and health. A majority of the medical establishment and public consider the body a complex machine that can be maintained and repaired by excellent mechanics—the doctors. It is assumed that breakdowns can be fixed if we spend enough money on medicine, surgery or other forms of treatment.

Both the church's concentration on the spirit and medicine's preoccupation with the body have overlooked the whole-person model presented in the Bible. Into this vacuum have rushed a variety of holistic cults from New Age mind control and biofeedback to hypnosis and Eastern meditation.[1] But in their search for a true humanity, the practitioners of these therapies have ignored the God who created it. Christians now have an opportunity to demonstrate God's power and desire to heal all dimensions of life. But that first requires a rediscovery of the biblical view of the whole person.

We will not attempt here to solve the agonizing problem of pain and suffering which crosses all boundaries of age and affluence, race and religion, paving the way for our last implacable enemy, death. In this chapter we will not explore why and how sickness arrives; our approach is not philosophical. Rather, we put the question another way: Given the suffering of human existence, is there any evidence that God cares and is willing to help? This practical approach takes us first to the Old Testament, then to the ministry of Jesus Christ. What was his commission to the church, and how has it fared over the centuries? Then in the two chapters that follow we will examine the practice of healing today.

Sickness and Health in Israel

"In the beginning God created the heavens and the earth. . . . God saw all that he had made, and it was very good" (Gen 1:1, 31). God's original creation was one of harmony and balance. Adam and Eve were responsible to obey God but had freedom of choice. They were innocent, free from evil; neither sin nor disease marred their life in Eden.

But they were tested. Genesis 3 recounts the intrusion of evil as the serpent sowed doubt about God. The man and woman disobeyed their Creator and reaped the consequences. Disharmony and alienation ensued. Their relationship with God now broken, Adam and Eve were separated from the Garden with a curse on their labor. Before long, family relationships were also fractured, and Cain murdered his brother Abel.

The Old Testament records the many ways sin further marred the lives of individuals, families and nations. The biblical writings also recount God's unceasing efforts through the prophets to reconcile people to himself and to each other. His activity culminated in the mission of his Son to restore the creation to its original harmony.

In the Bible a "Hebraic wholism" treats all elements of human nature as interrelated in the experience of any individual. The words for "body," "soul," "mind" and "spirit" do not represent separate parts of the person, but rather dimensions of a unified being. This model contrasts with the Greek view of a pure soul temporarily imprisoned in an evil material body from which it needs to escape. The high view of the body in Scripture is evidenced by the incarnation and resurrection of the Son of God. The Greeks' "immortality of the soul" is a far cry from the resurrection of the body.

The Old Testament conveys the unity of the person in the Hebrew cognates *shalem* ("healthy" or "whole") and *shalom* ("peace"). Health and peace coexist naturally, as we see in Psalm 29:11: "The LORD gives strength to his people; the LORD blesses his people with peace!" This peace is far more than an absence of conflict. It involves inner tranquillity, health, wholeness, perspective, integration of life—even when beset by external turmoil. This is God's desire for his people.[2]

Soon after the exodus from Egypt God revealed this purpose: "I am the LORD, who heals you" (Ex 15:26). This reality was recognized by psalmist and prophet alike. David declares that it is the Lord "who forgives all your sins and heals all your diseases" (Ps 103:3). Isaiah declares about the Messiah, "By his wounds we are healed" (Is 53:5). Jeremiah prays, "Heal me, O LORD, and I will be healed; save me and I will be saved, for you are the one I praise" (Jer 17:14). For these writers salvation and health are interrelated—a concept we need to recover for the church's ministry of healing.

The Old Testament prophets looked forward to a Messiah who would save them in every dimension of personal and national life. He would restore the health of the people as well as their lands (Is 35).

Jesus and the Early Church
We can never fully understand why God allows evil and suffering. But we know that he has demonstrated his compassion at great cost to himself. The heart of the gospel is not simply the inspiring *idea* that "God is love," but news of God's saving *action:* "God so loved the world that he gave his one and only Son" (Jn 3:16). God has revealed to us who he is, who we are and what his purpose is for us in prophetic message and redemptive action. Jesus Christ is the ultimate Word and Act of God. In him God became fully human, suffered with us and finally died and rose for us.

At Jesus' birth angels announced to the shepherds, "A Savior has been born

to you; he is Christ the Lord" (Lk 2:11). The Greek word *sōtēr* was applied
to philosophers, statesmen and physicians, implying salvation from meaningless existence and from political crises. In the New Testament this term is
applied uniquely to Jesus of Nazareth. The Savior came to deliver people from
their sins and sickness and to bring meaning to their lives. In his home synagogue Jesus announced as the keynote of his ministry Isaiah's prophecy:

> The Spirit of the Lord is on me,
>> because he has anointed me
>> to preach good news to the poor.
> He has sent me to proclaim freedom for the prisoners
>> and recovery of sight for the blind,
> to release the oppressed,
>> to proclaim the year of the Lord's favor. (Lk 4:18-19)

Jesus chose this Old Testament prophecy to announce his messianic ministry
of making people whole.

Luke records a visit Jesus made to Capernaum, where he taught in the
synagogue and healed a man of demon possession. Jesus then cured Peter's
mother-in-law of a high fever. "When the sun was setting, the people brought
to Jesus all who had various kinds of sickness, and laying his hands on each
one, he healed them" (Lk 4:40). Preaching and healing were the two legs on
which our Lord's ministry walked into every segment of society and the lives
of needy people.

Matthew links this ministry with another statement of Isaiah:

> He drove out the spirits with a word and healed all the sick. This was to
> fulfill what was spoken through the prophet Isaiah [53:4]:
>> "He took up our infirmities
>> and carried our diseases." (Mt 8:16-17)

Peter later testified to Cornelius how "God anointed Jesus of Nazareth with
the Holy Spirit and power, and how he went around doing good and healing
all who were under the power of the devil" (Acts 10:38). In his first letter the
apostle echoes this refrain: "By his wounds you have been healed" (1 Pet 2:24).

The close connection between salvation and healing appears in the Greek word *sōzō*. Usually translated "save," it also means "heal." The word was used for being saved from peril, death, shipwreck, dangers of war, judicial condemnation and illness.[3] This term, rich in medical and social as well as religious meanings, powerfully describes the purpose and scope of Jesus' ministry. Just as sin has ravaged every dimension of human life, salvation extends to the total person. Jesus declared: "I have come that they may have life, and have it to the full" (Jn 10:10). For this reason he healed all kinds of sickness—spiritual, emotional, physical and relational.

Why was healing a vital part of Jesus' ministry? First, it fulfilled the will of God, demonstrated in the Old Testament and predicted by the prophets, to make his people whole. If we ever wonder whether God wants to heal, we have only to look at his Son's actions. "Anyone who has seen me has seen the Father. . . . I do exactly what my Father has commanded me" (Jn 14:9, 31).

Second, Jesus healed out of his own compassion (Mk 1:41). His great love moved him to meet people's varied needs as they appeared to him like sheep without a shepherd. Third, Jesus' healings were a sign of the messianic age, the presence and power of the kingdom. He went about "preaching the good news of the kingdom and healing every disease and sickness" (Mt 9:35). The miracles were also considered signs that authenticated his message (Jn 2:18; 6:30), but this was neither the sole nor necessarily the most important significance of his healings.

Fourth, Jesus was sent to destroy the devil's work (1 Jn 3:8). Part of that evil work was to cripple and kill through disease. So when Jesus healed a badly crippled woman, he referred to her as a person "whom Satan has kept bound for eighteen long years" (Lk 13:16). Long before Marshall McLuhan, Jesus demonstrated how "the medium is the message": his actions as well as his words eloquently communicated God's desire to make people whole.[4]

After months of demonstration, Jesus gave his disciples some on-the-job training. "He sent them out to preach the kingdom of God and to heal the sick. . . . So they set out and went from village to village, preaching the gospel and healing people everywhere" (Lk 9:2, 6). Yet this ministry was not just for the select twelve disciples. Some time later "the Lord appointed seventy-two others and sent them two by two ahead of him to every town and place where he was about to go." He instructed them, "Heal the sick who are there and tell them, 'The kingdom of God is near you' " (Lk 10:1, 9).

After his resurrection the Lord commissioned his disciples to continue their ministry of preaching and healing: "Therefore go and make disciples of all nations, baptizing them in the name of the Father and of the Son and of the Holy Spirit, and teaching them to obey everything I have commanded you" (Mt 28:19-20). "Everything" included not only the words they had heard but also the actions they had been commanded to perform.

After Pentecost the church continued to preach and heal with power. Peter healed a lame man at the temple gate and then declared the gospel to the gathering crowd (Acts 3:1-16). For two years Paul spoke boldly at Ephesus, where he healed the sick and those possessed by evil spirits (Acts 19:8-12). Through the Holy Spirit, powerful words and actions spearheaded the Christian mission.

Nevertheless, the healing ministry was not limited to the apostles. As we have seen, Paul expected gifts of healings (various means for different kinds of illness), as well as other charisms, to be manifested through members of the Corinthian church. James instructed his readers, scattered throughout the Empire, about taking spiritual initiative when sickness struck. Neither he nor Paul gave any indication that the church's healing ministry was meant to end in a few decades.

> Is any one of you sick? He should call the elders of the church to pray over
> him and anoint him with oil in the name of the Lord. And the prayer
> offered in faith will make the sick person well; the Lord will raise him up.
> If he has sinned, he will be forgiven. Therefore confess your sins to each
> other and pray for each other so that you may be healed. The prayer of
> a righteous man is powerful and effective. (Jas 5:14-16)

It is significant that James connects physical and spiritual healing. In recent years we have learned much about the effects of attitudes and emotions on physical well-being; bitterness and resentment not only fracture interpersonal relationships but can also undermine physical health.

Some suggest that since the Greeks used oil as medication, this is what James had in mind. Admittedly, to the modern scientific mind a medical house call would be more effective than a visit simply for prayer. But the text does not support this conjecture. Anointing in the name of the Lord was a familiar *religious* act, and James explicitly says it is the believing *prayer* that heals.

The New Testament also reports a number of situations where immediate physical healing did *not* occur. For example, Paul writes that Epaphroditus was ill, apparently for some time, and almost died, although he was eventually restored to health (Phil 2:25-30). Timothy had recurring stomach trouble for which the apostle recommended drinking a little wine (1 Tim 5:23).

It is clear that the early Christians looked to the risen Christ for freedom from sin and sickness, not as a right to be demanded but as a gift to be received. To them the body had a value in the present as well as a glorious resurrection in the future. *This understanding of human life and God's salvation in Christ made healing an integral part of the church's message and mission.*

The Church's Record

During the second and third centuries, as the church continued to grow, healing was practiced and taught to new converts. Most Christian writers of this period witnessed some instances of healing.[5] Irenaeus, who lived in Gaul around A.D. 198, attested the full range of healings recorded in the Gospels and Acts. He noted that often these miracles led to conversion.[6]

Early in the second century, however, a revival of Plato's philosophy began to undermine the church's healing ministry. Contrary to the biblical writers, who viewed the person as a whole, Neo-Platonists drew a line between spirit and body. They taught that the person has a higher nature of soul, reason and will, and a lower nature of body, emotions and appetites. As a result, some theologians were influenced to emphasize the soul at the expense of the body.

For a time church leaders successfully resisted this philosophy, maintaining that salvation involves the whole person. Special prayer for a bishop entreated: "Grant him, O Lord, to loose all bonds of the iniquity of demons, the power to heal all diseases and quickly to beat down Satan under his feet." For many centuries Christians commonly participated in healing prayer for relatives and friends. Oil was distributed to the people for anointing their sick.

One of the greatest figures in the ancient church was Origen of Alexandria in Egypt (c. 185-254). This brilliant theologian and spiritual leader witnessed how Christians "expel evil spirits, and perform many cures. . . [T]he name of Jesus can still remove distractions from the minds of men, and expel demons, and also take away diseases."[7]

During the two centuries after the apostolic period, small bands of Christians took the gospel of Christ to the far corners of the Roman Empire and beyond. A significant part of their vital faith was a conviction that their God expected a healing ministry from his followers.

Nevertheless, that fire gradually died down, but hardly because gifts of healings were no longer needed in a vital church that had the New Testament canon. Around 250 Cyprian (c. 200-258), as bishop of Carthage, wrote that sometimes through baptism a serious illness was cured. But he noted with sorrow that the church had become soft and flabby. He expressed concern over Christians being "eager about our patrimony and our gain, seeking to satisfy our pride, yielding ourselves wholly to emulation and to strife."[8] He believed that the persecution by Emperor Decius was God's judgment on the moral laxity and division in the church.

Constantine's Edict of Milan in 313 marked a new era for the church. Persecution ceased, Christianity became the established religion, worship was more structured, and nominal Christianity became the rule. As a result, spontaneous manifestations of spiritual gifts through members of the body waned along with other basic New Testament teachings.

Still, the Eastern church continued its healing ministry under the leadership of several outstanding bishops. Basil the Great (c. 330-79), who had some medical training, founded a large hospital outside Caesarea—the first public institution devoted to caring for the sick. He also believed in and practiced healing though prayer. Gregory of Nyssa (fl. 335-95) developed a theology of healing in his book *The Making of Man,* based on the healing miracles of Christ. As he witnessed the effectiveness of healing ministry, he concluded that it is the main door through which people come to a knowledge of God.[9]

In the West, unfortunately, Augustine (354-430) rationalized the decline of spiritual power by teaching that certain extraordinary gifts were given for founding the church and then withdrawn because they were no longer necessary. Even this great theologian was not immune to tailoring Scripture to fit the status quo. Ironically, toward the end of Augustine's life the Holy Spirit challenged his theology with many remarkable healings. In 424, as *The City of God* was nearing completion, Augustine wrote: "Once I realized how many miracles were occurring in our own day and which were so like the miracles of old, how wrong it would be to allow the memory of these marvels of divine power to perish from among our people. It is only two years ago that the keeping of records was begun here in Hippo, and already, at this writing, we have nearly seventy attested miracles."[10]

Not only did Augustine witness miraculous healings, but on at least one occasion he laid hands on a sick man who went away well. Unfortunately, these events did not lead to a revision of the bishop's earlier doctrine about the cessation of miraculous gifts; that teaching prevailed after his death.

During the Middle Ages monasteries were centers of medical care as well as learning. Miracles of healing became associated with outstanding individuals. Yet reform and renewal were sporadic. In 1123 the Lateran Council forbade clergy to attend the sick except as spiritual directors. A century later surgery and dissection were declared sacrilegious, since the body was thought to be a prison of the soul and to have little importance for a person's spiritual well-being. The Western world (and the church) had effectively split the human person in two, setting up the double standard noted at the outset of this chapter.

By the thirteenth century the practice of prayer and anointing with oil for healing (Jas 5:14-15) had become "last rites" for the dying. New Testament concern for the whole person in this life had given way to simply making sure that the soul was saved for eternity. Although the Protestant Reformation changed many elements of church life, it perpetuated this concept: once the saving work of Christ and the canon of Scripture were completed, miracles and healings were no longer considered to be needed. It was considered sufficient that faith in Christ secured salvation of the soul while the indwelling Spirit provided power to obey biblical rules for living.

Sickness had come to be viewed as a specific punishment given by God for a person's own good. How ironic that the church had turned things upside down! In the New Testament it is Satan who sends sickness, while Christ and his followers heal through the power of the Holy Spirit. But now the church assures the sufferer that it is God who has certainly sent the sickness. The minister visits not to anoint for healing but to ensure the salvation of the soul.

As the twentieth century dawned, no major denomination had a theology affirming the direct healing activity of God through gifts of the Spirit. No wonder that so many today believe God is responsible for sickness, sending it as a punishment to bring sinners to repentance or as a "test" to produce patience in the saints.

Healing Rediscovered

Nevertheless, the healing ministry did not entirely disappear. During the nineteenth century it was rediscovered in parts of the Roman Catholic Church and in the ministry of well-known evangelical Protestant leaders. For example, A. J. Gordon, a Baptist minister in Boston, published his *Ministry of Healing* in 1882. He describes the history of healing and gives examples from his own ministry. Gordon notes that "the most powerful effect of such experiences is upon the subjects themselves, in the marked consecration and extraordinary anointing which almost invariably attend them."[11] A. B. Simpson, founder of the Christian and Missionary Alliance in 1877, wrote *The Gospel of Healing* as a result of his study of Scripture and his own ministry.[12] Andrew Murray of South Africa also taught: "The pardon of sin and the healing of sickness complete one another."[13] Theologian Donald Dayton has traced the rise of the divine healing movement in the Wesleyan, Holiness and Pentecostal churches.[14]

In the twentieth century several movements have contributed to the contemporary resurgence of healing ministries. For example, in 1910 Henry Wilson, an Episcopal minister in Asheville, North Carolina, founded the Order of the Nazarene to foster a ministry of healing. This movement, which became inactive with his retirement, inspired John Banks to devote the last thirty years of his ministry to healing. In 1947 he founded the interdenominational Order of St. Luke the Physician, comprising clergy and laity committed to a healing ministry. During the next decade the order spread to hundreds of churches in the United States and abroad.

Since World War II the healing ministry in America has moved in two major streams. The first flowed from classical Pentecostal churches but soon spread far beyond its banks to become an independent movement. Oral Roberts initiated his ministry in 1947 and gained a widespread audience among non-Pentecostals. Kathryn Kuhlman also began her healing ministry that year. Her weekly program became one of the CBS network's longest-running as it transcended denominational barriers. She and Oral Roberts were primarily responsible for bringing respectability to healing revivalism in North America. Unfortunately, many individualistic leaders, ranging from genuine to counterfeit, moved the fire out of the fireplace into their own organizations. The charlatans among them brought the activities of so-called faith healers into disrepute.[15] (For a study of healing in the prosperity gospel see chapter thirteen.)

Unlike independent revivalistic ministries, which often feature miraculous physical healings as each meeting's high point, a second stream has flowed responsibly within the mainline churches. These services emphasize prayer for the whole person, whose healing in various dimensions may be gradual, especially when the illness involves strained or fractured relationships. Among the early pioneers of this ministry were Episcopalians Alfred Price, Agnes Sanford, Donald Gross and Emily Gardiner Neal, as well as Roman Catholics Francis MacNutt and Michael Scanlon. Their teaching and healing services, initiated largely within the local church, demonstrate their purpose to strengthen the body of Christ for its life and service. This context also offers guidance and requires accountability in the use of healing prayer.

Many mainline Protestant and Roman Catholic churches now have regular healing services. Vatican II revolutionized the Catholic Church's practice of healing. Instead of Extreme Unction to prepare the soul for death, the Rite of Anointing now recognizes healing prayer for wholeness as a normal dimension of Christian life. Various sectors of the church are recovering, in a variety of ways, the powerful healing ministry intended by their Lord.[16]

Kinds of Illness

At the outset a healing ministry needs to recognize the major varieties of sickness and different kinds of treatment in the practice of "gifts of healings." We also must take account of developments in medicine during recent decades.

Since World War II and the advent of readily available antibiotics, the biomedical model has dominated the practice of medicine. It assumes that disease is due primarily to physical problems and treats them apart from emotional and spiritual factors. Modern science has fostered the idea that the body is a machine, disease is the result of a breakdown, and the doctor's task is to repair it.

Although this model has been successful with many physical disorders, its use has raised several critical questions. In becoming experts at treating diseases, have we forgotten how to heal persons? Why is so little attention given to the prevention of sickness? How can we hope to keep the machine running with so little concern for the way it is driven?

Only recently have we begun to recapture the ancient thought that health is a mosaic of physical, emotional, spiritual and sociological factors unique for each person. The evidence shows that our health is largely influenced by our behavior, nutrition and environment. Self-control, good diet, sufficient exercise, expression of feelings, stress management and a sense of self-worth foster well-being. Health is more than lack of disease; it is a way of living.

In some hospitals a majority of the patients suffer from diseases of lifestyle involving smoking, alcohol or drug abuse, inadequate diet, overeating or promiscuous sex. These diseases are preventable, but they persist because the habits that cause them are too pleasurable or hard to give up.

Emotional factors also figure in disease. Charles Mayo, founder of the Mayo Clinic, estimates that the spiritual and psychological element in illness varies from 65 to 75 percent of illness. No wonder that such a high proportion of people come home from the hospital unhealed! The prevailing biomedical model cannot cope with some important dimensions of their sickness. In fact, it often does harm by indicating medical or surgical procedures for diseases that can be cured only through marked changes in lifestyle or relationships.

Not that it is wrong for a doctor to focus on the body and to analyze physiological causes of disease. Or for a psychiatrist to concentrate on the emotions, or a pastor on spiritual issues. It is important to *distinguish* among physical, emotional and spiritual dimensions. But we should not *divide* them as if each could be treated in isolation from the others. No longer can the church settle for custody of the spirit and leave the rest to medicine and psychiatry. Increasingly, Christians involved in healing ministries are dealing with the whole person to provide appropriate means of aid—through prayer and medicine or surgery or counseling where necessary.

In the next chapter we turn to basic principles and practice of healing, including obstacles, mistaken beliefs, objections and the importance of healing within the Christian community.

9 Healing of Persons

*R**emember David Hadley, from the previous chapter? When his ulcers* were discovered, he was admitted to the hospital for further testing that indicated that immediate surgery was not required. He was given medication and sent home with instructions for a restricted diet. Meanwhile, several friends suggested specific prayer for his healing. While he appreciated their concern, David wondered whether it was God's will for him. That crucial question looms large in the minds of many, including the church members who were reluctant to pray for his healing. How can we be sure that God wants to heal our illness?

Is Healing God's Will?

We have already seen the prevailing double standard in dealing with this issue. If it is healing through medicine or surgery, the question is not even asked. It never occurred to Laura Nelson and her husband (our second example in chapter eight) to pray, "Lord, show us if it is your will for Billy to be healed, so we can know whether to call the doctor." Her unhesitating reach for the phone to get medical help showed her confidence that God wanted her to act on behalf of her child's healing.

Yet when it is a matter of healing through prayer, two questions frequently arise: Is this healing God's will? And if so, why is there so much persisting illness? These questions—roadblocks across the path to healing ministries—must be squarely faced.

First, we have already noted that healing of the whole person was an integral part of Jesus' ministry and training of his disciples. It continued in the teaching and practice of the church. Paul includes "gifts of healings" in his lists of charisms (1 Cor 12:9). James instructs the sick person to "call the elders of the church to pray over him and anoint him with oil in the name of the Lord" (Jas 5:14).

Healing of persons is rooted in the character of our God. Scripture consistently affirms that God is the source of all good (Gen 1:31), including truth (Jn 17:17) and health (Ex 15:26). On the other hand, Satan is the source of all evil (1 Jn 3:8), including falsehood (Jn 8:44) and sickness (Lk 13:11). God sent his Son into the world to destroy the evil works of the devil, to free us from his power and to make us whole. In the midst of evil and suffering, the apostle Paul assures us: "And we know that in all things God works for the good of those who love him" (Rom 8:28). We derive our theology of healing from the self-revelation of God in Scripture, not from the circumstances of life in our fallen world. *God is always on the side of good, truth and health.*

Nevertheless, we need to face the second question: If God desires healing, why does so much sickness persist? Like many other "why" queries about God's actions, it has no pat answer. Yet this is parallel to other cases where we have learned to cope with an apparent contradiction between a divine desire and observed results. In evangelism, for example, Peter writes that God desires "everyone to come to repentance" (2 Pet 3:9); Paul teaches that God "wants all men to be saved and to come to a knowledge of the truth" (1 Tim 2:4). If that is true, why do we see so many, even in our own country with all its opportunities to hear the gospel, spurning God's offer of salvation in

Jesus Christ? Then there is sanctification: Paul declares that "it is God's will that you should be sanctified" (1 Thess 4:3). Yet we see in our churches many professing Christians whose lives are far from holy.

Does our inability to account for the gap between God's will and its fulfillment cause us to give up our preaching and teaching? No. We continue our efforts on behalf of evangelism and sanctification. By the same token, then, we can affirm that God wants people to be well, and we can confidently pray for healing despite the fact that it sometimes doesn't occur as expected. God is just as much on the side of healing as he is on the side of salvation and holiness.

Here we can learn from Agnes Sanford, whose pioneering ministry of spiritual healing in the 1940s and 1950s has profoundly influenced the church in this area. She urged that when praying for healing we say not "*if* it is your will" but "*according to* your will"—that is, we ask that God answer in his own way and time. Between those two phrases lies a wide chasm. On one side hesitates wavering doubt; on the other stands a confident faith. As in the Lord's Prayer, we can pray "Your will be done"—not as an escape clause but with expectancy. After all, Jesus didn't teach his disciples to ask, "Give us today our daily bread, *if it is your will.*"

We know that ultimate healing—wholeness in every dimension of our being—does not take place in this life. Each of us must eventually die. Even Lazarus eventually departed this world permanently. Yet although complete health and holiness will come only with the resurrection body, we can be assured that here and now God is constantly working toward these very goals.

Principles and Practice
At the outset we face a significant semantic difficulty. What should we call a biblical healing ministry that involves spiritual gifts? The term *faith healing* starts with two strikes against it: (1) the unsavory reputation of many so-called faith healers and (2) an implication that other kinds of healing, such as medicine, surgery and counseling, do not require faith. The term *divine healing* can also be misleading, since it may seem to imply that only charismatic

healing comes from God, when in fact every kind of healing is his gracious gift.

Since we are focusing on spiritual gifts, we could call it *spiritual healing*. But that term might seem to refer to healing only in the spiritual arena and not the emotional or physical dimension. We will call this ministry *healing prayer* since prayer is basic in this ministry to the whole person, whatever kinds and means of healing are called for.

A strategy for healing must recognize many kinds of illness, various means of healing and different degrees of health.

1. Kinds of illness. Sickness works its destructive effects in all dimensions of life—physical, emotional, spiritual, relational. Physical illness takes such diverse forms as heart disease, cancer and diabetes. Emotional strain is evident in depression, fears and anxiety. Jesus recognizes the power of evil spirits to afflict people in many ways. He also lists various kinds of spiritual disease: evil thoughts, greed, envy, malice, deceit, slander, arrogance (Mk 7:21-22). These in turn generate anger, resentment, bitterness and guilt, which strain and fracture human relationships. They can also precipitate chronic physical ailments, the kind that medical science with its emphasis on crisis intervention is least able to cope with. (In their battle against sickness the big guns of drugs and surgery successfully search out and destroy specific enemies—bacteria, viruses, cancer cells—that make people sick. But doctors are far less successful in dealing with the many ailments that do not strike as a crisis but surreptitiously sneak in and refuse to go away—arthritis, allergies, the common cold.)

Since these dimensions of life are not isolated, illness is often more complex than we realize. Such was the case with David Hadley. His ulcers were a physical problem detected by x-rays and treated with medication. But the biomedical model failed to diagnose the cause and prescribe its cure; at best it produced a temporary holding pattern. Eventually David understood the effects of friction in family relationships, pressure at work and emotional wounds of childhood—areas his doctor had ignored. His complete healing had to come through means other than prescribed drugs and restricted diet.

2. Means of healing. In his list of nine charisms in 1 Corinthians 12 Paul includes gifts of healings, a significant double plural overlooked by many modern translations. We need to recognize that God heals in a variety of ways through different gifts.

The most important means of healing is prayer. It should come first. Yet we often respond like a patient whose painful symptoms baffled the doctor. When thorough examinations failed to yield a diagnosis, the physician said, "I am sorry; I can do nothing now but commend you to God." Thereupon the patient cried out, "Oh no! Has it come to that?"

In prayer we align ourselves with the desire and power of God our Healer. When we pray, we should not only request healing for a specific observed illness but also consider the person's pattern of living. What could have caused the illness? What corrective action needs to be taken? Prayer for healing of a physical disease often brings to light some emotional or spiritual sickness of which the sufferer is not aware. (We will consider this situation in the next chapter on inner healing.)

On one occasion Agnes Sanford received a telephone call from a distant city requesting prayer for a friend who was in the hospital with bleeding ulcers. Knowing his hard-driving temperament, she replied, "I have no liberty at this point to pray simply for his physical healing, because unless he is willing to change his lifestyle he will soon produce a new set of ulcers."

Two incidents in the Gospels illustrate this point. On one occasion a man was carried to Jesus by four friends who were concerned about his paralysis; he walked home with spiritual as well as physical healing (Mk 2:1-12). Another time, however, ten lepers were physically cleansed, but only the one who returned to give praise to God was spiritually healed (Lk 17:17, 19).

Through prayer we can also overcome demonic influence. Exorcism was a major part of our Lord's ministry. The apostle Paul viewed this dimension of spiritual conflict as vitally important (Eph 6:12). (We will gain an understanding of the long-overlooked relationship between sickness and evil spirits in chapter eleven, "Spiritual Warfare.")

Sometimes a sufferer has been overwhelmed by sorrow that has washed away hope. The demonstration of loving concern and faith by those who pray replaces fear with hope (1 Jn 4:18) and releases the body's recuperative forces. Emily Gardiner Neal observes that healing prayer results in a divine hastening of the entire healing process; it is like baking a potato in a microwave oven rather than an ordinary oven.[1]

While at times healing comes through prayer alone, often an illness needs to be addressed with medicine or even surgery. Long-standing emotional illness and fractured relationships may require counseling over a period of time. However it may come, we accept the healing as God's gift. The great French surgeon Ambroise Paré declared: "I care for the wound; God cures it." We should not emulate ancient Israel, about whom the Lord said, "They did not realize it was I who healed them" (Hos 11:3).

The wholistic approach I have outlined bridges the unbiblical gulf between "supernatural" and "natural," a dichotomy that causes many to thank God for healing through prayer but credit modern science for curing with penicillin. Scripture teaches that although God performs miracles, he is equally active in recurring events that we can explain and predict (see, for example, Ps 65). We do not worship a "God of the gaps," needed temporarily for phenomena we cannot yet explain. Our God is One in whom "we live and move and have our being" (Acts 17:28), who is "sustaining all things by his powerful word" (Heb 1:3). We should gratefully receive healing by whatever means God chooses to give it.

3. Degrees of healing. Overlooked or denied in some forms of healing ministry is the fact that healing may be incomplete. None of us in this life will become entirely whole in every dimension. Francis MacNutt's extensive ministry has shown that there is a "more or less" element in healing through prayer.[2]

□ Among us there is *varying power or gifts* to pray for healing. We do not yet understand how to pray for the unimpeded influence of the Holy Spirit.

□ For the sickness itself there can be *degrees of difficulty* in healing through prayer.

□ Healing is often a *process* involving a *time element* that can vary from a few seconds to many months.[3]

☐ There are also *degrees of improvement,* from slight to total healing. We must get out of the habit of categorical thinking that either a person is completely healed or the prayer was futile.

☐ There seem to be *degrees of the miraculous,* events that lie beyond the explainable or predictable.

We should note that the first four principles are comparable to the healing factors accepted in modern medicine and surgery. Everyone recognizes that the doctor's ability to diagnose an illness, the effectiveness of prescribed medication, the time needed for the healing process and the completeness of recovery may all vary from one case to the next. Why, then, should we be surprised to find variations in the effects of healing prayer? In both approaches the sick person is encouraged by a reasonably good diagnosis and a remedy that begins to bring improvement. MacNutt has found that understanding this "more or less" variability produces a greater appreciation of God's compassion and wisdom in healing.[4]

With a strategy for healing based on the above principles, we can move confidently in prayer without a simplistic formula that guarantees immediate preconceived results. It keeps us looking to God himself, who gives "every good and perfect gift" (Jas 1:17), to heal in his own time and way.

Obstacles to Healing

The first hurdle to be overcome is fear of failure. If we pray for healing and it does not occur, won't the person's faith be undermined? This question is answered by Don Gross, a research physicist turned parish priest, on the basis of extensive pioneering experience with healing prayer:

> Disappointments can come when detailed predictions of healing fail to materialize. . . . So we should wait and see, openmindedly, just what God will do. We can increase our faith, hope and expectancy by concentrating on what God has done, on his promises, in a clear visualization of the healing we desire, and by thanking Him for the healing He is giving in His perfect way.

Gross reports that over the years no one has expressed regret over his praying for healing because it did not occur as initially expected.[5]

Physicians and surgeons follow much the same path. None has a perfect record. Yet they have the faith and courage to act with the best resources at hand. Sometimes the medicine or surgery doesn't succeed, and the patient dies. But doctors do not give up, disillusioned with the practice of medicine—nor do their patients.

Why can't concerned Christians act in the same confidence with spiritual resources provided by their Lord? The answer to fear of disappointment is not to minimize expectancy but to maximize believing prayer and so demonstrate the compassion of Christ for the sick.

Once we start praying for physical healing, how do we explain apparent lack of results? One person with a visible tumor on the neck is prayed for; within ten minutes it has shrunk and disappeared. For another person with the same kind of tumor and expectancy, no observable change takes place. We naturally ask, "Why is the second person not healed?"

Our response is that we do not know. We should certainly not accept either of two prevalent pat answers: "It was not God's will"; "The person did not have enough faith." The first is contrary to biblical teaching; the second loads a burden of guilt on one who is already suffering.

When Jesus' disciples saw a man blind from birth, they inquired about the cause: Was it his sin or that of his parents? Jesus did not explain the past—why or how the man became blind. He looked to the future—what he intended to do about it (Jn 9:1-3). Although we cannot explain why a person is not immediately healed, we can try to identify possible barriers that lie across the path and help remove them.

First is *lack of faith,* primarily on the part of those praying for healing. When the disciples could not cure an epileptic boy, Jesus said it was "because *you* have so little faith" (Mt 17:20). On the positive side, when four men carried a paralytic into his presence, Jesus saw *their* faith and healed their friend spiritually and physically (Mk 2:1-12).

A second reason an illness may not be cured is a *wrong motive.* Why do I want to be healed? So that I can continue my self-centered way of living?

James reminds us, "When you ask, you do not receive, because you ask with wrong motives, that you may spend what you get on your pleasures" (Jas 4:3).

A third obstacle may be *sin in our lives:* unforgiveness, bitterness, destructive habits, involvement with the occult. When we start to pray for healing, the Holy Spirit sometimes puts his finger on one of these barriers that needs to be cleared away. On occasion a chronic physical or emotional malady, apparently incurable, disappears once a sinful habit is confessed and forsaken.

Fourth, people *don't persevere* over a period of time in what Francis Mac-Nutt calls "soaking prayer." Some illnesses take a long time for complete healing. For example, Emily Gardiner Neal persisted in seeking her own healing of intense back pain in the midst of her ministry that brought healing to hundreds of others.

A fifth reason is strange but true: some people *don't really want to be healed.* Ruth came to a prayer service for healing of depression. She had a loving husband and two loyal sons who waited on her hand and foot. When it became clear that the Holy Spirit was going to heal her gradually, Ruth backed off. She preferred being taken care of by her family to assuming responsibility for running her life. This attitude may explain Jesus' unexpected question to an invalid for thirty-eight years at the pool of Bethesda: "Do you want to get well?" (Jn 5:6).

Let's return to the case of David Hadley. After leaving the hospital, he encountered another situation that impeded his healing. Several friends introduced him to a charismatic group who impressed him with their assurance that God would heal his ulcer. They quoted Isaiah 53:3 as evidence that Christ bore our physical as well as spiritual sickness on the cross.[6] David was urged to claim this promise and exercise faith for immediate healing; he should continue to claim his cure even though the symptoms might persist. To demonstrate his faith, he was also instructed to stop taking his medication. One person told David, "It sometimes takes more faith to keep your healing than to get it."

During the following weeks David's pain returned. Now he was not only burdened by his illness but also weighed down with guilt. Perplexing questions battered his mind and conscience: *Am I really healed? If so, why do these symptoms continue? If I am not, where did my faith break down so that I lost the healing? Will I be sinning to go back to my medicine?* What was supposed to be a gift of grace had turned into an albatross of guilt.

It took David a while to sort out these questions. As he read the Gospel records, he found that when Jesus healed a person, the symptoms disappeared. The paralytic in Mark 2 stood up, picked up his mat and walked away. The formerly violent Gerasene demoniac of Mark 5 sat quietly, dressed and in his right mind. No one had to assure these people that they were healed!

And there was no indication that anyone whom Jesus healed had to exercise faith to "keep the healing." As he read up on ulcers, David began to see how they can be caused by emotional or relational disorders that may take time to treat.

Because healing prayer recognizes the interaction of physical, emotional, spiritual and relational illness, it reaches far beyond the simplistic models of both biomedical medicine and the prosperity gospel. Roy Lawrence, who has pioneered healing ministry in several English Anglican parishes, affirms: "Christian healing is not just a flash in the pan, a magic moment; it is a way of life, a lifelong process. Who needs healing? We all do. You do. I do. And I shall need it tomorrow, and the day after, and the day after that."[7]

Objections to Healing Prayer

Despite the weight of biblical, historical and current evidence, arguments against the church's healing ministry persist. Several major objections are represented in the critique of Peter May, a British Christian physician, in "Focusing on the Eternal," a chapter in a symposium that presents conflicting views of "signs and wonders."[8]

At the outset May recognizes that health involves physical, mental and social well-being, not merely absence of disease. In a fallen world, he reminds us, we can experience only relative health which fluctuates by degrees. Although in each dimension there can be some improvement, "renewal is real but it is not complete by any means." Christians cannot expect to be immune from life's stresses. May counters what he considers unwarranted claims by the Vineyard "signs and wonders" movement (which we will evaluate in chapter twelve). Unfortunately, his critique perpetuates several widespread misinterpretations of Scripture.

1. Argument from silence. May notes that we do not read in the Gospels of the disciples' healing diseases and driving out demons apart from the special commissions in Luke 9 and 10. Furthermore, "when Jesus commissioned the church after the resurrection, healing was not mentioned" (see Mt 28:18). May further notes that "the silence [about health and healing] in Ephesians and the Pastoral Epistles (which concern the church and its ministry) is *deafening.*" He concludes that healing ministry was no longer operative by the time of Paul's letters.

Biblical scholars, however, recognize that conclusions based on what is *not* said or done are speculative at best, since other explanations are possible.[9] For example, we can just as well conclude that since Jesus did not command the disciples to stop the healing ministry he had given them, it was meant to continue—as, in fact, it did in the early church's teaching and activity.

2. Unsupported evaluation. Two specific references to healing in the Epistles are dismissed with faulty arguments. May sets aside "gifts of healings" (1 Cor 12:9, literal translation) as an "*ambiguous* reference in *only one* of the lists of gifts." Yet he fails to show why he considers the double plural to be ambiguous, or how many times the apostle Paul must mention a gift—or any other doctrine—to make it significant.

May concludes that the mention of healing gifts in 1 Corinthians 12 and the instruction in James 5:14-15 to anoint the sick with oil and pray over them for healing "have to be weighed against the recorded instances of illness"—as if the latter nullified these two explicit apostolic teachings. The fact that many people during Jesus' time remained ill hardly undermined the importance of his healing ministry or the expectancy of the crowds who came to him for cures.

3. Misinterpretation of suffering. May makes the common mistake of assuming that "suffering" in the New Testament refers to "illness." He sees God's "good purpose" and "positive value" in illness, based on Paul's statement that "we rejoice in our sufferings, because we know that suffering produces perseverance . . . character . . . hope" (Rom 5:3-4). But a concordance shows that in the New Testament all eleven occurrences of *pathēma,* the word translated "suffering," connote pain due to persecution or death—of Christ, or of his followers for the sake of the gospel—and not to illness.[10]

4. Spirit-body dichotomy. May's concept of what it is to be human reflects the Greek philosophical and biomedical dichotomy between spirit and body more than Hebraic wholism, which teaches the essential unity of the person. After defining the nature of humanity in purely spiritual terms, he declares, "This consideration of the image of God has set an agenda for the restoration of shalom ('wholeness, well-being') in man which excludes man's physical body." This surprising conclusion is based on a novel interpretation of Paul's statement "Though outwardly we are wasting away, yet inwardly we are being renewed day by day. . . . So we fix our eyes not on what is seen, but on what is unseen. For what is seen is temporary, but what is unseen is eternal" (2 Cor 4:16, 18). May concludes, "The current emphasis on healing encourages a neuroticism that focuses attention on the outward, the visible and the temporary to the neglect of the inward, the invisible and eternal. It distracts us from the positive value of suffering."

At this point two questions come to mind. First, to what extent does May consistently apply this concept in his medical practice with patients deeply concerned over persisting illness? To what extent does he urge them not to have a neurotic concentration on the physical that keeps them from appreciating the "positive value" of their suffering? Second, what evidence can he adduce that the growing ministry of healing prayer is producing a large crop of neurotics who neglect eternal values?

Other critics express concern over what they see as dangers of preoccupation with signs and wonders and with the demonic in exorcism. But although the ministry of healing prayer—like other gifts such as prophecy, teaching and evangelism—suffers from misuse, we must look at the other side of the coin. What are the perils of *not* practicing it?

First is the danger of failing to carry out the full ministry our Lord desires for his church. Second is the risk of denying Christian love to the sick by failing to do all we can for their healing through believing prayer. Third is a weakening of our witness to a secular world that denies the existence of the "supernatural" as it worships the "natural" realm of human achievement. Those with such a worldview are hardly impressed by our staunch claim that Jesus Christ healed two thousand years ago though he is apparently unable or unwilling to do so today. Many people assume that if there is a God, it is he who sends sickness (along with natural disasters, which insurance policies call "acts of God"), while it is modern science that cures disease and restores health.

Healing in Community

In our Western world the individual has become increasingly isolated from community support. The family doctor has largely been replaced by a variety of specialists. Often a person is separated from family and friends for treatment in the hospital. Much counseling has focused on the individual apart from family relationships. Even the church seems to have lost its ability to function as a community of faith.

Yet there are signs of hope. A new field of family medicine has emerged, and counseling now usually treats the individual in the context of family. We have belatedly begun to realize that more than 50 percent of all healings take place through and within the family. In the last analysis, however, the fundamental sicknesses are those of the spirit. Even the best medicine is often ineffective for a person who has given up hope, while serious diseases beyond medical help are sometimes cured through a will to live. The most effective therapy is a strong sense of meaning and purpose in life. Yet neither medicine nor psychology can deal with ultimate questions of life and death.

The answers are found in Jesus Christ, proclaimed by his church. Here is the power for healing in all dimensions of life. Catholic scholar Henri Nouwen writes: "We can never leave the task of healing to the specialist. In fact, the specialists can only retain their humanity in their work when they see their professions as a form of service which they carry out, not instead of, but as part of, the whole people of God. We are all healers who can reach out and offer health, and we are all patients in constant need of help."[11]

We need to realize that true healing is *centered in the body of Christ,* with medicine, surgery, psychiatry, public health and social services each making its appropriate contribution.

Across the country many churches now have regular healing services and a team that carries out ministry through prayer and anointing with oil or laying on of hands. Gifts of healings are manifested through many members of the body, who are learning through trial and error (as in past renewals) how this ministry can be fulfilled. Sometimes there is a full cure, often there is relief, always there is comfort. Not only is the Christian community strengthened by these gifts, but it also serves as a guide, and corrective where needed, in their practice.

Like other renewals in the church's history, healing ministry has its share of aberrations and extremes. Many of them are due to "lone-ranger" entrepreneurs with their own organizations and TV programs, responsible to no one except boards of their own choosing. The results are a painful reminder of G. K. Chesterton's observation: "The only incontrovertible evidence against Christianity is the Christians." The fire of healing ministry belongs in the fireplace of responsible Christian community, not out in the middle of the floor with a potential for burning out of control.

Once more, back to David Hadley. Eventually David started to attend a church that practiced biblical healing prayer along the lines we have sketched. The healing team first suggested that he resume the medication and diet his doctor had prescribed. Prayer for a physical cure of his ulcer led to discovery of emotional wounds from childhood abuse and long-repressed anger that called for inner healing (which we will consider in the following chapter). Sessions with a counselor helped David understand and begin to cope with pressures at work and at home. Members of the fellowship understood his need for gradual healing in these dimensions over a period of time, during which they supported him in prayer and love.

David's six-month checkup indicated that the ulcer was healed and required no more medication. The whole-person healing process resulted in more than a physical cure; it enabled David to experience healing in other related dimensions of his life.

Where Do We Begin?

For churches wishing to start a ministry of healing prayer, the following steps can prove helpful.[12]

1. Study the biblical teachings relevant to healing prayer and ask the Holy Spirit to give confidence that God desires to heal in all dimensions of illness. "Faith comes from hearing . . . the word of Christ" (Rom 10:17), who declared that he had come to give life "to the full" (Jn 10:10) here and now.

2. Whenever sickness arrives, whether it is a cold or cancer, a headache or high blood pressure, first begin to pray for healing. At the same time suggest that the person check with a doctor if the symptoms (like David Hadley's severe abdominal pain) warrant such a visit.

3. Ask the person what healing is being sought. Pray that God will give insight into attitudes or elements of lifestyle that may be contributing to the illness and need changing. Be prepared to deal with any underlying spiritual problems.

4. Persevere in thanksgiving and prayer through encouragements and difficulties (Phil 4:6-7). To foster a climate of faith, picture the person well—the goal of your prayer—rather than focusing on the disease itself. Paul encourages such a positive attitude in his command to keep our minds on whatever is true, noble, right, pure, lovely, admirable (Phil 4:8).

5. Continue to be sensitive to the Spirit's guidance as you pray, remembering the "more or less" described earlier in the chapter. If healing does not occur or is limited, bring the situation to mature Christians experienced in discernment and soaking prayer.

While biblical teaching about healing emphasizes faith, both love and hope are also important. Love builds Christian community and a healing climate through caring relationships that continue to support the sick, whose faith and patience are stretched thin by constant pain. Hope ultimately looks to the future, to the return of our Lord Jesus Christ and our resurrection life in his presence. Then, finally, the whole creation will know complete healing.

10 *Inner Healing*

*A*fter several years of internship and general practice, George finally arrived in the Caribbean with his family to serve as a medical missionary. He joined several other doctors at a clinic in a small rural town. During the week he saw patients; on most Sundays he preached in small outlying chapels.

An overseas missionary assignment had been the last thing in George's mind when he entered university. He had grown up in a nonreligious family that considered Christianity a relic of the past. Yet through the friendship and witness of students in a chapter of InterVarsity Christian Fellowship, he had a profound conversion to Jesus Christ that led to a commitment to serve his Lord overseas.

In George's new ministry, his low-key manner quickly won the people's confidence. The variety of sicknesses calling for immediate treatment was incredible. His practice was far more general than he had ever imagined it could be. Often people came to him as a last resort after their own "bush medicine" didn't work. George became a versatile diagnostician and counselor; no specialists were available for referral.

George was also a good husband and a caring father to his two children, who adapted well to their new school system. The family seemed ideal to face the opportunities and difficulties of serving God in a new culture far from home. But toward the end of the second year, George's affair with a local woman suddenly came to light. He resigned and returned home, where his fractured family soon fell apart with disastrous consequences. George left his family and the Christian faith.

Friends, in shock, were at a loss to explain this catastrophe. It was the last thing they would have expected of George. Some wondered whether he had really become a Christian. Only later did they learn about the traumatic childhood abuse that had inflicted deep wounds of anger and insecurity. Those wounds had never been dealt with and healed.

Emotional Wounds

In recent decades the emotional dimension of health has drawn increasing concern. It is evident that unhealed wounds of the past warp behavior in the present. When we bury a negative feeling, it is not dead; it is only dormant and will eventually revive to cause trouble. Memories of past hurts have powerful influences on current attitudes and actions.

For example, a person with a deep feeling of inferiority developed in childhood continues to hear an inner message: "Everything I do is wrong. No one could love me." When this person becomes a Christian, the mind accepts God's love and forgiveness, but something within cries, "Don't believe it. How could God love someone as bad as you?"

The person afflicted by perfectionism produced by demanding parents hears, "I can never do anything well enough to please others and God." Driven by inner "oughts" and "shoulds," this person keeps climbing toward, but never reaches, expected levels of performance.[1]

Failures to love, to forgive, to accept others and ourselves are symptoms of deep emotional wounds. Exhortation to perform in these areas—an appeal to the mind and will—is as counterproductive as urging a person with a broken leg to drop his crutches and run. It only increases a sense of guilt and fosters further repression.[2] The repair of damaged emotions requires a special kind of healing suited to the nature of the illness.

The term *inner healing* has become a catchall for a variety of approaches to "holistic health" and New Age therapies. If you have discovered the phrase *healing of memories* in that context, don't be put off. Like *meditation* and *mysticism,* the term has an honorable Christian meaning that should not be tarred with the brush of secular versions.

First we will consider the biblical meaning of memory and its implications for the healing of memories. We will then look at the practice of inner healing and current criticisms of it.

The Biblical Meaning of Memory

The Bible deals with memory in the same way it treats other concepts—with little if any theoretical discussion of how it works. While the noun *memory* appears only five times, when it becomes something concrete, *memorial,* the number rises to thirty-two. On the other hand, verbs for *remember* occur about 250 times. About 75 of these refer to God's memory; many of them are requests for him to remember his covenant, his promises, his people. Other requests are for God *not* to remember their sins and failures. The remaining 125 refer to the memory of God's people, also both positively and negatively.

In all cases, remembering is meant to influence present attitudes or actions. When biblical writers command us to "remember the Lord," they mean more than a mental exercise; we are instructed to center all our thoughts and actions in God and our relationship to him. To "remember the Sabbath day by keeping it holy" (Ex 20:8) is to live according to God's principles of worship and action. Scripture considers memory, both God's and ours, as one of the most important functions of a person.

We have seen how the biblical writers recognize the full *unity* of the person, of which body, soul and spirit are dimensions and not separate compartments. This reality underlies the importance of memory as a function of the whole person. Memories do more than produce mental pictures of the past; they exert an influence on present experience—feelings, attitudes, concepts and unconscious behavior. The tragedy of hurtful memories lies not simply in their emotional pain but also in their impact on how we cope in the present with life and relationships with others. Even from infancy, painful memories have power in adult experience.

We often say, "Time heals all wounds." Although the passage of time can heal some emotional hurts, others, like an infection, are so deep that they turn inward, spread and worsen with the years. What cannot be faced and resolved is often denied; bad memories can be repressed into our subconscious, only to appear disguised as physical illness, unhappy marital relationships, cycles of spiritual defeat. Repressed memories hinder our love to God, our neighbor and ourself.

That is why it's essential to discover and consciously deal with the *roots* of the problems we face. Simplistic approaches to the mind and will simply mow off the tops of the dandelions, removing visible effects but leaving the roots intact to blossom again in similar or different ways.

Unfortunately, as we will see in the following chapter, many churches prevent people from honestly facing past realities of abuse, lovelessness and misunderstanding by warning against "negative confession." After a brief prayer, sufferers are exhorted to "claim your healing," when in reality it may require ministry over a long period from other members of the body of Christ.

Tim was terribly afraid of dogs. Every time he saw one, his heart started pounding. He couldn't recall any traumatic experience with a dog, and he had no fear of other animals. So Tim asked for prayer that God would show him the root problem. One day his mother unexpectedly said, "Don't you remember when as a child you were chased and bitten by a bulldog?" Prayer for healing of that repressed memory then freed Tim from the fear, though dogs never did become his favorite animals.

Sarah found it almost impossible to make decisions. When faced with a choice between two jobs, or about getting a new car, she was overcome with anxiety and almost immobilized. She put off the decision as long as possible, to the exasperation of others, and her own sense of inadequacy increased.

Through prayer she was helped to trace the root to her childhood, when her mother habitually criticized her hesitation: "You can never make up your mind!" Sarah was freed from that ingrained negative image of herself and gradually became more decisive in daily choices.

Emotions can be damaged by a specific traumatic incident like the dog bite or by prolonged criticism that plants indecisiveness deep in the psyche. There is also a third kind of emotional damage, the "wounded personality," recently identified by Episcopal rector Mark Pearson.[3] It can be experienced by a child growing up in a caring Christian home—not by mistreatment, but through misplaced love.

Paul's parents, for example, wanted to set an example and to teach their son to be a responsible, mature Christian. They were introverts—reserved, proper and disciplined in their conduct. Paul, however, was an extrovert— outgoing and exuberant. By forcing him to express his Christian values in their way, his parents squeezed him into a mold too narrow for his personality. Although well motivated, they confused virtue with style, as if there were only one manner of Christian living.

As an adult, Paul was shocked to learn that the emotional distress he was experiencing was due to his upbringing. He protested, "My parents were always wonderful to me." Then he admitted, "It's gotten so bad that every time I talk or laugh loudly, I have a feeling deep in my soul that I've offended God."

Healing of memories is a form of Christian counseling and prayer that focuses the Holy Spirit's healing power on certain kinds of emotional/spiritual problems. The major pioneer of this long-overlooked ministry for inner healing was Agnes Sanford (1897-1982). She grew up in China, the child of Presbyterian missionaries, and married Episcopal priest Edgar Sanford. Her interest in inner healing developed after she was healed of long-standing depression. Her pioneering ministry was vigorously opposed by many clergy. But in 1955 the Sanfords launched the School of Pastoral Care—residential conferences on the ministry of healing for clergy and their spouses and for medical professionals. Agnes Sanford was a foremost encourager of healing ministry within the charismatic renewal. Her 1958 book *Behold Your God* was an early presentation of biblical principles and practice of inner-healing ministry.[4]

Prayer for healing of memories goes back to reclaim the past—not to change or erase it, but to remove its present negative influence. It goes to the source of the problem and brings release from the pain of past events.

Memories are stored away as if they were true pictures of reality. The child of an abusive father preserves a distorted view of life: that all fathers, including the heavenly Father, are harsh and unloving—that's the way life is. Our feelings about God affect our ideas of God. This crucial fact is overlooked by many pastors and teachers who assume that if the doctrines they present are biblically sound, they will automatically correct a person's concept of God and generate trust in him. In reality, appeals to the facts and the mind alone are often futile to change a "taped message" that is stored deep in the subconscious.

Here it must be affirmed that damaged emotions from past hurts do not excuse wrongdoing. A person's sin cannot be blamed on heredity or past environment. We are not mature until we stop blaming others and take responsibility for ourselves and our actions. Nevertheless, awareness of past damage reminds us of our particular recurring tendencies to sin and helps show us what further healing prayer is needed.

A hurting person needs the presence and power of Jesus to face the damaged experience or image and receive a new perspective. This process does not rewrite the past or imply that an event or experience didn't happen; nor does it attempt to create a new reality, as claimed by New Age groups. It accepts the reality of Jesus' promise to be there in all circumstances (Mt 28:20). He is present in loving concern amid all our suffering. As he heals our painful memories, they lose their crippling power over us.

Ministry of Inner Healing
Usually a person with negative feelings or a damaged self-image needs the help of others to identify a hidden hurt or unmet need. This ministry has three main phases: diagnosis, healing prayer and follow-up.

1. Diagnosis. The first step is opening up to a pastor or trusted friend. The apostle James writes, "Confess your sins to each other and pray for each other so that you may be healed" (Jas 5:16). This phase may last a considerable time. A mystery of memory is our ability to block out of our mind things we are not able to face, selectively forgetting what is painful. We need to uncover the situations, experiences and attitudes that are causing the negative emotions so that the Holy Spirit can deal with them specifically. In fact, the very act of remembering and feeling the pain can be a breakthrough that begins, and often effects, healing.

During this phase the prayer minister looks for indications that healing of memories is needed. Pastor David Seamands identifies several major categories of such signs:[5]

a. Rejection. At the heart of many hurts is a sense of rejection. The more significant the rejecting person, the greater our hurt. The most painful experiences occur in the earliest years of life because children cannot understand this treatment and cope with it. Many rejections result from accidents, illnesses, delays or death, as parents, family members, relatives or friends choose or are forced to give attention to someone or something else. Intentional or not, the hurt can take its toll in later life.

b. Humiliation. Another common experience is embarrassment and shame: an insensitive parent, teacher or other authority figure, in private or public, puts down a child by ridiculing mistakes or weaknesses. Humiliation is often used as discipline or a way of changing behavior. But it is a devastating blow to the fragile self-esteem of children, robbing them of self-confidence in the years to come. Humiliation may also result from living with an alcoholic parent; to cover up for a parent's drinking problem, the child learns to make excuses for not inviting friends home or for the parent's inadequacies. A life marked by half-truths fills the child with the shame of deceit.

c. Fear. A wide spectrum of fears and anxieties can call for healing: fears of failure, being alone, trusting others, rejection, sex, serious illness or injury, the future, death. For many Christians, fears are intensified by guilt over feeling fearful. After all, doesn't the Bible declare, "Perfect love drives out fear" (1 Jn 4:18)? But many fears are rooted in frightening experiences, intimidating teachings or fractured relationships in the past, often during early childhood. They may have been pushed down into the subconscious so often that the person has no specific remembrances, only a vague, gnawing anxiety that attaches itself to one thing after another.

d. Anger. Anger often masks feelings of rejection, humiliation and fear because it seems more socially acceptable. Frozen and buried resentment often causes depression and various kinds of physical illness. When people fail to express their true feelings, their bodies often cry out through emotional or physical pain. Most disturbing and long-resisted by sincere Christians is an admission of their anger at God for allowing such painful experiences. Healing of such anger can lead to an understanding of, then freedom from, their distorted and destructive concepts of God.

2. Healing prayer. This distinctive element of healing memories invites the Holy Spirit to take us back in time to the actual experience and walk with him through the painful memories. From that perspective we pray and allow God to minister in the manner needed at that time. Here the healing miracle begins. It is not the autosuggestion or feeling therapy of New Age "positive mental attitude," but a redeeming, liberating work of God's grace.

We pray about the memory of a specific event or relationship thought to be the heart of the problem. But the Holy Spirit, our Counselor, leads to deeper levels to discover the real issue. At times it may be through a spiritual gift for the occasion—a word of knowledge, word of wisdom or discernment.[6] This guidance is especially needed when the memory of an experience is blurred or distorted because of the intensity of the emotions connected with it. Specifics are also shielded by defense mechanisms: denial that the experience happened, rationalization to justify the behavior, projection or blaming others for our problem. It is essential for memories to surface for confession of specific feelings and actions at the time and, where necessary, to receive forgiveness.

Yet forgiveness is a two-way street. Our Lord emphasizes the importance of a forgiving spirit: "And when you stand praying, if you hold anything against anyone, forgive him, so that your Father in heaven may forgive you your sins" (Mk 11:25). "Forgive, and you will be forgiven" (Lk 6:37). When Peter asked if he should forgive his brother up to seven times, Jesus answered, "I tell you, not seven times, but seventy-seven times" (Mt 18:22).

Continuing unforgiveness not only blocks God's grace but also takes an emotional and physical toll. The person who has been hurt needs to forgive, not just in the present as an adult who can understand, for example, alcoholism's strong grip on an abusive father. The forgiveness must also come as the person stands in the place of the small, terrified child whose world was being shattered.

Often Jesus himself appears to be there in the midst of the trauma. The person can be encouraged to picture the Lord standing alongside, demonstrating his love and concern, and to tell Jesus about the hurt and receive his love and grace for freedom from its present effects. Use of the imagination to visualize such a scene is thoroughly biblical, as we will see later in this chapter, and radically different from New Age "imaging." Christian visualization is always based on specific biblical truths, never on the invention of "truth." Furthermore, it lets God be sovereign in the process. This prayer time brings new perceptions and power. It is the probing, freeing action of the Spirit that heals and makes this experience radically different from "positive thinking" or "feeling good about yourself."

3. Follow-up. Healed memories of damaged emotions do not automatically change present behavior. Distorted images of God and others have produced aberrant patterns of thought and action that need to be re-created. During the follow-up phase the prayer minister and counselee work with the Holy Spirit to reorient or readjust to develop new attitudes and behavior.

Positive memories are invested with new meaning and integrated into life to ensure permanent changes. The process is somewhat like the restoration of a broken leg: after your immobilizing cast is removed, it is possible for you to walk freely again, but first you will probably need exercise therapy.

Jesus promises, "If you hold to my teaching, you are really my disciples. Then you will know the truth, and the truth will set you free" (Jn 8:31-32).

Free from those pains and compulsions, we can grow in grace and holy living. The ultimate goal of healing is not simply a higher level of emotional health but an effective life of discipleship for our Lord.

Episcopal rector Len Cowan, who recently started a healing ministry in his church, remarked to me, "I don't think you can emphasize this follow-up phase enough. So often we see people who want a 'quick fix' from the pain, who want *us* to do the healing for them. At St. David's we have been called to be a *healing and teaching* fellowship. Many people who have experienced God's healing grace need encouragement to walk in newness of life, taught from the Scriptures what it means to do so."

Is Healing of Memories Biblical?

Unfortunately, the phrase *healing of memories* now has a variety of meanings. For some Christians inner healing is an expected shortcut cure-all to emotional and spiritual maturity. Others identify its use of imagination with New Age "imaging" or "mind over matter" techniques. As a result of this misunderstanding and misuse, some people have abandoned healing of memories as unhealthy and even unscriptural. So here we will consider biblical support for the healing of memories, then examine objections to its use of visualization.

Once again we need to define our terms. What is meant by *biblical?* Justifying everything by a "chapter and verse" quotation? Or practice that is not contradictory to but consistent with biblical principles? The first criterion obviously rules out many current church activities: Sunday school, youth programs, evangelism workshops, weekend conferences, choir practice, use of organs and pianos, to mention a few. Clearly, that criterion is impractical. So we will consider healing of memories in terms of its harmony with biblical principles.

We saw in chapter nine that our God, who is always on the side of truth, goodness and health, desires that we become whole. We need to be concerned for healing in every dimension—emotional as well as physical and spiritual. Full healing involves dealing with damaged emotions of the past which influence current attitudes and actions. On this basis, healing of memories has a solid foundation in Scripture, our final authority in matters of faith and conduct.

Christ Our Present Helper

Before he died, Jesus promised his disciples another Counselor: "I will not leave you as orphans; I will come to you" (Jn 14:18). After his resurrection Jesus demonstrated that he can appear anywhere and anytime. He assured his disciples, "I am with you always, to the very end of the age" (Mt 28:20). Yet he transcends our linear time-space continuum, the finite limitations within which we live. He is the Lord of time, our eternal contemporary and helper through the Holy Spirit. The writer to the Hebrews declares: "Jesus Christ is the same yesterday and today and forever" (Heb 13:8). It is from our limited perspective that we figuratively say the Lord "walks back through time" to minister to a hurting person.

The distinctive part of healing of memories is the time of prayer in which we recall the painful memory and visualize the experience as it once took place. The Holy Spirit makes the transcendent Christ present to us. We pray as if we were on the spot, asking him to do for us what we would have asked if we had prayed there and then. We ask him to heal the little child or teenager who experienced the pain that has been present ever since. Our prayer doesn't _produce_ his presence; it simply recognizes that he was there even though we didn't know it. We are open to Jesus to change our _perception_ of the experience, to invite him into that memory to heal it.

David Seamands notes: "The _form_ of the mental images by which we visualize Jesus' presence is the product of our imaginations. But the _fact_ of his presence pictured by these images is guaranteed by the promises of Scripture."[7]

Our immediate reaction is to ask, "How can this be possible when the events happened many years ago?" Behind this question lies our Western scientific rationalism, which demands an explanation of _how_ things work before we can accept _that_ they are valid. Yet the Bible does not give explanations of how God works in history and nature. The writers are concerned about the _who_ and *what for*—God and his purpose. Belief that biblical events and experiences occurred is based on historical facts reported by reliable witnesses and recorded in Scripture. We are not told how Jesus rose from the dead, how the Holy Spirit regenerates or how healing of past memories occurs through this kind of prayer. Those who experience inner healing are like the blind man who could not answer the Pharisees' questions but resolutely affirmed, "One thing I do know: I was blind but now I see!" (Jn 9:25).

Prayer for healing of memories is grounded in our being members of the body of Christ to strengthen one another with spiritual gifts, including gifts of healings (1 Cor 12:9, 26). We have the privilege and responsibility to pray for healing and to confess our sins (Jas 5:15-16). In Matthew 18:19-20, the Lord teaches us to pray by "agreeing" on specific requests and expecting answers from God. The verses that follow contain crucial teachings on the importance of forgiveness and being forgiven. These passages teach that some kinds of healing—physical, emotional and spiritual—come through ministry by other members of the body.

We may wonder how the results of this ministry are to be tested. They should not be only subjective, just "feeling better about myself." As with other experiences in the Christian life, we check to see if the results are consistent with Scripture and are confirmed by other Christians in the body of Christ. A ministry is ultimately known by its fruit: does the end result glorify our Lord Jesus Christ and promote holy living in the fellowship of the Christian community?

Visualization and the New Age

Healing of memories has been attacked for its use of the imagination. Given the prevalence and growth of various New Age practices, this criticism needs to be squarely faced. We will review biblical visualization within a Christian worldview, then examine visualization within the New Age worldview. After defining the terms we can assess current criticism of this procedure.

1. Biblical visualization. Imagination—the ability to visualize—is a God-given faculty that, like other gifts, can be misused. Visualization is a prominent biblical method of teaching. Much Old Testament revelation came in the form of visions and dreams. Some prophets, such as Ezekiel, Jeremiah and Amos, taught through an enacted parable, taking an action whose interpretation required the use of imagination. In the New Testament Jesus constantly teaches through parables—the good Samaritan, the prodigal son, the absent landlord. These word pictures of people and events get through cognitive defenses, challenging and convicting as they invite his hearers (including us today) to imagine themselves as one of the characters. The book of Revelation, except for its letters to the seven churches, is mainly a panorama of visions on a vast cosmic scale.

For the world's people outside our Western culture, stories that draw on imagination have been a preferred means of communication. Not merely illustrations of eternal truths, these stories make their own unique impact; the medium itself is the message.

We have seen how hurtful memories are stored away as if they were a true picture of reality—for example, the abusive father can produce in a child a distorted image that is projected on all fathers, all men, even God himself: harsh, demanding, angry, unloving. Imagination is a projector that rewinds the memory, allowing us to go back and relive the hurt as it actually happened. Healing of memories is the process of making the presence of God accessible to that hurt. It invites Jesus into that memory to heal the damaged emotion. We allow him into our life to change our perception of the hurt so we can face it, with him, and be freed from its power.

2. New Age visualization. Diverse philosophies and spiritualities thrive under the umbrella of the New Age movement, whose worldview conflicts with the following basic concepts of the biblical worldview:

☐ The Creator transcends his creation; everything was originally good, and humankind was made in the image of God.

☐ Evil—including demons and a spiritual realm—is a universal reality that has defaced the image of God in people.

☐ Redemption through Christ not only re-creates that image in us but also will ultimately defeat all the forces of evil.

In contrast, the New Age worldview denies the distinction between God and his creation. Its monism holds that there is only one ultimate substance or principle. In everyday terms, "everything is one, everything is God, all humanity is God."⁸ A corollary is pantheism, the teaching that God is not a personality but the sum of all beings, things and forces in the universe. Most New Age groups consider "god" or "the divine" as an impersonal force or consciousness. Coupled with this view is syncretism: all religions are essentially one; they are simply different paths leading to the same truth. Thus the uniqueness of Christianity is denied. Jesus of Nazareth is only one of many religious leaders who have possessed the "Christ Spirit."

Second, New Age groups deny the reality of evil; they teach that all spiritual reality is good. Our problem, they say, is not sin but ignorance of our essential goodness and of the oneness of the universe; Western culture has held our consciousness captive to the illusions of everyday limitations.

Third, according to New Age thinking, the solution is not redemption in Christ but a "change in consciousness" to become aware of our oneness and spiritual power. Here various groups advocate different meditation techniques that generally involve emptying oneself so that one can hear wisdom through spirit guides, channels, an inner voice or humanistic psychology. Some offer "consciousness-raising" experiences through drugs, group therapy or occult practices. Whatever the path, the goal is to *be* what we *know,* our divinity through which anything is potentially possible. We create our own reality; in popular terms, it is "mind over matter." We stand at the threshold of a "new age" that is rising out of the ashes of the old, limited Western worldview.

Holistic health is a related movement that goes beyond the biomedical model of illness to address spiritual as well as physical and mental needs. In that respect it is consistent with the "Hebrew wholism" we have considered. Nevertheless, it offers a mixture of beliefs and practices, some of which are based on New Age concepts. Since holistic healers rarely say what religious ideas are implicit in their techniques, those ideas usually go unchallenged. Many of them assume that all healing is basically self-healing; in other words, each of us possesses unlimited potential and thus we all need to get in touch with our own inner resources. For that reason it is necessary to uncover the underlying presuppositions of any practice claiming to heal the whole person and test it against biblical teachings.[9]

Objections to Inner Healing

In recent years the ministry of inner healing has come under increasing criticism for its supposed practice of New Age principles. The 1985 book *The Seduction of Christianity* begins with a concerted attack on various forms of pantheism, paganism, shamanism, sorcery, the occult and self-idolatry. These beliefs and practices have in common the underlying New Age worldview we have sketched. Authors Dave Hunt and T. A. McMahon also explain the way some prominent scientists promote their own philosophy under the guise of science.[10] For example, in his television series *Cosmos,* which presented good science, professor Carl Sagan stated confidently, "The Cosmos is all there is, or was or ever will be." He failed to tell his listeners that this statement is not science but "scientism," the popular philosophy of naturalism. They are led to think this must be a scientific concept when in reality it is a statement of his faith.

Hunt and McMahon then turn their attention to "visualization" and "guided imagery," long recognized by shamans (sorcerers, medicine men, witch doctors) as a powerful means of contacting the spirit world to acquire supernatural power, knowledge and healing. Hunt and McMahon also recognize legitimate, nonoccultic uses of imagination—seeing mental images of written descriptions, designing, planning, remembering a place or event. These are "normal aids to everyday activities and do not involve an attempt to create or control reality through mind-powers."[11]

Yet they express concern about what they see as shamanistic inroads into Christianity through inner healing. In chapter nine, "Shamanism Revived," they set their sights on Christian leaders who have pioneered this ministry, which Hunt and McMahon charge is a "seduction of Christianity." The authors assure readers that they are not criticizing the teachers, only their unbiblical teaching and practice: "It should be clearly understood that we are not making a blanket condemnation of anyone."[12]

Agnes Sanford is singled out as the person most influential in bringing occult methodologies into the church. The authors quote from two early books to demonstrate her use of "metaphysical/Jungian terms" to explain the way God works in redemption and healing. Yet after 121 pages devoted to New Age phenomena, the evaluation of Agnes Sanford's important writings receives a scant three pages in *The Seduction of Christianity*. On the basis of only a few paragraphs and a dozen phrases lifted out of context, the authors conclude that her books are "blatantly pagan." Her "prayer through imagination" was "rooted in her basically pagan beliefs onto which she merely superimposed Christian and psychological terminology, especially Jungian. . . . Agnes Sanford was a pantheist."[13]

Admittedly, some of Sanford's statements attempting to explain *how* God's healing works are not consonant with biblical concepts. But she hardly warrants such a blanket condemnation. Her autobiography, *Sealed Orders,* reveals her commitment to the authority of Scripture, her unflagging lifelong service to her Lord and her effective ministry in the salvation and healing of hundreds of others.

Hunt and McMahon comment negatively on other ministers of inner healing who have expressed appreciation for Sanford's pioneering work. For example, using brief, misinterpreted quotations lifted out of context, they accuse Francis MacNutt and Rita Bennett of attempting to re-create the past and change history in "a Christianized form of the mental alchemy that lies at the heart of shamanism."[14]

Given the wide circulation (more than half a million) and influence of this book, it is unfortunate that the authors consistently misunderstand and misrepresent the Christian use of visualization in healing of memories. Their evaluation is flawed by two basic errors. First, there is faulty logic in their syllogistic reasoning:

Shamans use visualization to effect healing.

Shamans are pantheistic pagans.

Therefore all visualization used in inner healing is pantheistic paganism.

The same kind of reasoning can lead to a conclusion that is more obviously fallacious:

Medicine men pray for bountiful harvests.

Medicine men are animists (they believe that every natural object has its own spirit).

Therefore all prayer for bountiful harvests is animistic.

Second, the authors make a fundamental error in failing to recognize that *visualization* has two entirely different meanings. In the context of the biblical worldview, the source of power is the Holy Spirit; visualization perceives the reality of Jesus' presence in a past painful experience; the healing is a gracious gift; its goal is a fuller life to serve and glorify the God of Scripture. In the New Age worldview, however, the source of power is an impersonal force; visualization itself produces the healing; it is the result of using our own inner human potential; its goal is self-realization.

New Age visualization is a counterfeit of the Christian use of the imagination. Like a counterfeit twenty-dollar bill, it succeeds only when it closely resembles the original. When that occurs, two losses can follow. Carelessness takes the fake for the real thing, only to discover later that it is worthless. On the other hand, ignorance rejects the original because it is thought to be counterfeit. *The Seduction of Christianity* correctly warns against the first error—accepting New Age counterfeits. Unfortunately, its unwarranted condemnation of the biblical healing of memories has caused many Christians to forgo the emotional health God offers through this means.[15]

The Apostle Peter's Healing of Memories

On the night of Jesus' arrest, Peter followed him at a distance to the courtyard of the high priest. Earlier that evening Peter had declared, "Even if all fall away on account of you, I never will" (Mt 26:33). Now he alone of the disciples sits with the guards and warms himself at a charcoal fire. While upstairs Jesus is being tried on trumped-up charges, Peter is accused three times of being one of his disciples. Each time he denies the relationship. When a rooster crows the second time, Peter remembers Jesus' prediction of the denial, and he breaks down and weeps. For the rest of his life, the sight and smell of a charcoal fire will surely spark the memory of his terrible failure and kindle an overwhelming sense of guilt.

John 21 tells us how after his resurrection, Jesus appeared to his disciples by the Sea of Tiberius. They had fished all night and caught nothing; but at Jesus' command they tried one more time, on the right side of the boat, and made a huge catch. One of the disciples exclaimed, "It is the Lord!" Peter immediately jumped overboard and swam to shore. There he found Jesus standing by a charcoal fire. (This is the only other time the word for such a fire is used in the New Testament.)

Two vivid memories leaped into Peter's mind—an experience of discipleship and one of betrayal. Three years earlier he had spent a night in fruitless fishing, given it another try at Jesus' command and drawn in a huge catch. Jesus then told him, "From now on you will catch men." (See Lk 5:1-11.) With James and John, Peter had then left everything to follow Jesus—until the night of his trial. The second memory, of Peter's denial by a charcoal fire, suddenly made him wonder what Jesus would say to him now.

After breakfast Jesus asks Peter three times, "Do you love me?" Thus he gives Peter the opportunity to reaffirm his love, once for each denial. Reliving that traumatic experience in the presence of his Lord, Peter receives a forgiving acceptance and a renewed commission of discipleship. Three times he hears Jesus say, "Feed my sheep." Never again will those painful memories of denial haunt him or hinder his ministry.

If you also desire the healing of a painful memory, you may be thinking, "But that was long ago, when a disciple could see and talk to Jesus." True, but the Lord declared to Thomas, "Blessed are those who have *not* seen and yet have believed" (Jn 20:29). In faith we can sing a hymn by Henry Twells that many years ago became a favorite among students and staff in InterVarsity summer camps:

> At even, ere the sun was set,
> The sick, O Lord, around Thee lay;

Oh, in what divers pains they met!
Oh, with what joy they went away.

Once more 'tis eventide, and we,
Oppressed with various ills, draw near:
What if Thy form we cannot see?
We know and feel that Thou art here.

O Saviour Christ, our woes dispel;
For some are sick, and some are sad,
And some have never loved Thee well,
And some have lost the love they had.

And none, O Lord, have perfect rest,
For none are wholly free from sin;
And they who fain would serve Thee best
Are conscious most of wrong within.

O Saviour Christ, Thou too art man;
Thou hast been troubled, tempted, tried;
Thy kind but searching glance can scan
The very wounds that shame would hide.

Thy touch has still its ancient power;
No word from Thee can fruitless fall;
Hear, in this solemn evening hour,
And in Thy mercy heal us all.

IV
New
Movements

11 *Spiritual Warfare*

*W*alter, *a thoughtful and gentle young man, is active in his church and* has a good reputation in the community. So his friends were shocked to hear that he had been arrested for accosting and fondling a woman in a bookstore. He admitted to the police that he had acted similarly several times in the past. In sessions with a counselor Walter told how he lived in a fantasy world, struggling against sexual compulsions. Eventually he revealed what he had earlier denied, that in childhood he had been a victim of incest.

Two members of his church's healing team began special prayer for Walter. During the second session he suddenly beat his head violently with his fist and cried out in an agonized voice, "I hate you! I hate you! Nobody loves me!"

At that point one of the team discerned that Walter was oppressed by an evil spirit. Thereupon the leader declared, "Spirit, you have no rights here with this child of God, who has been redeemed by the blood of the Lamb. I command you in the name of Jesus to flee into the abyss."

Immediately Walter stopped yelling; he began to sob and cry in a childish voice, "I need a daddy." The healing team assured him that he had a loving Father, "Abba," in heaven. They prayed for a special presence of the Holy Spirit, that he might know the peace of Christ. Soon he looked up quietly and reported that he was suddenly free from a heaviness of mind ("like a weight in the back of my brain") that had burdened him for a long time.

The healing team continues to keep in contact with Walter, but additional prayers for this specific problem have not been needed, since he is no longer harassed by temptation to act out inappropriate sexual behavior.

The Reality of Spiritual Warfare

A call to arms falls on deaf ears when people are not even aware that a war is going on. Though from beginning to end the Bible reveals relentless warfare between good and evil, in our century the Western church has been unaware of the extent to which demonic forces pervade society. In recent years, however, widespread incursions of evil into our culture have occasioned alarm.

Movies like *The Exorcist* honor the demonic. Occult bookstores feature Satanic Bibles and New Age accessories. Rock musicians adulate Satan and spread hatred. Drug dealers sacrifice the innocent to gain the favor of demons. Yet TV cartoons picture demons as harmless creatures for children's imaginations.

In reaction, the topic of spiritual warfare has become newly popular in Christian publishing. This development has heightened awareness of Satanic influence in daily life; it has also spawned deleterious side effects. Fast-selling sensationalism goes far beyond biblical teaching and accurate documentation. Some books promote fear that Christians can be possessed—completely controlled—by a demon. Others tend to see behind every bush an evil spirit they can blame for an attitude or action that is their own responsibility.

As the theological pendulum swings from one extreme to another, we need to understand biblical teaching on spiritual warfare. What are the forces and strategy of the enemy? How can we be equipped to withstand demonic assaults? What principles should guide our prayer and action? Yet as we answer these questions, we need to remember that the church is not only an army but also a family, a school and a hospital.

This chapter offers a brief introduction to spiritual warfare, not in morbid preoccupation with the demonic but with realistic recognition that opposition from evil forces is a central dimension of kingdom life in a fallen world. First we will look at the biblical account of this warfare and the available weapons. Then we will survey the current battlefields and identify three major strategies presently employed.

Biblical Encounters

Following Satan's victory over Adam and Eve in the Garden of Eden, the Lord God declared a continuing conflict: "And I will put enmity between you and the woman, and between your offspring and hers; he will crush your head, and you will strike his heel" (Gen 3:15).

The book of Job unveils this spiritual conflict in terms of interaction between God and Satan. When the Lord points out that his servant Job is "blameless and upright," Satan replies that Job has good reason to fear God, who has made him the wealthiest man in the East. "But stretch out your hand and strike everything he has, and he will surely curse you to your face" (Job 1:11). The unfolding story then shows how the devil has a wide but limited sphere to wreak havoc on earth as a tempter and deceiver.

The Old Testament prophets looked forward to a day when God would purge the world of evil and set up his perfect reign on earth. For example, Isaiah describes that situation when the Lord "will create new heavens and a new earth. . . . They will neither harm nor destroy on all my holy mountain" (Is 65:17, 25).

In the New Testament, Jesus' ministry from the outset is portrayed within a framework of spiritual warfare. The first three Gospel writers report that Jesus' baptism by John was immediately followed by his temptation in the desert. Mark writes, "He was in the desert forty days, being tempted by Satan. He was with the wild animals, and angels attended him" (Mk 1:13). Jesus won the battle against three crucial enticements designed to undermine his ministry before it even got started. But the war was not over; Luke records that the devil left him "until an opportune time" (Lk 4:13).

When Jesus announced his kingdom, it was "essentially one of conflict and conquest over the kingdom of Satan."[1] When he sent out seventy-two disciples on a preaching-healing mission, they returned with joy as they reported, "Lord, even the demons submit to us in your name" (Lk 10:17). In Luke 10:18-20 Jesus gave a threefold response. First, he revealed that as they carried our their mission he had watched Satan "fall like lightning from heaven"; the devil himself was now suffering defeat. Second, Jesus reaffirmed the disciples' authority to "trample on snakes and scorpions [symbols of demons] and to overcome all the power of the enemy; nothing will harm you." Third, the Lord tempered his disciples' enthusiasm with a reminder of their true status: "However, do not rejoice that the spirits submit to you, but rejoice that your names are written in heaven." Their identity derived not from successful service but from the gift of salvation.

One time when Jesus healed a demon-possessed man, the Pharisees claimed he did it through the prince of demons. Jesus replied that it is absurd to think that "Satan drives out Satan," since "every kingdom divided against itself will be ruined." He declared, "But if I drive out demons by the Spirit of God, then the kingdom of God has come upon you." Jesus had come to bind this "strong man" and "carry off his possessions"—that is, to release the captives in Satan's kingdom (Mt 12:22-29).

Peter proclaimed this good news in his sermon to Cornelius and his household: God had anointed Jesus with the Holy Spirit and power so that he "went around doing good and healing all who were under the power of the devil" (Acts 10:38). Later, writing out of his own bitter experience of denying his Lord, Peter warned his readers against Satan's attacks. "Be self-controlled and alert. Your enemy the devil prowls around like a roaring lion looking for someone to devour. Resist him, standing firm in the faith" (1 Pet 5:8-9). The devil continues to "strike the heel" of the body of Christ.

The apostle John also recognized Satan's current power and Jesus' mission: "The whole world is under the control of the evil one," but "the reason the Son of God appeared was to destroy the devil's work" (1 Jn 5:19; 3:8). John assures us that Satan and all his demons will ultimately be defeated. Isaiah's vision of a new heaven and a new earth will become reality in the Holy City, the new Jerusalem, where there is no more pain or death (Rev 20:10; 21).

Spiritual Forces of Evil
In his letter to the Ephesians Paul proclaims that Christ has been exalted "in the heavenly realms, far above all rule and authority, power and dominion, and every title that can be given" (1:20-21). God intends that through the church his manifold wisdom "should be made known to the rulers and authorities in the heavenly realms" (3:10). Two terms used in these verses are synonymous and interchangeable. *Archōn* is a "ruler, lord, prince"—in the plural, "authorities, officials." *Exousia* is "authority, ruling power, official power," also the bearers of authority, "authorities, officials," or "domain, jurisdiction."[2]

The term *power (dynamis)* has the connotation of "might, strength, force" which is exercised by rulers and authorities. It can mean a "personal supernatural spirit or angel,"[3] in this case a "spiritual force" of evil. All these terms have overlapping connotations that can apply to earthly or heavenly realms. Paul is not concerned to identify specific ranks in a hierarchy. He lumps the evil powers together as emissaries who attack the church but can be overcome through the power of the risen and ascended Christ.

What did these terms mean to Paul's readers? Theologian Clinton E. Arnold describes the background of first-century belief in the "powers." Paul's vocabulary reflects the Jewish demonology of his own day. Yet his use of these terms "does not mean that what he had to say about the powers of darkness would have been incomprehensible to the non-Jew."[4] Pagans also used them in their magical and astrological texts. Nevertheless, Paul gives them a new significance as he writes of Satanic forces marshaled against Christ and his kingdom.

Paul provides a classic description of our spiritual enemies and the weapons available for fighting them. First, he identifies our enemies: "For our struggle is not against flesh and blood, but against the rulers, against the authorities, against the powers of this dark world and against the spiritual forces of evil in the heavenly realms" (Eph 6:12). The battle is ultimately against malevolent spiritual forces. Here Paul is concerned not so much about evil persons and institutions as the powers behind them, for which he uses four terms.

Second, the apostle urges his readers in the face of these powerful enemies to use "the full armor of God," which he describes in Ephesians 6:13-18. He draws on Isaiah's picture of God as a warrior who vindicates his people: "He put on righteousness as his breastplate, and the helmet of salvation on his head" (Is 59:17). Paul's model is the Roman soldier, of whose equipment he has personal knowledge since he is chained to one as he writes this letter. Here the apostle identifies six major items—belt, breastplate, boots, shield, helmet and sword—as pictures of the Christian's equipment of truth, righteousness, good news of peace, faith, salvation and the word of God. (A detailed description of this armor appears in appendix F, "Weapons of Spiritual Warfare.")

Four times in these verses Paul urges us to *stand*. He depicts Christians as fully armed soldiers, standing firm on ground that has already been won by the Lord Jesus Christ in his defeat of Satan. This warfare passage is usually viewed in terms of individual Christians armed for battle. Actually, Paul depicts the arming process in corporate terms; all his admonitions are in the plural. The apostle James affirms this picture with his command "Resist the devil, and he will flee from you" (Jas 4:7).

Although spiritual warfare involves resistance to Satan's attack, it is also a demonstration of Christ's power against enemy territory. Paul also declares, "The weapons we fight with are not the weapons of the world. On the contrary, they have divine power to demolish strongholds" (2 Cor 10:4).

Dimensions of Evil Influence

In Ephesians 2:1-3 Paul identifies three major sources of evil: the world, the devil and the flesh. Although interrelated, these have distinct characteristics. Before they became Christians the Ephesians had "followed the ways of this world." Paul has in mind the whole pagan worldview—powerful patterns of thinking, customs, traditions and institutions.

The Ephesians had also followed the ways of "the ruler of the kingdom of the air." This is a powerful spirit in charge of a host of demons who exert a compelling influence; he "is now at work in [among] those who are disobedient." Paul portrays Satan's method as immediate and personal. Finally, the Christians formerly had been "gratifying the cravings of our sinful nature and following its desires and thoughts." Paul calls this sinful nature "the flesh," by which he means not the physical body (considered evil by the Greeks) but an inner motivating force, hostile to God, behind sinful thoughts and actions.

Satan achieves his goals through all three channels: the environment and social structures, direct personal action and the inner impulse to sin. While in a particular situation one of these may play a leading role, all three need to be considered. In the last analysis Paul considered Satan the chief opponent of Christ and his kingdom. The demonic element is the thread that ties together all other evil influences.

Discussion of ways to counteract that element is often clouded by a debate over whether a Christian can be "possessed by" a demon. The problem is accentuated by a misinterpretation of Gospel accounts of varied demonic influences—physical, mental and spiritual—in the exorcisms of Jesus. Vineyard leader John Wimber notes that English translations are misleading when they describe people as "having a demon" or being "demon-possessed" (such as in Mt 4:24; Mk 1:32; Lk 8:36; Jn 10:21). Such translations are unfortunate because the word *possession* conjures up images of demons indwelling and controlling people at all times—a situation not true of Christians, who are under the lordship of Christ. Wimber points out that the Greek word *daimonizomai* should be translated "demonized," which simply means "influenced, afflicted or tormented by a demonic power." He describes a wide variety of demonic influences and ways of deliverance from their power.[5]

Although Paul does not use the language of "demonization" found in the Gospels, he exhorts the Ephesians, "Do not give the devil a foothold *[topos]*" (4:27). This Greek word can also be translated "opportunity" (RSV) or "chance" (TEV). So the verse can be expressed, "Do not give the devil a chance to exert his influence."[6] In Romans 12:19 Paul uses *topos* in a similar way: "Do not take revenge, my friends, but leave room [give a chance] for God's wrath."

Frontline Ministries pastor Thomas B. White has developed from biblical terms a model of three "levels of evil influence."[7]

1. General warfare against the believer. It may take the form of "temptation": enticement or compulsion (from an external source) to violate God's law. An example is the experience of Jesus in the desert after his baptism by John. The solution is resistance (Jas 4:7; 1 Pet 5:9). Or the attack may come as "flaming arrows," external influence of evil spirits intended to attack weaknesses or hinder ministry.

2. Specific bondage, demonization. This is "oppression": persistent, ongoing bondage, affliction of body or soul that may be outward ("vexation") or inward ("demonization"). The solution is deliverance (Acts 10:38).

3. Deception and bondage in unbelievers. This is "control" (1 Jn 5:19): dominance of a person by Satan, either generally (covertly) through deception and disobedience (Eph 2:2; Rev 12:9) or specifically (overtly) through the direct control of evil spirits (Mt 8:28-33).

Following a description of principles and practices for dealing with each level, White gives a detailed checklist for testing spiritual bondage. He also has a chapter of patterns for effective prayer.

Like a medical doctor diagnosing a physical illness, we can learn from symptoms what spiritual forces are at work to cause a specific distress. From many years of experience with victims of the occult, Anglican pastor Russ Parker has come to appreciate the importance of "discernment before ministry." Of the many who have asked him to pray for release from evil spirits, only about a third actually needed freedom from evil oppression. "The others had equally genuine needs but they were not demonic in origin; they ranged from emotional hurts to obsession with evil, from long-standing guilt and mental disturbances to plain disobedience to the Word of God."[8]

Parker looks for signs of mental or emotional problems, projection, speech problems, addictions or physical ailments that may be mistaken for demon oppression. "Counseling before ministry" is essential to clarify issues and decide on the form of ministry required.

The Weapon of Prayer

Paul concludes his teaching on the armor of God with this admonition: "And pray in the Spirit on all occasions with all kinds of prayers and requests. . . . [A]lways keep on praying for all the saints. . . . Pray also for me" (Eph 6:18-19). Christians are to arm each other through prayer so that the church may be prepared for its spiritual warfare.

It is one thing to be fully armed, but quite another to fight effectively. Ultimately our strength is "in the Lord and in his mighty power" (v. 10). In spiritual warfare, prayer is vital as an attitude of expectancy and openness to God's power on our behalf.

What does it mean to "pray in the Spirit"? We find an answer in Paul's letter to the church in Rome. "In the same way, the Spirit helps us in our weakness. We do not know what we ought to pray for, but the Spirit himself intercedes for us with groans that words cannot express. And he who searches our hearts knows the mind of the Spirit, because the Spirit intercedes for the saints in accordance with God's will" (Rom 8:26-27). Here the word *helps* means "comes to the aid" of a person, takes hold on the other side. Effective prayer is a *two-party* communication that recognizes our own weakness. This is our starting point; alone and unaided, we cannot pray effectively. Why? Because we do not know how to pray. So at the outset, counting on the Spirit's help, we cry out to God for wisdom for this specific situation.

As Vineyard pastor George Mallone has discovered, "Praying in the Spirit is incredibly important during spiritual warfare. Often, as I pray for people in need, the Holy Spirit reveals the source of the battle and the particular strategy needed for the person."9 He identifies three ways of praying in the Spirit. First, we can pray with words we understand—as Paul puts it, "with my mind" (1 Cor 14:15). Our minds are filled with God's character and love, a sense of his presence and guidance in the requests we make. Second, we can pray with words we do not understand. The apostle says, "If I pray in a tongue, my spirit prays" (1 Cor 14:14). As we have seen, this is nonconceptual (not irrational) speech that enables us to keep on praying when words or ideas run out or seem inadequate in a particular situation.

Third, the Spirit can also lead us to pray without words in groans and sighs. For example, on one occasion when Jesus healed a deaf-mute, he "looked up to heaven . . . with a deep sigh" (Mk 7:34). Without words a burden was communicated to his Father. At times we too may have this experience under the pressure of a great need.

Paul also commands us to pray on all occasions. He writes to the Thessalonian church, "Pray continually; give thanks in all circumstances" (1 Thess 5:17-18). With practice we can develop a "running conversation" with God as we go about our daily tasks, as well as in specific times devoted to prayer.

As we pray, we need to confess known sin and receive forgiveness (1 Jn 1:9). We also want our minds to be filled with Scripture so that the "word of Christ" dwells in us and flows through our prayers. Our petitions should be made in the context of praise, with thanksgiving and expectancy that the Holy Spirit will empower our prayer as we engage in spiritual warfare.

Distinguishing Between Spirits

Battlefield tactics must always be suited to the kind of attack we are experiencing. Too often a nation's armed forces are well prepared to fight the "last war," but they are unprepared for a new conflict. The European trench tactics of World War I were hopelessly ineffective against Rommel's flexible desert warfare in North Africa during World War II. American World War II tactics failed in the jungle combat of Vietnam. Success in spiritual warfare likewise requires understanding of the specific enemy we face and selecting appropriate tactics to engage and defeat him.

In 1 Corinthians 12:10 the list of spiritual gifts includes "distinguishings between spirits" (a double plural; literal translation). The word *(diakrisis)* conveys the idea of differentiating or judging correctly between good and evil (as in Heb 5:14). In 1 Cor 6:5 the word connotes a legal judgment.[10] Distinguishing between spirits may be a complementary gift to prophecy, just as interpretation is to glossolalia, as they are listed together in verse 10. The apostle John stresses the need for such discernment: "Dear friends, do not believe every spirit, but test the spirits to see whether they are from God, because many false prophets have gone out into the world" (1 Jn 4:1).

Nevertheless, this gift has a wider scope in spiritual warfare. Theologian David Prior observes that it could refer specifically to discerning "the presence and the nature of evil spirits in a person, a place or a situation. More widely . . . from what source any purported spiritual manifestation comes."[11] The Bible indicates three possible sources: the Holy Spirit, the human spirit and evil spirits. For an appropriate response to a specific situation it is crucial to know what has motivated the troublesome behavior.

Christine was suffering from a depression that sapped her energy and caused the loss of her job. In desperation she came to the healing team of her church for help. Week by week they prayed for her, with no discernible results.

Eventually one team member became convinced that Christine was under demonic influence and needed prayer for deliverance. But as the others prayed for the Holy Spirit's guidance, they perceived that her problem was not demonic. As they learned more about her past, the team recognized a need for inner healing. Long-repressed anger over childhood abuse had now expressed itself in depression. As the team applied principles of inner healing, Christine was released from the grip of her past and emerged from her depression.

As with other gifts and ministries of the Spirit, spiritual warfare must be waged *within the body of Christ.* This context provides guidance and correction by the Spirit, feedback on action taken and accountability for follow-up support when deliverance is not immediate. Although charisms for these purposes can potentially be manifested through any member of the body, often special ministry is called for.

Demonization can come in different forms and degrees of control. Michael Scanlan, president of the University of Steubenville, and his colleague Randall J. Cirner have written out of long experience in this ministry. They describe four levels or means of deliverance: the personal or self-deliverance that is available to every Christian; fraternal deliverance through a Christian brother or sister; pastoral deliverance through someone who has spiritual responsibility for others; and the special ministry of "spiritual gifts of discernment, revelation, and authority to overcome Satan and evil spirits at their most profound levels of activity."[12]

Spiritual warfare today seems to be waged with three major, and somewhat overlapping, strategies. Mainstream evangelicals are moving into this arena in new ways. A variety of groups are involved in fighting "territorial spirits." Charismatic/Third Wave Christians are combating evil forces with the whole arsenal of available weapons. (We will discuss the "Third Wave" further in chapter twelve.)

Mainstream Evangelical Strategy

A good representative of the mainstream group is Timothy M. Warner, former missionary and professor in the School of World Mission and Evangelism at Trinity Evangelical Divinity School. His book *Spiritual Warfare* offers an excellent introduction to his principles and practice. He views mainstream evangelicalism on this subject as middle ground between those who want to solve every problem through spiritual warfare and those who reject spiritual warfare entirely.

Warner begins with the basic concept of "worldview," the thought system we develop for explaining the world and our experiences in it, the lenses through which we view the world around us. The *biblical* worldview envisions three orders of beings in constant functional contact: Deity, angels and demons, and human beings. Satan and his forces are always at work to mar the reflection of God's glory in humanity and nature through enmity, perversion and catastrophe.

The Western worldview, however, has two functional orders: the "supernatural" realm of God and other spirits, and the realm of the created world, which operates on its own according to "natural" laws. It is assumed that the two realms are separated from each other. For any phenomenon in the natural realm, except for an occasional "miracle," there is a natural cause. For all practical purposes most Western Christians have adopted this worldview, becoming functional deists who believe that although God created the great world clock, it continues to tick along on its own.

Warner calls for a return to the biblical worldview. We must understand Satan's strategy for attacks in both the spiritual and physical realms, as he uses the weapon of deception and lies. "One of the great needs of the church today is to bring the truth about the victory of Christ and the power of the Holy Spirit from the realm of theory or professed belief into the realm of practical experience."[13] Christians need to recognize and live out the reality of their being new persons "in Christ" (2 Cor 5:17). We need not fear demons but should treat them like the defeated enemies they are.

Warner breaks new ground for many evangelicals by recognizing that "the demonstration of Jesus' power over demons and his ability to do miracles were not just to validate His identity and message; they were actually part of His message." Victory over the demons evidenced the presence of the kingdom of God (Mt 12:28). "The work He began in relation to the Kingdom, we are to continue."[14] Proclamation and demonstration go hand in hand.

Another dimension of ministry that involves a demonstration of power is healing. Warner is not impressed by arguments that healing miracles were unique to the first century. He makes the perceptive comment that "our faith must be based in truth, not just in miracles; but part of the truth is that God does indeed work in power in all areas of life."[15]

Currently Warner conducts seminars and consults with churches and mission agencies. While he finds increasing openness to his message, some pastors and missionaries are interested but reluctant to become involved in the practice of spiritual warfare.

Another recent book that has gained widespread influence is *The Bondage Breaker* by Neil T. Anderson, chairman of the Practical Theology Department at Talbot School of Theology of Biola University. He conducts seminars for Freedom in Christ Ministries. His book also notes that the Western world sees reality in two tiers: (1) the transcendent world of God and spiritual forces understood through religion and mysticism, and (2) the empirical world understood through the physical senses and science. The former is considered to have no practical bearing on the latter. Anderson calls Christians to recognize the biblical teaching that spiritual forces are constantly at work in the physical world.

Anderson offers two chapters full of practical steps toward finding freedom in Christ and then helping others along the same path. He explains that "in Christ's death and resurrection every believer is made alive with Him and is now seated with Him in the heavenlies" (Eph 2:5-6). In order to experience freedom from Satan's bondage, we need to "understand and appropriate [our] position and authority in Christ."[16] Basic to freedom from bondage is our "identity in Christ."

Anderson's central thesis is that "Satan is a deceiver, but the truth of God's word exposes him and his lie. . . . When his lie is exposed by the truth, his plans are foiled. . . . *Truth* is the liberating agent." Freedom from spiritual bondage is not a power encounter but a "truth-encounter." In other words, the essential conflict is in the mind, a battle between truth and falsehood.

So how do we defeat Satan? "You just have to *outtruth* him. *Believe, declare, and act upon the truth of God's Word,* and you will thwart Satan's strategy. . . . The power of the believer is in knowing the truth. We are to pursue *truth,* not power."[17] This principle is based on Jesus' statement, "You will know the truth, and the truth will set you free" (Jn 8:32).

However, Anderson's concept of spiritual warfare as mainly a conflict between truth and error has several flaws. First, Satan not only deceives, he attacks in all dimensions of our lives—physical, emotional and relational as well as intellectual. For that reason we need both *proclamation of truth* and *demonstration of power* in each of those dimensions. Jesus' ministry consisted of both teaching and healing. After the resurrection he commissioned his disciples to proclaim the *truth* of the gospel when they had been clothed with *power* by the Holy Spirit (Lk 24:45-49; Acts 1:8).

Paul reminded the Corinthians that he came not only preaching but "with a demonstration of the Spirit's power" (1 Cor 2:4). The apostle also reported to the Romans what he had *said* and *done* to free the Gentiles from the dominion of Satan to obey God—"by the power of signs and miracles, through the power of the Spirit" (Rom 15:18-19). The New Testament consistently teaches the truth that power is essential to proclaiming the gospel and waging spiritual warfare.

Second, Anderson ignores the context of the statement "The truth will set you free." Jesus was speaking to those who now believed and were really his disciples. Jesus then said, "If the Son sets you free, you will be free indeed" (Jn 8:36). It is not simply the knowledge and acceptance of biblical truth that liberates. (That concept reflects and reinforces the rationalism that has long influenced Western Christian theology.) Freedom is experienced in the context of a learning relationship with the Lord who both teaches and empowers his disciples through the Holy Spirit.

That leads to the third and most serious flaw of Anderson's book. Surprisingly, he presents a theology of spiritual warfare without a role for the Holy Spirit. Throughout 247 pages, except for some passing comment, there is no recognition of the Spirit or the gifts through which he empowers the church. Anderson not only sets aside the Gospels and Acts as histories with little if any theological value for our spiritual warfare, he ignores the truth in the Epistles about spiritual gifts. He declares that in helping others find freedom, it is wrong to expect "an unusual giftedness or calling instead of character and the ability to teach."[18]

Many mainstream evangelicals recognize the reality of spiritual warfare and want to be effective against Satan and his demons. But they seem reluctant to rethink their view that certain so-called supernatural spiritual gifts ceased at the end of the first century. As a result, they lose the benefit of significant weapons available for this conflict.

Territorial Spirits

A dimension of spiritual warfare largely neglected until recently is the confrontation of demons associated with specific geopolitical areas such as cities or nations. A leading proponent in the field of spiritual warfare is C. Peter Wagner, professor of church growth at the School of World Mission, Fuller Theological Seminary. In his recent study of "spiritual territoriality," Wagner examined the one hundred books listed in the Fuller Seminary library card catalog under "angelology" and "demonology." Only five so much as mentioned the issue of territoriality; three had helpful information, but none was valuable enough to include in his study of this subject.

Wagner's 1991 book *Engaging the Enemy: How to Fight and Defeat Territorial Spirits* has seventeen articles by veterans of spiritual warfare from a diversity of denominational and international backgrounds.[19] They comment on biblical examples of territorial spirits and report current activities against them in a variety of situations.

A vision in Daniel 10 pictures this warfare as a struggle between angels and demons. As Daniel fasted and prayed for three weeks, God's messenger sent to explain the vision was opposed by "the prince of the Persian kingdom" (v. 13), apparently a demon exercising evil influence over that realm. But this demon was overcome by the archangel Michael, "the great prince who protects your people" (12:1). The messenger then described to Daniel future political and military struggles among the powerful nations of his day.

The Old Testament has many references to "high places," or certain trees identified by pagan nations as locales for particular gods (Deut 12:2; 1 Kings 20:23). Images that represent spirits and gods are called evil (2 Kings 17:17). When the Hebrews entered the land of Canaan, they were afraid to trust the Lord for its fertility; they turned repeatedly to worship the Baals, the local agriculture-fertility deities.[20]

Although in the New Testament many demons were confronted, only a few were attached to a specific location. In Mark 5:1-20, for example, the evil spirits Jesus cast out begged to stay in that area of the Gerasenes; they were allowed to enter a nearby herd of pigs. In Ephesus Paul conducted open warfare against evil spirits and preached with power so that "the word of the Lord spread widely" (Acts 19:12-20). Soon a riot against Paul and the gospel was generated by the cult of the goddess Artemis (Roman Diana), to whom "unsurpassed cosmic power" was attributed. Called "Savior," "Lord," "Queen of the Cosmos," she was worshiped throughout Asia.[21]

These are all biblical examples of spirits associated with or controlling cities or areas. During the Roman occupation, the Israelites considered demonic personages to be located in certain political powers in specific places.

Engaging the Enemy reports many current encounters with territorial spirits around the world, especially in connection with evangelistic efforts. These insidious powers work through governments, religions and powerful personalities to promote Satanism, the provision and use of drugs, terrorism, sexual perversion and pornography. Consistently, a key to the spread of the gospel is a power encounter through intercessory prayer that breaks the power of the local spirits.

Pursuing this dimension of evangelism and church growth, Peter Wagner has continued his research in three areas: strategic-level intercession, intercession for Christian leaders and the relationship of prayer to the growth of the local church. The first book in this trilogy is *Warfare Prayer,* which describes frontline spiritual warfare in Argentina, maps out a biblical strategy and indicates courses of action. Wagner concludes with rules for taking cities and pitfalls to be avoided.[22]

This growing movement is attracting Christians from a variety of theological persuasions. It has also sparked some criticism, not so much about the biblical basis and reality of territorial spirits but concerning the current emphasis in fighting them. For example, Timothy Warner cautions that they should not be a primary focus of our ministries since they are not so presented in Scripture.[23] John Wimber notes that while Daniel was praying, it was *God* who deployed the angels to do spiritual battle. He warns against a misguided focus on Satan.[24]

Charismatic/Third Wave Strategy

Participants in the charismatic/Third Wave renewal generally accept the biblical principles enunciated by the first two groups and much of their practice. The major difference lies in two fundamental emphases of the charismatic renewal: the full range of spiritual gifts and their primary purpose to empower the body of Christ.

Satan and his demons are waging war on all fronts: spiritual, intellectual, physical, emotional, interpersonal and societal. To repulse these varied assaults, the soldiers of Christ need as weapons the wide range of gifts provided by the Holy Spirit—for example, wisdom, knowledge, distinguishing between spirits, prophecy, evangelism, teaching, physical and emotional healings, miracles, contributing to needs, showing mercy (Rom 12:6-8; 1 Cor 12:8-10). Soldiers armed only with rifles can inflict limited damage in a skirmish; in a major battle, however, they need the support of heavy artillery.

The use of spiritual gifts and the armor of God is usually explained in terms of individuals. But the New Testament context of both is the community. Charisms are meant to empower the body of Christ for its worship, witness and service. Likewise, soldiers don't go into battle alone; they fight together as an army. Ephesians 6 depicts the armor in corporate terms: the whole church is involved in the process of arming. Although we experience individual attacks, Satan's objective is to damage the whole body of Christ. Both the fire and the firepower are meant for the fireplace.

Christus Victor

The coming of God's kingdom in Christ has both present and future implications. It is "already" here, as Jesus declared, but "not yet" complete in its reign. Even though the decisive battle was won by the Lord in his death and resurrection, his servants will be engaged in costly warfare with Satan's kingdom until its final defeat.

Christ's once-for-all victory over the powers of darkness finds vivid expression in Colossians 2:15: "And having disarmed the powers and authorities, he made a public spectacle of them, triumphing over them by the cross." Through his death and resurrection Christ won a victory with eternal consequences over the powers. By shedding his blood on the cross he brought forgiveness and freedom from the sin that had kept people in bondage. By his resurrection he overcame death, Satan's ultimate weapon. The "public spectacle" was a triumphal procession of a Roman general and his soldiers celebrating their victory. Bringing up the rear in chains were the defeated king and his surviving warriors, their subjugation paraded for all to see and ridicule.

The Christian must know that every conceivable god or goddess, power, spirit or demon falls under the dominion of Christ. Satan launches both frontal attacks and subtle infiltrations; battles can be fierce. But they should be fought with confidence that the decisive victory has been won by our Lord Jesus Christ in his death and resurrection. Ultimately he will preside over the total defeat of Satan and his minions.

Looking to the future, the New Testament sees a point in history when the tyranny of all evil spirits with their leader Satan will be terminated: "Then the end will come, when he [Christ] hands over the kingdom to God the Father after he has destroyed all dominion, authority and power. For he must reign until [God] has put all his enemies under his feet" (1 Cor 15:24-25).

Therefore God exalted him to the highest place
    and gave him the name that is above every name,
that at the name of Jesus every knee should bow,
    in heaven and on earth and under the earth,
and every tongue confess that Jesus Christ is Lord,
    to the glory of God the Father. (Phil 2:9-11)

12 *The Vineyard Fellowship*

*J*ohn and Carol Wimber came to faith in Christ by widely different routes.
A fourth-generation unbeliever, John had received no Christian training and
did not attend church regularly. At twenty-nine, a jazz musician with a "soar-
ing career and a diving marriage," he found that his life was in shambles.
Carol, on the other hand, had been raised in church and had attended paro-
chial schools. A young mother with three children and another on the way,
she had a gnawing sense of guilt over abandoning her Christian heritage. Both
turned to Christ out of deep personal need; in him they found freedom from
guilt, a purpose for living and a renewed marriage.[1]

As the two also plunged into personal evangelism, John recognized their
different approaches. Carol gave a clear presentation of the gospel and answered questions to lay a solid intellectual base for conversion. John, however,
relied more on intuition, a spiritual guidance that told him when people were
ready to give their lives to Christ. During the following years, as pastor of a
Friends church, he felt a tension between the intellectual and intuitive aspects
of evangelism.

On his subsequent pilgrimage—personal and pastoral—Wimber encountered an emerging renewal movement. It was called the "Third Wave," a term coined by C. Peter Wagner.[2] As Wagner explains it, the First Wave was the Pentecostal movement which began at the turn of the century. The Second Wave was the midcentury charismatic renewal in three streams: mainline Protestant, Roman Catholic and independent churches. Wagner defined the Third Wave in the September 1984 issue of *Christian Life* magazine: "It is a new moving of the Holy Spirit among evangelicals who, for one reason or another, have chosen not to identify with either the Pentecostals or the charismatics. . . . I see the third wave as distinct from, but at the same time very similar to, the first and second waves."[3]

Wagner noted that a majority in the Third Wave prefer to use the term "filled with the Spirit" or "empowered by the Holy Spirit" instead of "baptized in the Spirit." Although many in this movement report a "life-changing" encounter with the Spirit, it is not necessarily accompanied by speaking in tongues. Participants are committed to "power ministry" such as healing, prayer, deliverance and prophecy. In that connection the phrase *signs and wonders* has become closely associated with the movement.

This chapter traces the rapid growth of the Vineyard Fellowship under John Wimber's leadership. What are its strengths and weaknesses? To what extent can it be considered a "third wave" in the empowering movement of the Holy Spirit during the twentieth century?

Power Evangelism

In 1971, after returning from missionary service in Bolivia, C. Peter Wagner succeeded Donald McGavran as dean of the Fuller School of World Mission in Pasadena, California. Four years later he met John Wimber, who enrolled in his doctor of ministry church-growth course. At the time Wagner was in the process of establishing what became the Charles E. Fuller Institute of Evangelism and Church Growth. He persuaded Wimber to resign as copastor of the Yorba Linda Friends Church and join the institute to take the lead in applying church-growth principles at the grassroots. The two became fast friends; both were traditional evangelicals who admired Pentecostal and charismatic groups—from a distance.

Soon John Wimber discovered the "Engel Scale." This model describes stages in thinking (from little knowledge to considerable knowledge) and attitudes (from hostile to responsive) that people go through in conversion. In every society there is a group of people on the verge of becoming Christians; their openness involves both intellectual and attitudinal factors. Wimber realized that both he and Carol had been right in their evangelism methods. Effective evangelism requires both the *message* (the content of the gospel) and the *right timing* (readiness for harvest). He saw how Western evangelicals frequently stress the intellectual element to the exclusion of the intuitive.

Wimber also ran across Peter Wagner's book *Look Out! The Pentecostals Are Coming.*[4] He had always avoided Pentecostal and charismatic Christians, partly because controversy seemed to surround their ministry; also, as a dispensationalist, Wimber believed that the extraordinary gifts of prophecy, healing and tongues had ceased at the end of the first century. But in Wagner he found a credible witness, an experienced missionary and academician who reported gifts of healing and deliverance from evil spirits in twentieth-century South America. These miraculous encounters had resulted in large evangelistic harvests and church growth. Although skeptical about the validity of such gifts today, Wimber was forced to reconsider his views.

With new openness he read books by English Pentecostal Donald Gee, *Concerning Spiritual Gifts,* and American Episcopalian Morton T. Kelsey, *Healing and Christianity.*[5] Their writings, combined with firsthand testimonies of the miraculous from Third World students at Fuller, gave Wimber new understanding of the Holy Spirit's role in evangelism. He also reevaluated his own experiences in personal evangelism. Slowly he realized that what he had considered merely psychological insights into people's concerns as they neared conversion were really spiritual gifts such as words of knowledge and wisdom.

As he studied the Gospels from this perspective, Wimber discovered that Jesus always combined a proclamation of the kingdom of God with its demonstration: healing the sick, casting out demons, raising the dead. Teaching and healing were integrally related; for example, the first half of Mark's Gospel (which covers the major portion of Jesus' ministry) has about the same number of verses for each. Spiritual gifts took on new meaning for Wimber. They authenticated the gospel, cutting through people's resistance and opening them to the good news of Christ.

By 1977 Wimber's thinking regarding personal evangelism was significantly altered. He concluded that the key to effectiveness is a combination of *proclamation* and *demonstration*. He made a distinction between traditional "programmatic evangelism" and "power evangelism." The former is usually message-centered with rational arguments—one-way communication through a prepared message. Often there is an emphasis on a technique of presentation—several spiritual laws or steps needed to enter a relationship with Christ. Programmatic evangelism generally assumes that a potential convert's major reservations about the gospel are intellectual.

Power evangelism, however, presents the gospel message accompanied by spiritual gifts such as a word of knowledge, healing or discernment of spirits. It is more confrontational in that "each evangelism experience is initiated by the Holy Spirit for a *specific* place, time, person or group." In his 1986 *Power Evangelism* Wimber declares, "A divine appointment is an appointed time in which God reveals himself to an individual or group through spiritual gifts or other supernatural phenomena."[6]

During the following years, this distinction between "programmatic" and "power" evangelism stirred vigorous controversy as it was both embraced and excoriated. The 1993 revision of *Power Evangelism* drops that contrast and affirms, "*The heart and soul of evangelism is proclamation of the gospel. . . .* Preaching and demonstrating the gospel are not mutually exclusive activities; they work together, reinforcing each other."[7] Power evangelism *consciously* cooperates with the Holy Spirit's anointing, gifting and leading.

Nevertheless, Wimber lacked a biblical theology to integrate his understanding and practice of evangelism, the Holy Spirit and church growth. His search for a solid evangelical theology culminated in a study of the book *Jesus and the Kingdom* by George Eldon Ladd of Fuller Seminary.[8] Ladd points

out that every kingdom has three essential elements: a king, authority and
subjects. Jesus is our King; all authority in heaven and earth has been given
him by his Father; Christians are his subjects. The gospel is a call to the
lordship of Christ and membership in his kingdom, not the prevalent self-
centered message to come to Jesus to meet all your needs and fulfill your
potential. It is a costly calling that involves spiritual warfare on many fronts.
For this conflict the King equips his subjects with "power and authority to
drive out all demons and to cure diseases . . . to preach the kingdom of God
and to heal the sick" (as in Lk 9:1-2).

Power Healing

John Wimber began to consider whether the signs, wonders and rapid church
growth prevalent in the Third World were possible in the United States, where
Western rationalism and materialism inhibit the practice of power evangelism.
In 1978 he resigned from the Institute of Evangelism and Church Growth to
become a more active member of the Friends congregation that had been the
Wimbers' home base. John and Carol began to participate in a group of some
fifty people already meeting in their home to worship and study Scripture. By
the second year, two hundred people were meeting in a high-school gymnasium.

But differences arose. After being asked to dissociate from the Friends
congregation, Wimber's group linked itself to Calvary Chapel. They were
eventually asked to leave because Wimber and the other leaders could not
commit themselves to Calvary Chapel's strict eschatology. They then affiliated
with Vineyard Christian Fellowship, a church established by Kenn Gulliksen
in West Los Angeles in 1974.

In his book *Power Healing* Wimber describes how he overcame his bias
against spiritual gifts and how God led him into a healing ministry.[9] During
its first year the church did not experience any of the signs and wonders
described in the New Testament. So he began a series of sermons on healing,
based on the Gospel of Luke. During the next ten months not one person was
healed, and half the members left the church. But Wimber kept preaching and
praying for healing.

That long dry period taught him several lessons. First, there is more to being equipped and empowered to do God's work than studying the Bible. Second, there are different kinds of faith. As an evangelical, Wimber thought of personal Christian growth as having two components, doctrinal faith and faithfulness. Now he recognized another dimension of Christian growth, an exercise of faith for spiritual gifts such as healing and words of knowledge. It is essential to know when God's anointing has come for a task like healing in a particular situation. Although biblical knowledge and character development are essential, this other dimension is needed to empower ministry.

At the end of ten months, when John Wimber was at his lowest point, his prayer for the healing of a woman's life-threatening illness was answered and she got out of bed completely whole. That first healing soon led into a steady stream.

In *Power Healing* Wimber presents a comprehensive exposition of biblical principles of healing and practical models for its implementation, based on experience in Vineyard churches. Besides an emphasis on physical healing, attention is given to the healing of the "demonized" person, inner healing and spiritual warfare. Wimber contends that the believer has been given the same power and authority to heal and cast out demons that Jesus proclaimed and demonstrated.[10] A section of the book deals with the question whether physical healing is inherent in Christ's atonement for sin. Wimber leans toward the view that although physical healing is not *in* the atonement, it comes to us *through* the atonement, which is the basis of all healing.[11] Three appendixes list the many biblical references to healing, usually overlooked in standard commentaries: Old Testament, 80; Jesus' healings, 41; disciples' healings, 28.[12]

John Wimber stands in awe of God's sovereignty, desires to move only in response to divine initiative, and is deeply moved by the grace and compassion of Christ. He is convinced that following conversion (when the Holy Spirit enters a Christian's life), no "second work of grace" is necessary for empowering. Predominant in Wimber's ministry is the concept of power to carry out the Great Commission, which involves both evangelism and gifts of healing, proclaiming and demonstrating the gospel. The in-breaking of the kingdom by the Spirit of God through "miraculous signs and wonders" strengthens the faith of believers and brings nonbelievers into contact with God (Mk 16:17; Acts 5:12; Heb 2:4; for a note on Mk 16:9-20 see appendix E).

Basic to Wimber's understanding of spiritual gifts is the biblical teaching that all of them (including the entire list in 1 Cor 12:8-10) can potentially be manifested by any believer, as the Holy Spirit ordains, to empower the worship and service of the body of Christ. As we have seen, charisms are not permanent possessions. Nor is their manifestation—whether message of wisdom or healing or prophecy—limited to a select few, even though the Holy Spirit often works frequently and consistently through certain individuals to empower a specific ministry. John Wimber's more recent book *Power Points* is a practical theology that instructs Christians in basic biblical doctrines and their application to daily life.[13]

MC510 at Fuller Seminary

John Wimber had returned to the pastorate from the Fuller Institute of Evangelism and Church Growth to become more personally involved in power evangelism and healing. Nevertheless, he volunteered to give a lecture in the Church Growth II class on "Signs, Wonders and Church Growth." About this time Wagner learned that his predecessor Donald McGavran, world-renowned founder of the church-growth movement, had lectured on divine healing and church growth in one of his advanced classes. If it was all right for McGavran, it was all right for his disciple!

In January 1982 a new School of World Mission course appeared in the Fuller catalog: MC510, "The Miraculous and Church Growth," taught by adjunct professor John Wimber. The course was designed to deal with both theory and practice of the miraculous in the proclamation of the gospel. It was welcomed by President David Allan Hubbard and launched with considerable fanfare.

The course was held on Monday evenings in the basement of a church just off campus. A class of about 130 typified the diversity of those enrolled in MC510. Students varied greatly in age and denominational affiliation; theology students predominated; psychology majors were a minority; a third were older men and one woman from Third World countries, many with considerable pastoral experience. Most students came with an open attitude, mixing healthy skepticism with a desire to learn.

Three major theological areas were studied in light of Jesus' life and teaching: the nature of evil in general, the nature of sickness in particular, and the kingdom of God. For their understanding of the kingdom the instructors drew heavily on the writings of George Eldon Ladd and Lutheran theologian James Kallas: The term *kingdom* signifies rule or dominion. The kingdom of God has arrived in Jesus to take dominion over Satan and all demons. Jesus' teaching and miracles went hand in hand to proclaim and demonstrate his sovereignty. He rebuked forces of nature, cast out demons, cured diseases and raised the dead. Christ's authority over these evils was passed on to his followers. Signs of the kingdom's presence are proclamation of the gospel, regeneration, healing, exorcism, a people united and manifesting the gifts and fruit of the Spirit.

Two hours devoted to theological discussion were followed by an hour of laboratory designed to help the students put into practice what they had learned. Over time a variety of healings occurred. As the course proceeded, skepticism diminished as the majority of students became actively involved in healing outside class time.

Peter Wagner attended an early MC510 class as a spectator, with no intention of participating. But in the third week his role unexpectedly changed. When the teaching part was over Wimber asked, "Is there anyone here who needs prayer for physical healing?" Wagner put up his hand; for several years he had been taking three pills a day for high blood pressure. As he sat on a stool in front of the class and Wimber began to pray, a deep sense of peace came over him. After about ten minutes he was told that God was ministering to him but he should not go off medication until he had medical permission. A few days later Wagner's doctor was surprised to see that his blood pressure had fallen considerably; he reduced the medication gradually and a few months later discontinued it. Wagner, too, started laying hands on the sick and learning how to minister to them in the name of Jesus. Healing happened often enough to encourage him to pray for the sick as a regular part of his Christian life.

Popularly called "Signs and Wonders," the course broke all enrollment records at Fuller; it stirred national attention when *Christian Life* devoted an entire issue to it. (An expanded version of this issue was edited by Peter Wagner.[14]) During the following three years MC510 also encountered a variety of criticisms, including objections to conducting healing services in an academic setting. In March 1986 the School of World Mission declared a moratorium on the course pending seminary faculty review of the issues. Later that year the task force reported its findings, which were soon published.[15]

This book was introduced into the curriculum of a new course, MC550, "The Ministry of Healing in World Evangelization," taught by Peter Wagner and offered in the spring 1987 quarter. Students were able to study the miraculous in off-campus class assignments in churches where healing was being practiced. To undergird his concern for world evangelization and church growth, Wagner developed a "theology of power" in his 1988 book *The Third Wave of the Holy Spirit.*[16]

Addressing the Critics

The Fuller faculty's study, *Ministry and the Miraculous,* examines the biblical, historical, theological and pastoral implications of conducting sessions of healing in the context of a seminary course. It does not attempt a critique of healing ministries but rather reflects on the place of the miraculous in seminary curriculum. The tone is more irenic than polemic, with gratitude expressed for current healing activities of the Spirit, yet concern about the role claimed for New Testament "signs and wonders today." The study attempts to "tack between the shoals of denying the possibility of miracles in our day and the rocks of presumption that demand miracles according to our need and schedule."[17]

Discussion covers the coming of the kingdom of God and healing ministry, differences of worldview on the supernatural, the place of suffering in Christian experience, verification of claimed miracles, miraculous healing and responsible ministry, and Fuller Seminary's distinctives. The study is strongest in the last area, clearly spelling out the seminary's responsibilities as an academic, theological institution serving an evangelical, multidenominational constituency. Academic, pastoral and faculty accountability, based on faculty consensus, is essential for curriculum offerings. The study urges faculty to support critical exploration into all the dimensions of miraculous healing and exorcism. But it states that consensus would be threatened if a classroom practice became a *cause célèbre* and a public signal that Fuller had changed its character. Any future course on the subject of the miracles in ministry should be taught by a full-time faculty member and take its practical ministry component off campus.

Despite its reasonable tone, the study has a strong bias against the manifestation of gifts of healings and miracles today. The objections are based on frequently used arguments that violate basic principles of biblical interpretation. (See the section titled "Objections to Healing Prayer" in chapter nine.)

First is the fallacious *argument from silence,* the attempt to infer a writer's view on a subject from what is *not* said about it. For example, the first chapter of *Ministry and the Miraculous* states that when Mary prophesies about the mighty works of her Son, "she does not so much as mention temporary healings of individual bodies" (p. 26). After his resurrection, Jesus "gives no mandate to undertake a healing ministry."

Second is an *unsupported conclusion* about the value of healing: As time went on after Pentecost, "gifts of healing became subordinate to moral and spiritual transformation" (p. 32).

Third is a *misinterpretation of suffering,* which is defined as "the experience of any condition one most sorely wishes were absent" (p. 52). Several pages of general observations on the human condition in a fallen world show how suffering is to be accepted as the common lot of all people. Unfortunately, the study fails to take account of two distinctive New Testament terms for a particular kind of suffering: the noun *pathēma* and the verb *pascho,* which occur eleven and fifty times, respectively. These words consistently connote experiences of persecution, pain and death externally perpetrated, first on Christ and then his followers. Unlike sickness (for which these terms are *not* used), *pathēma* is voluntary, an experience of those who choose to take up their cross and do the will of God. Statements about pain from persecution for Christ's sake therefore should not be gratuitously applied to suffering from sickness.

The above weaknesses also reflect a fourth characteristic: a *spirit-body dichotomy*. The study reflects a Neo-Platonic dualism that emphasizes the importance of the eternal spirit and disparages the temporal body. This perspective runs contrary to Hebraic wholism, which expresses the unity of the person and concern for all dimensions of well-being. The Fuller study also offers as a possible interpretation of James 5:14-15 that the promise of the Lord's raising up the sick person refers to "the perfect and permanent healing that comes with life after death" (p. 33). This conjecture is clearly unsupported by the context of the passage and a plain reading of the text.

A fifth argument is based on a *reductionism* that fails to recognize that a word or phrase can have more than one meaning and an action or event can have more than one significance. The study affirms that "the primary motive for divine miracle is not compassion but revelation" (p. 27). Yet Mark, for example, reports that when a leper begged for healing, Jesus was "filled with compassion" as he reached out to touch and heal him (Mk 1:41). Are we to believe that the Lord's primary motive was actually to use this man as an object lesson to win acceptance for his message? Such reductionism denies the multifaceted meaning of Jesus' healing ministry emphasized in chapter five. It also reflects a rationalism that emphasizes the words of revelation at the expense of its acts. Jesus revealed God in word *and* deed as he taught and healed. The healing medium is its own message, a demonstration of God's present concern for the whole person that speaks louder than words.

Despite its welter of arguments against the MC510 course, *Ministry and the Miraculous* affirms: "Gifts of healings and miracles, just as gifts as healing and prophecy, are part of the life of the body of Christ today, and should be used, under the guidance of the Holy Spirit and the instruction of the Scriptures"

(p. 33). The modified signs and wonders course, MC550, has continued with less controversy.

A Question of Worldviews

In *The Universe Next Door,* James Sire defines *worldview* as "a set of pre-suppositions (or assumptions) that we hold (consciously or subconsciously) about the basic makeup of our world."[18] Lying at the heart of each culture, its worldview explains how and why things are, evaluates events and experiences, and integrates new information, experiences and values. A worldview is necessary to form and maintain a culture.

Our Western worldview, derived largely from the eighteenth-century Enlightenment, is naturalism or secularism, the assumption that the natural world is the sum total of reality. By the nineteenth century, materialism and rationalism had also prevailed in Western thought. Materialism grants reality only to the natural world; rationalism accepts as valid only reasoned explanations of observable phenomena.

Christian theism, on the other hand, holds that the ultimate reality is God, the Creator and Sustainer of the universe, the Lord and Judge of history. Human beings are made in his image with moral responsibility. Holy Scripture is our final authority and trustworthy guide in all matters of faith and conduct. The biblical worldview includes a transcendent spiritual world beyond our observable universe, with God, heaven and hell, angels and demons.

Those who want to preserve belief in God have drawn a line between the so-called natural and supernatural realms (see appendix E). According to their definitions, the physical world—our autonomous universe—is controlled by natural laws which science has the potential to explain completely. The spiritual world is the abode of God, who has occasionally intervened with a miracle that breaks or suspends the natural laws.

John Wimber is concerned that many Western Christians neatly divide up their lives between the categories of "natural" and "supernatural," with the latter removed from everyday life.[19] They exclude God's miraculous power from their theology and practice of the Christian life. They accept spiritual miracles of regeneration and growth in character, but not physical miracles of healing or other New Testament "signs and wonders." Many evangelicals believe that their thinking on issues of healing and power evangelism is formed by the Bible alone. They are unaware of the powerful influence of the Western secular worldview on their perception of the "supernatural" in Scripture.

One California church that had relegated miraculous gifts to the first century suddenly faced a problem. Raymond Smith was told by the doctor that his hospitalized wife would not live through the night. When he called the church elders to pray and anoint her with oil, they did so—not in faith but out of obligation. To their amazement, she walked out of the hospital the next day. The doctors called it a "miracle." But the elders never told the congregation what had happened! This remarkable healing did not stimulate more prayer for healing the sick. Why? Because the elders' worldview screened out the possibility that Mrs. Smith's healing was a miracle in answer to prayer. They lacked a theology for the practice of healing.

Wimber notes that we see according to our expectations. Since what we expect is often a result of conditioning, we miss what God is doing outside our expectations. We need to recover the biblical worldview of a God who is constantly at work, sometimes in surprising ways.

Signs and Wonders
We have noted that in the Bible miracles are called "signs" and "wonders." They are *wonders* because these events make people stop, look and think; they are also *signs* that God is alive and well, actively demonstrating his kingly rule, carrying out his purposes in history and nature. Furthermore, miracles are meant to involve the observers. We should evaluate miracles in terms of their intended effect on the observers, called to repentance and holiness of life. The biblical writers are mainly concerned with what an object or event *does,* its concrete effects in daily life, rather than what it *is* in abstract terms like *supernatural.*

The crucial question for Vineyard Fellowship teaching is whether the signs and wonders that were prominent in the ministry of Jesus and his disciples were meant to be continued in the church and operative today. Here we have examined the case for the affirmative made by John Wimber and Peter Wagner; it is based on both their interpretation of Scripture and their witness to its reality in their lives. On the other hand, the Fuller study *Ministry and the Miraculous* concludes that the phrase *signs and wonders* connotes only the unique revelatory events of salvation history in the life, death and resurrection of Christ and the advent of the Spirit. Therefore, when our prayers for healing are answered, "we may best honor the unique acts of God in Jesus" by not calling them "signs and wonders."[20] (See appendix E.)

Before we settle on either of these opposite views, we need to consider several factors. The term *signs and wonders* is both biblical and dramatic; it makes a good watchword, a label for the whole package of demonstrating the power of God through miraculous spiritual gifts. At the same time it runs a risk of oversimplification and thus can alienate many who are basically attracted to this movement. For example, the biblical and historical case for healing prayer today, reviewed in chapters eight through ten of this book, does not depend on the "signs and wonders" concept, although it allows ample room for miraculous healings. Francis MacNutt's model of "more or less" covers a wide spectrum from immediate, complete healing to long-range or partial relief. Do only *immediate, miraculous* healings qualify as a sign or wonder? If not, how far along the scale is the cutoff point?

To what extent does the use of this label to connote the church's healing ministry prove divisive? The Vineyard Fellowship avoids using the controversial phrase *baptism in the Spirit* because it unnecessarily alienates evangelicals who equate it with the Pentecostal theology of a second stage in Christian experience evidenced by speaking in tongues. What message, then, does the Vineyard have for charismatic congregations that are involved in a healing ministry but have problems, for one reason or another, with "signs and wonders" theology?

If a picture is worth a thousand words, as Confucius said, an apt label or slogan can be valuable as shorthand for a complex product. Yet it runs the risk of oversimplification and becoming a liability. To what extent does *signs and wonders* now face that situation, unnecessarily turning people off? Perhaps it is inevitable that every renewal will have a distinctive, long-neglected doctrine and label that both attract and alienate would-be participants. As in the case of Pentecostalism, further theological reflection and experience may provide new insight into the semantic "signs and wonders" question.

Evaluation of the Vineyard Fellowship
In the last two decades the Vineyard Fellowship has made several significant contributions to charismatic renewal.

  1. Philosophical framework. The Western worldview of naturalism (secularism) is being widely challenged by cultural forces. The Enlightenment rationalism that denies the reality of spiritual forces is coming apart at the seams. New Age, occult and drug movements affirm the reality of the spiritual realm in daily life. From the perspective of biblical theism, the Vineyard Fellowship challenges the natural-supernatural dichotomy that still dominates not only the culture but large segments of the Christian church—both liberal and evangelical—which have denied the observable miraculous activity of the Holy Spirit in the physical realm.

  2. Theological foundation. The Vineyard provided a theological underpinning that the charismatic renewal did not yet have: the biblical doctrine of the kingdom of God. In this respect it went beyond the Pentecostal and early charismatic focus on spiritual renewal as a second stage in the pilgrimage of the individual believer. Vineyard Fellowship leaders are committed to a biblical worldview within which a doctrine of the empowering ministry of the Holy Spirit advances the kingdom of God.

  3. Equipping all Christians. Wimber's book *Power Encounters* reveals another of the Vineyard's fundamental contributions to charismatic renewal. It is an *equipping* movement "in which *all* Christians are encouraged to pray for the sick and experience *all* the gifts. This is why I conduct training seminars, not healing campaigns; my goal is to release the healing ministry throughout the entire body." Wimber's aim is to reform the training system in most

Western churches. "It is moving the ministry from the pulpit to the pews, from clergy to laity, from the few to the many . . . training all Christians for power ministry, especially personal evangelism and divine healing."[21]

4. *Evangelical appeal.* John Wimber wanted to transcend controversy and division over "baptism in the Spirit" as a second stage in Christian experience. He has appealed to Christians with an evangelical or Reformed theology who cannot accept that Pentecostal assumption. The Vineyard churches are largely made up of conservative evangelicals, who have learned that they too can be open to the full range of spiritual gifts within their theological heritage.

The Vineyard Fellowship also has manifested a crucial weakness that illustrates the maxim that most movements tend to be the lengthened shadow of their founder.

For many years John Wimber functioned as a "benign dictator." There was no doubt about who was in charge. This leadership style became a crucial weakness during his involvement with the Kansas City Fellowship prophets. Before Paul Cain visited the Vineyard's Anaheim headquarters in December 1988, he predicted that earthquakes would occur on the day he arrived and the day after he left. They took place on schedule, the first in Pasadena, the second in Armenia. Wimber considered them a validation of Cain's ministry, which emphasizes predictive prophecy. He took the KCF prophets on a world tour of conferences featuring their message.

In the fall of 1989 Wimber described how he was taking prophecy seriously for the first time in his life: "Prophecy is now assuming center stage in the Vineyard." Regarding Paul Cain, Wimber concluded, "He is a model of maturity. I highly recommend his character and ministry to you."[22] In May 1990 Wimber announced that KCF had become part of the Vineyard Fellowship as he undertook mediation of its controversy with Ernest Gruen.

During this period several of Wimber's key associates became deeply concerned over the new teaching on prophecy. They could not accept the Kansas City model featuring the ministry of a few authoritative prophets who focused on predicting events. This elitist practice contradicted a most distinctive and valuable element of the Vineyard renewal: the rediscovery and practice of spiritual gifts through all members of the body of Christ. The biblical model in 1 Corinthians 14 teaches that prophecy can come through any member and its major purpose is the "strengthening, encouragement and comfort" of the church. Furthermore, each prophecy is to be "weighed carefully." As a result of the KCF concept of prophecy, several influential Vineyard pastors and their churches left the fellowship.

In early 1992, after a long silence in the face of strong criticism, John Wimber published a paper explaining why he believed that he should now respond to criticism. Two additional position papers defending the Vineyard against unwarranted attacks were written by theologians Jack Deere and Wayne Grudem.[23] Wimber has admitted that he was wrong about the KCF model of prophecy and its eschatology, and he has been steering the Vineyard back to its evangelical roots. His current understanding of the biblical principles and practice of prophecy is set forth in "The Gift of Prophecy" in the November 1992 issue of *Charisma.* Meanwhile, on its own, the Metro Vineyard Fellowship in Kansas City has moved toward the "cell group church" model advocated by church planter Ralph Neighbour.[24] Paul Cain has left Kansas City for other arenas of ministry, including Westminster Chapel in London.

For the Vineyard this "time of troubles" has been a costly lesson in the dangers of authoritarian leadership. As national director, Wimber now works more closely with a team of regional pastoral coordinators. They are back to basics in church planting, with a goal of two hundred new congregations in two years.

A Third Wave?

As noted above, the term *Third Wave* was coined by Peter Wagner. He sees the "signs and wonders" movement as a third wave of the Holy Spirit distinct from, but related to, two waves earlier in the twentieth century: the Pentecostal and charismatic movements. In his 1986 book *Power Evangelism* John Wimber describes the Third Wave as "the next stage of development in the charismatic renewal. . . . [All three waves] are part of one great movement of the Holy Spirit in this century."[25] Like the first two movements, it is characterized by the full range of spiritual gifts, but its leaders avoid speaking about "baptism in the Spirit" or giving glossolalia a special place among the charisms.

Nevertheless, there are several questions about the validity of the "Third Wave" terminology for the Vineyard Fellowship.

Once such question concerns origin and leadership. The first two waves were sovereign explosions of divine grace. Unlike other revivals in the history of the church, they did not arise from the ministry of any one pioneer. Although Pentecostalism is considered to have started at Charles Parham's Bethel Bible School in Kansas in 1900, it did not become a movement under his leadership; the renewal went public in 1906 at Azusa Street. Yet Azusa pastor William Seymour did not really lead it; rather, he presided in a general way over a movement of the Spirit that spread primarily through visitors who returned home, in the United States and abroad, to continue seeking the Spirit in their own way.[26]

The charismatic renewal of the 1960s has had many different leaders— Episcopalian Dennis Bennett, Lutheran Larry Christenson, Roman Catholics Kevin Ranaghan and Leon Joseph Cardinal Suenens, to name a few. But even within mainline churches, Protestant and Catholic, charismatic renewal sprang up spontaneously at the grassroots in different parts of the country and different situations. The Vineyard Fellowship, however, like other church movements in the United States, has one major leader. John Wimber pioneered its ministry; he has continued to steer its course and alter its focus from time to time.

In several respects the Vineyard Fellowship is not all that distinct from the charismatic renewal. For example, the charismatic renewal encompasses many who accept the full range of spiritual gifts but do not feel a need to speak in tongues. Many are evangelicals experiencing the empowerment of the Holy Spirit in gifts of healings, prophecy, messages of wisdom and knowledge, but without Pentecostal connotations.

David Barrett's *World Christian Encyclopedia* adopts the term *Third Wave* to designate not just the Vineyard Fellowship but also many other groups around the world that do not call themselves Pentecostal or charismatic.[27] They are energized by the Spirit, exercise gifts of the Spirit and emphasize signs and wonders, although they do not recognize Spirit baptism as a second stage evidenced by speaking in tongues. Since they remain in their mainline, non-Pentecostal denominations, Barrett terms the movement "mainstream church renewal." For 1988 in North America he lists about 12 million participants, including "many unorganized individuals, but also increasingly organized intradenominational bodies with their own periodicals such as Fullness movement (2,000 Southern Baptist pastors)."[28]

As Barrett's categories are defined, the Vineyard Fellowship has much in common with other Third Wave groups. But its 325 churches and about 100,000 members in North America (even with an equal number of churches worldwide) hardly *constitute* this wave. In recent years there has been growing charismatic renewal in evangelical churches, through both Wimber's message and that of others, accompanied by a divergence of interpretation and emphases regarding the Spirit's empowerment.

Given these facts, would it not be more accurate to recognize the Vineyard Fellowship in North America as a new "current" (among others) within the continuing charismatic wave? In other words, its distinct contribution has a continuity with the renewal that preceded it.

Although the wave metaphor is apt in its picture of surging power, in one respect it is inappropriate. Ocean waves follow one another in sequence, each reaching the shore and then receding to make way for the next. But Pentecostal renewal did not ebb and give way to charismatic, nor mainline charismatic renewal to newer forms. All three "waves," which now constitute 21 percent of organized global Christianity, continue to move and grow. Barrett observes: "Even with these three waves and 38 categories, an underlying unity pervades the movement. This survey views the Renewal in the Holy Spirit as one single cohesive movement into which a vast proliferation of all kinds of individuals and communities have been drawn in a whole range of different circumstances."[29]

Unfortunately, recent debate over charismatic renewal often seems to be a struggle between theologians on one side and practitioners (evangelists, pastors, church planters) on the other. Each party tends to operate from its limited perspective without listening to the other. A forum and medium are needed so that genuine dialogue can take place. Surely the several movements have enough shared theology, common concerns and mutual respect to produce substantive discussion in the near future.[30]

13 *The Prosperity Gospel*

P

eter and Cathy Thompson had served as missionaries in Africa for about ten years when Peter developed a malignant tumor. They returned home for radiation and chemotherapy. The prognosis was bleak. Their church gave the couple all the support they could but without much hope for recovery.

But several friends in the next town offered to pray for Peter's healing. The Thompsons were impressed when the friends confidently showed them from the Bible why Christ's death had provided for physical healing. These friends prayed over Peter and declared him healed. When he returned to the hospital that week, tests showed the cancer had disappeared. Since then, except for occasional recurrences of symptoms which Peter says he resists by faith, he has been in vibrant health.

Rita was a college student afflicted with cerebral palsy. She had never been able to walk without leaning heavily on crutches. Since walking was so difficult, she spent most of her time in a wheelchair. Several friends in a Christian fellowship on campus taught that physical healing was among the blessings secured by Christ's death. One night they encouraged her to step out in faith, believing that God would heal her. After they prayed with Rita, she stood up and for the first time walked twenty steps, unaided, before stumbling. The fervent friends assured her that God would manifest a complete healing in the days to come if she continued to walk in faith.

In spite of determined efforts, however, Rita never matched the initial twenty steps. And a burden of guilt was added to her perplexity. Where had she failed? If God really promised to give healing, as her friends declared, why was she still crippled? How could she cope with this deep disappointment and plan for the years ahead?[1]

Prosperity Promises

In recent years a rapidly growing movement has confidently proclaimed that we have been created for an abundant life in Christ that includes physical health and material prosperity based on unwavering faith. This movement has many names—"word of faith," "health and wealth," "positive confession." Here we will use the term *prosperity theology* for the beliefs that date from the nineteenth century and *Faith Movement* for its widespread promotion in recent years.

The father of the Faith Movement is Kenneth Hagin, whose ministry blossomed during the 1970s. He has a daily radio program, *Faith Seminar of the Air*. In 1974, with his son Kenneth Jr., Hagin founded the Rhema Bible Training Center in Tulsa, Oklahoma. By 1980-1981 it was enrolling more than two thousand. A year later the school's correspondence courses were being sent to 11,400 students, while the Hagins' summer camp meeting had as many as 20,000 participants.

Kenneth Hagin's influence also persists in the ministry of other major "faith" teachers whom he has directly affected, especially Kenneth and Gloria Copeland. A Hagin teaching tape revolutionized the Copelands' lives in 1967. Their own large cassette collection now presents major Hagin views but with an emphasis on financial prosperity. A circulation of 500,000 is claimed for their free newsletter. Four years after the start of a radio program in 1975, the Copelands' ministry expanded into television.

In turn, the Copelands inspired another faith teacher, Jerry Savelle, who has reported an annual distribution of about 300,000 copies of his books and tapes. Frederick Price also gives Hagin credit for changing his life. His Los Angeles church grew from 150 members in 1972 to 14,000 in 1985. Dallas-based Bob Tilton's Word of Faith network beams revivals and seminars into two thousand churches. In 1985 one seminar turned into a two-month revival, with healings and miracles reported across the country.

The rapidly growing Faith Movement has produced both converts and controversy. How should it be evaluated? On one hand, in two major respects it is not a part of the mainstream charismatic renewal. First, prosperity theology is based on a worldview that became popular in the late 1800s (before the rise of Pentecostalism) and is not accepted by most participants in charismatic renewal. Second, its rapid growth can be traced to one influential leader who has left his stamp on the movement.

On the other hand, many adherents of the Faith Movement are also participants in charismatic renewal and advocate the use of spiritual gifts such as healing and prophecy. So we need to explore the prosperity gospel in more depth to see what relationship it has with the charismatic renewal.

Historical Roots
Like every large river, the Faith Movement has a variety of tributaries that have influenced its content, shape and size. One stream of divine healing goes back to several influential evangelical leaders, among whom we have already noted A. J. Gordon, A. B. Simpson and Andrew Murray.[2] John Alexander Dowie, an Australian who carried his message of healing to Chicago in 1893, eventually bought a large tract of land north of the city. He attracted ten thousand people to build Zion, a theocratic colony. As a father of healing revivalism in America, he influenced many early Pentecostal leaders.

A second contributing stream was the Pentecostal movement.[3] In 1900 Charles Parham opened Bethel Bible College in Topeka, Kansas, and soon his students began to manifest gifts of healing as well as prophecy and tongues.

Within a few years his "Apostolic Faith Missions" attracted twenty-five thousand Midwest followers. In 1906 William Seymour started meetings at 312 Azusa Street in Los Angeles. His daily interdenominational, interracial meetings attracted many from around the country and Europe; the visitors returned to their home communities to share the manifestations of long-neglected spiritual gifts.

A third stream ran largely underground until the late 1960s, when it emerged to provide a doctrinal framework for Kenneth Hagin and the Faith Movement. The essentials of prosperity theology stem primarily from the teaching of Essek William Kenyon, who was born in April 1876 in New York State.[4] He was converted to Christ in his late teens and was ordained a deacon in the Methodist Church. In 1892 Kenyon moved to Boston and attended Emerson College, where he learned about New Thought, a metaphysical cult that appeared in a variety of groups such as Unity, Divine Science and Christian Science.[5] The system taught that true reality, which is spiritual, causes all physical effects; the human mind through positive mental attitude and positive confession can create physical benefits such as health and wealth. Although there is no evidence that Kenyon openly converted to New Thought, he admitted his indebtedness to its concepts.

Kenyon was appalled by the sad state of the historic churches, torn by controversy and giving way to liberal theology. He indicted the church for failure to carry on its supernatural healing ministry as it reduced the gospel to pious platitudes and ethical demands devoid of power to deliver and heal.

Although he traveled in Pentecostal circles, Kenyon was not a member of a Pentecostal church. In Seattle he founded the New Covenant Baptist Church and began a radio ministry that continued until his death at the age of eighty in 1948. Yet it was Kenyon's books that have had the greatest influence on the Faith Movement over the years.

The spread of Kenneth Hagin's prosperity theology beginning in the 1970s was also due largely to more recent events that prepared a soil far beyond the constituency of Pentecostalism. In 1947 Oral Roberts initiated a healing ministry; in 1974 he went on television, gaining a widespread audience among non-Pentecostals. Kathryn Kuhlman also began a healing ministry in 1947. Her ministry of miracles, transcending denominational barriers, took place on one of the CBS network's longest-running programs. She never made high-pressure appeals for financial support. She attributed any miracles to the power of the Holy Spirit and insisted on medical verification of healings before including the stories in her books.

The burgeoning charismatic renewal of the 1960s also prepared soil for the seed of prosperity theology throughout mainline Protestant and Catholic churches.

Father of the Faith Movement

Kenneth Hagin, the widely acknowledged originator of the Faith Movement, was born in 1917. He reports that at age seventeen, bedridden with an incurable heart deformity, he received a "revelation" that has become a hallmark of his ministry.[6] He meditated on Jesus' statement in Mark 11:24: "Therefore I tell you, whatever you ask for in prayer, believe that you have received it, and it will be yours." Hagin suddenly saw that "the *having* comes after the *believing.*" Still lying on his back, he began to confess that the paralysis had gone. Within a few minutes he struggled to his feet, and after two days of practice, he joined his family at breakfast.

In 1937 Hagin received the "baptism of the Holy Spirit" and became an Assemblies of God pastor. In 1943, without formal education or theological training, he was "anointed" with a teaching gift through a mystical experience. Nine years later he felt called to the office of prophet, which he defines as one who has visions and revelations. He reports that during the following decade he had eight personal visitations from Jesus and many more visionary experiences. The dual role of prophet and teacher is crucial to understanding Hagin's role in the Faith Movement. As a prophet he communicates divine revelation; as a teacher he expounds Scripture. The combined offices produce a ministry that appears both supernatural and biblical.

Yet Hagin's theology, like every other teacher's, has historical roots that can be traced. It is a distinctive blend of evangelical orthodoxy, biblical fundamentalism, charismatic experience and metaphysical thought. The last he has borrowed from Essek Kenyon, taking many passages word for word without citing his source. When asked about this evidence of plagiarism, Hagin replied, "When individuals are speaking on the same subject they will virtually say the same thing. This is because it is the same Spirit that is leading and directing."[7]

It is apparent that Hagin found in Kenyon's teaching a ready-made theological system to strengthen and help promote his view of a Christian life that is healthy, wealthy and wise in the ways of God. Let's take a closer look at the basic concepts of that system—revelation knowledge, positive confession, divine healing and material prosperity.

Revelation Knowledge—The Only Way to Know God

E. W. Kenyon's worldview posits two mutually exclusive realms—the spiritual and the material. The former, under the governance of God, is superior and the proper domain for people. The latter, ruled by its own god (Satan), is in eternal conflict with the former. All people start in the material realm and aspire to the spiritual, which can be attained only with help from the spiritual realm.

Within that framework Kenyon made a radical distinction between what he called "revelation knowledge" and "sense knowledge." The latter comes from the five senses and so is limited to the physical environment. It is the source of all rational and scientific knowledge and is responsible for modern technology, including the advances of medicine. But sense knowledge cannot answer the deepest questions of human existence or allow us to know God. To know God we need supernatural "revelation knowledge" from the Bible which enables us to transcend the limitations of sense knowledge and to act in faith.

Kenyon's distinction between the two kinds of knowledge has important parallels with New Thought. Both are based on a spiritual-material dualism and teach that possession of one type of knowledge demands denial of the other when they seem to conflict. For example, an illness is understood to be healed even though its symptoms persist. Kenyon insists, "Real faith is acting upon the Word independent of any sense evidence."⁸

Kenneth Hagin believes that God cannot communicate with us through the senses. This anti-intellectual position appears in his statement that "one almost has to by-pass the brain and operate from the inner man [the heart or spirit] to really get into the things of God."⁹

Prosperity theology as well as New Thought creates two classes of Christians, ordinary believers and the "miracle class," who, according to Kenyon, have "gone outside of the realm of Sense Knowledge and passed over into the realm of God, the spiritual realm."¹⁰ Hagin explains that through revelation knowledge, Faith Movement "supermen" become "kings in life" and the "bondage breakers for the rest of the human race."¹¹ Other leaders also teach that Christians are "little gods." Tilton writes, "You are . . . a God kind of creature. Originally you were designed to be as a god in this world."¹²

Positive Confession—Creating Our Own Reality

The most distinctive doctrine of the modern Faith Movement, positive confession, was also taught by E. W. Kenyon. It insists that what we believe and confess determines what we get from God: "What I confess, I possess." Confession is affirming something we believe. Kenyon teaches that sooner or later we become what we confess; the powers of mind and word have the ability to reshape reality.

This concept is based on a two-realm view. God is a "faith God" because he had faith that his words would bring forth creation ex nihilo (out of nothing). "Faith-filled words brought the universe into being, and faith-filled words are ruling the universe today."¹³ The "law of faith" in the spiritual realm is like the "law of gravity" in the physical realm; whenever the law is set in motion, it works.

Hagin explains how to use the faith formula based on the spiritual laws of the universe: "If anybody, anywhere, will take these four steps or put these four principles into operation, he will always receive whatever he wants from Me or God the Father. [With these steps] you can write your own ticket with

God: (1) Say it, (2) Do it, (3) Receive it, and (4) Tell it."[14]

The believer claims a divine promise (usually in a Scripture verse), demands that God do what he has promised, then gives thanks for receiving it. Faith is released through prayer to activate God to do something. So the key to healing, for example, is to get the word (spiritual reality) to the body (material) via the soul (mind) by its positive confession. Kenneth Copeland has popularized the term "faith-force," through which believers can make the laws of the spirit world do their bidding. This is how Christians can regain their proper authority over the earth—the control of circumstances influencing their bodies and society.

Divine Healing—Finding Health in the Cross

Prosperity theology's doctrine of healing is based on its understanding of the nature and purpose of Christ's atonement. Like the evangelical and Holiness-Pentecostal movements noted earlier, Kenyon believed, on the basis of biblical passages such as Isaiah 53:5, Matthew 8:17 and 1 Peter 2:24, that the purpose of the atonement is to provide complete physical healing of disease as well as forgiveness of sin. But as the years went on, he incorporated New Thought concepts.

Kenyon believed that Jesus died two deaths—physical on the cross and spiritual as he descended into hell. "His physical death was but a means to an end."[15] Although that death fulfilled perfect obedience, it could not eradicate sin and sickness, which are essentially spiritual. Fred Price concurs: "Do you think that the punishment for our sin was to die on a cross? . . . No, the punishment was to go into hell itself and to serve time in hell separated from God."[16]

Healing is to be accepted as an accomplished "faith fact," even though it is not immediately manifested as a physical fact. Admitting the reality of continuing physical symptoms is a "negative confession" that forfeits healing. Kenyon writes, "Confession always goes ahead of healing. *Don't watch the symptoms*—watch the Word. . . . You are healed. The Word says you are."[17] (This was the basis on which Rita was assured of a complete healing as she continued to walk "in faith.") Kenyon believed that it is wrong for us to have diseases in our bodies when God laid them on Jesus. The believer who is not healed is out of God's will; sickness is caused by unbelief or sin.

Following his mentor's lead, Hagin teaches that because all disease is spiritual in origin, God's healing method must be spiritual. The test of faith comes when one must deny pain to make a positive confession. A sure way to become ill is to utter a "negative confession," any mental or verbal acknowledgment of disease in one's body. Since negative confessions also have the power to infect others, conversation about one's illness must be severely restricted.

In this view, what is the right attitude toward doctors and medication? Most Faith Movement leaders stop short of ruling out the use of medicine when it is necessary, but they consider it a sign of weak faith. At this point there is ambiguity in their teaching. Fred Price believes that medicine is not opposed to divine healing, but it should be considered a stopgap. "If you need a crutch or something to help you get along, then praise God, and hobble along until you get your faith moving to the point that you don't need a crutch."[18] The implication is that anyone who needs medicine doesn't yet have strong faith.

Material Prosperity—The Principle of Seed Faith

Kenyon defined prosperity in terms of deliverance from poverty and the power to deliver others. He believed it is abnormal for believers to be in bondage to poverty. But far from encouraging materialism, Kenyon stated that the biblical concept of prosperity is more than "prosperity of the senses, which thinks gold and political favor is prosperity";[19] it is the presence of God himself. Ironically, however, his concept of positive confession was later applied to material wealth.

The Faith Movement has gone far beyond Kenyon. Although "seed faith" was a late addition to Hagin's doctrinal system, he claims to have learned it directly from God. Yet the prosperity doctrine had appeared many years earlier among prominent Pentecostals, especially Oral Roberts. He popularized "seed-faith giving," which guarantees that donors will soon reap rich returns on their investments.

In the 1960s Hagin and other Faith Movement leaders embraced this message of material prosperity. For them it has been very profitable, providing the large-scale funding required for expensive radio and television programming and worldwide travel. Even more than promises of divine healing, keys to financial success have attracted millions of supporters.

Their teaching on this subject is purportedly based on several biblical passages. In Genesis 17 we read God's promise to make Abraham a father of many nations with great wealth. The apostle Paul promises Christians the "blessing of Abraham" in Galatians 3:13-14, 29. Hagin writes, "Abraham's blessing is ours. . . . [T]he first thing God promised Abraham was that he was going to make him rich."[20]

In Mark 10:29-30 Jesus promises that those who leave home and fields for him will receive a hundred times as much. Gloria Copeland explains this spiritual law: "You give $1 for the Gospel's sake and $100 belongs to you; give $10 and receive $1000. . . . In short, Mark 10:30 is a very good deal."[21]

The Copelands have become concerned about excesses of individualistic greed. They and Jerry Savelle emphasize the importance of giving. Gloria Copeland urges looking beyond your own needs to believe God for a surplus of prosperity in order to help others. Savelle insists that God mainly wants his people to have money so they can give to reach millions with the gospel.

The Bible and Prosperity Theology

An essential but often overlooked principle for studying Scripture is that what the message meant for the original readers determines what it may mean now. Otherwise there is no control over proof texting—taking a statement out of its original context to make it support whatever teaching we want to promote. This procedure attributes to the biblical writer a meaning he did not intend and thus overlooks the intended message inspired by the Holy Spirit.

Important elements of biblical promises for divine healing and material prosperity are the specific conditions laid down for their fulfillment. Let's look, then, at the four main teachings of prosperity theology in this light.

Revelation knowledge. We have seen how E. W. Kenyon's prosperity theology is based on a dualism that has hovered around Christianity since its beginning—a Neo-Platonic concept of two mutually exclusive realms, the good spiritual world opposed to the evil material world. This worldview was adopted in the first few centuries A.D. by various Greek sects that took Jesus Christ as the "outside agent" of salvation. Those groups became known as Gnostic since they stressed salvation through *gnosis* (knowledge) that produces an elite class of people.[22] Early church fathers attacked Gnostic teachings as heretical.

The concept of revelation knowledge as entirely spiritual in origin and opposed to sense knowledge reflects the Gnostic spirit-matter dualism, which is contrary to the biblical doctrine of revelation. In the Bible, revelation is both physical and spiritual: God reveals himself in mighty *acts* of judgment and mercy as well as in *words* of the prophets. The ultimate Word of God ("revelation knowledge") appeared in the physical realm in the incarnation, death and resurrection of Jesus Christ. Furthermore, Jesus' coming was clearly heard and seen by the physical senses (Jn 1:14; Col 2:9; 2 Pet 1:16; 1 Jn 1:1).

Nor is the biblical revelation contrary to reason, calling us to "by-pass the brain . . . to really get into the things of God." Jesus commanded his disciples to love God "with all your soul and with all your *mind*" (Mk 12:30). Paul calls for the "renewing of your mind" (Rom 12:2), and Peter urges believers to "prepare your minds for action" (1 Pet 1:13).

The New Testament also knows nothing of an elite class of Christians— "supermen," "little gods" or "pneumatics" (spiritual leaders) who dispense saving knowledge as if it were their own possession. The biblical model is the body of Christ in which each member has a significant role as the Holy Spirit manifests a variety of spiritual gifts for the common good (1 Cor 12:4-11). *Charisms are not a personal possession but a means of grace for others.* In that context Christians are expected to love, serve and strengthen each other as the occasion requires. For Christians—contrary to our rationalistic scientific culture—knowledge is not the supreme value, the key to open all doors. Paul reminded the church at Corinth, "Knowledge puffs up, but love builds up" (1 Cor 8:1).

Positive confession. Prosperity theology teaches that God has built into the world both physical and spiritual laws which even he must now obey. God is bound by his laws to perform when their conditions are met; he no longer has freedom of choice. This view is based on misunderstandings of both modern science and the God of the Bible. So-called natural laws do not *prescribe* what must happen, they simply *describe* what is happening and explain how the forces of nature work.[23] Although God usually acts in familiar, predictable ways, he is certainly not "bound" by them. At times, as Scripture reveals, he works in unpredictable ways (miracles, signs, wonders). "Our God is in heaven; he does whatever pleases him" (Ps 115:3; see also Dan 4:34-35). (See appendix E.)

In describing faith as a "force" with which the believer can "move things as it works for you," the Faith Movement makes the sovereign God a servant who must obey human commands. The "force of faith" becomes "faith in the Force." As Luke Skywalker in *Star Wars* learned to manipulate the "good side of the Force" through mind control, the Faith Movement teaches how to use the prosperity god through positive confession.

But the God of the Bible is a person, not a principle; biblical faith is a trusting relationship, not a formula for success. A central theme of Scripture is covenant—God's establishment of a personal relationship with his people who love and serve him. In that context faith is not a possession I have in sufficient quantity to produce results. It is an attitude of trust in a loving Father to do what he knows is best for me, a partnership in which we work together to do his will.

Divine healing. The Faith Movement should be appreciated for helping the church to recover its healing ministry—too long ignored and denied. For fifteen hundred years, as we saw in chapter nine, the command of Christ to heal the sick was obscured by prevailing theological tradition. We can be grateful that the healing ministry is now being widely practiced across denominational boundaries.

Nevertheless, Faith Movement teaching regarding healing is unbiblical in several respects. First, it perpetuates the philosophical dualism of opposing spiritual and material realms through the division of the person into three components: spirit, soul and body. That concept is contrary to Hebraic wholism, which views all dimensions of human nature as interrelated.

Second, the Faith Movement view that atonement was effected by Jesus' "spiritual death" in hell, not his physical death on the cross, contradicts New Testament teaching. Many scriptures affirm that atonement was essentially a physical act involving the shedding of Christ's blood (for example, Col 2:13-15; Heb 2:14-15; 9:22-23; 1 Pet 2:24; 4:1). The "double-death" theory is actually based on a mistranslation of one word in a single text of Scripture: "deaths" in Isaiah 53:9.

Third, although Christ's atonement is the basis for making people whole, in our fallen world complete healing doesn't always take place. It is not a "universal, immediately available privilege."[24] The Faith Movement's emphasis on the individual's right and responsibility for healing places a heavy burden of guilt on the sick person. Even to say "I am ill; please pray for me" is often considered a "negative confession" by which one forfeits the right to healing. When a "claimed" cure doesn't occur, the sufferer is blamed and must then bear guilt as well as pain. Just when encouragement is most needed, the person—like the leper in old Israel—is thrust "outside the camp," lest negative confession infect others. A decision to forgo medical aid sometimes results in a death that could have been avoided. And prosperity theology fails to provide compassionate support for the terminally ill; at a time when the dying most need faith, they are told they least have it.

The New Testament presents a model of burden-sharing in sickness. When the four men brought their paralyzed friend to Jesus, it was "when Jesus saw *their* faith" that he forgave and healed the man (see Mk 2:1-12). Another time, when the disciples couldn't heal the epileptic boy, Jesus gave the reason for their failure: "Because *you* have so little faith" (Mt 17:20). If a healing is thought to be hindered by lack of faith, let the Christian community point the finger first at themselves!

Material prosperity. How does the "blessing of Abraham" relate to Christians? The apostle Paul declares that "Christ redeemed us . . . that the blessing given to Abraham might come to the Gentiles" (Gal 3:13-14). The context shows that the *only* part of Abraham's blessing of concern to Paul is that the Gentiles would be included in God's people. By faith they would be justified and "receive the promise of the Spirit" (v. 14). Nothing is said here about wealth or freedom from sickness.

For his faith and obedience Abraham did become "very wealthy in livestock and in silver and gold" (Gen 13:2). God also gave him servants, slaves and a concubine. If his blessing is to be ours today, why not the whole package, including a few slaves and a mistress? Or are we to claim only those elements that are now considered acceptable?

The Faith Movement also bases its teaching of material prosperity on promises made to Israel in Deuteronomy 7:13-15 and 28:1-14. But like many other promises, these have specific conditions: "If you *fully* obey the LORD your God and carefully follow *all* his commands I give you today . . . the LORD will grant you abundant prosperity" (28:1, 11). How many Christians now obey those scores of commands regarding religious, civil and personal life to qualify for the affluence they expect?

Old Testament promises of prosperity were made to a covenant people dwelling within particular geographical boundaries and obeying detailed regulations for their way of life. The relationship between wealth and God's blessing was radically altered with the new covenant in Jesus Christ, which is international in scope. Nowhere in the Gospels does Jesus teach that God intends all Christians to be materially rich. On the contrary, Jesus consistently warns about the *dangers* of wealth and its misuse, and he shows concern for the poor rather than criticizing them. He himself was poor, without even a home of his own.

Faith Movement teaching about the hundredfold return promised in Mark 10:29-30 ignores both its context and its conditions. Jesus has just told the rich young ruler to sell everything and follow him. The Lord presents the cost, not the financial advantages, of discipleship. It is to disciples *who have left everything* that Jesus promises the hundredfold return—and with it persecutions (overlooked by the prosperity gospel). Actually, Jesus' promise to his disciples would be fulfilled not individually but corporately in the experience of the Christian community, within which they found far greater family than ever they had left.

The apostle Paul followed his Lord in both teaching and lifestyle. He wrote that often he had been hungry, poorly clothed and homeless. He took the Corinthians to task for pursuing riches (1 Cor 4:8-17). Paul later described in graphic detail a life far from perfect health and material prosperity (2 Cor 4:7-11; 6:3-10; 11:21-29). In fact, the apostle warned Timothy against those "who think that godliness is a means of financial gain. . . . People who want to get rich fall into temptation and a trap" (1 Tim 6:5, 9).

The Faith Movement's use of 3 John 2 as a proof text for its doctrine of wealth is based on a misunderstanding. The writer's wish that the reader may "prosper" (KJV) should be translated "that all may go well with you" (NIV). Far from a timeless guarantee of financial blessing, this is simply a standard form of greeting in letters of antiquity.

The movement also tends to degrade the poor, claiming that their poverty is the result of "dishonoring" God through lack of faith rather than oppression inflicted upon them by the greedy and selfish. Rich *and* poor Christians should trust God for their needs, realizing that "godliness with contentment is great gain" (1 Tim 6:6).

Beliefs and practices vary widely among the leadership of the Faith Movement. Although the practice of many may not be as extreme as some of the foregoing quotations would suggest, those statements have not been repudiated by the leaders and are widely quoted. Although largely orthodox and evangelical in most biblical doctrines, the prosperity gospel's dualistic worldview and its teaching on human nature, Christ's atonement and deification of the believer constitute major deviations from historic Christianity.

The Faith Movement, although influenced by the charismatic renewal, is unlike it in another significant respect: its origin. While the charismatic renewal from its very beginning has been a grassroots movement largely within the major denominations, the Faith Movement has been typical of most others in history. It began with one influential leader, Kenneth Hagin, who in this case adopted a theological system, attracted colleagues and developed an independent following through radio, conferences, publications, a school and correspondence courses.

Christ and Culture

The burgeoning of the Faith Movement poses a basic question: Why, despite opposition from Pentecostal, mainline charismatic and evangelical Christians, has it blossomed?

For seed to bear fruit two elements are essential—fertile soil and a favorable climate. Earlier in this chapter we saw how the classical Pentecostal and charismatic movements of the post-World War II decades served as fertile soil for the seed of Kenyon's prosperity theology. And a favorable climate has been provided by prevailing winds in Western society.

In every age the church, like a chameleon, tends to take on the colors of its culture. To what extent do the characteristics of our society explain the phenomenal growth of the Faith Movement? What cultural and religious needs does this movement address?

Every culture creates a view of reality that gives its members a feeling of security and importance based on the things they can control. Even though they have widely different customs, cultures present their gods as responsive to human manipulation, giving religious status to the people who control society. In that respect every Western culture since the Enlightenment has denied the fact that our lives are given and sustained by an all-powerful and gracious God who is beyond our control. Our culture teaches that we can determine our lives and make ourselves secure by taking matters into our own hands.

Our society has become preoccupied with material prosperity and obsessed with concern for health. The "good life" of TV commercials is defined by possessions—well-furnished house, late-model car, high-tech imports. In the 1980s public and private sectors ran up an incredible six trillion dollars of new debt and charged it to future generations. Americans now spend $900 billion annually on health care, equating health with the traditional rights of "life, liberty and the pursuit of happiness."

Obsession with our health is producing a nation of "bionarcissists"—people relentlessly absorbed with their own sense of physical well-being. In the midst of social change and disruption, the one thing left that we think we can control is our bodies. There we take our stand, even though perfect health is an illusion.

Why has the self become the all-important center of attention? Robert Bellah observes that Americans are unable to determine who they are in the context of their society.[25] Having lost faith in traditional communities and institutions, they look within themselves for answers. This narcissism signifies not so much self-assertion as a loss of selfhood.

The seeds of prosperity theology flourish in the climate of modern culture. The Faith Movement promises its followers the best of both worlds: the blessing of God and the respect of society. Members join a community that defines who they are as "children of God"; at the same time they can realize the American dream of material prosperity and perfect health. Instead of standing against secular values of our culture opposed to Christian principles, the Faith Movement—along with many other Christians—has embraced them.

Lessons to Be Learned

Lutheran theologian Susanne Heine notes, "The rise of heretical groups is always a sign that orthodoxy has become heretical."[26] In other words, history shows that most basic doctrinal deviation arises from the church's denial of a biblical truth—in practice if not in preaching. Efforts to remedy this lack then send the pendulum to an opposite extreme. It was Kenyon's concern for the loss of spiritual power in the churches of his day that motivated him to preach a "new Christianity." Hagin, after his experience of healing, shared a similar concern.

Consequently, it is not enough to point out the errors of Faith Movement teaching; we need to identify the lacks in contemporary church life that it endeavors to remedy. One area of impoverishment is the church's ministry of healing, commanded by our Lord but largely abdicated for more than a millennium. Although resurgent in recent decades, this ministry is still widely ignored or opposed by many American churches—but not in the so-called mission fields of Africa, Asia and Latin America, where the church is growing by leaps and bounds.

Another element in the Christian life emphasized by the Faith Movement, all too rare in our churches, is a faith that is willing to take risks. Biblical faith is more than intellectual assent to correct doctrines. It is obedient trust in the living God to fulfill his promises as we venture forth, like Abraham and Paul, beyond the limits of our present experience into uncharted territory.

V
A Look to the Future

14 *Charismatic Renewal Today*

*L*ong ago there was an innkeeper by the name of Procrustes. He offered only one bed of fixed length, on which all guests were forced to lie. Procrustes cut off the feet of those who were too long and stretched the bodies that were too short. The result each time was a perfect fit to the bed.

Emissaries of church renewal often suffer the same fate as the travelers in this Greek myth. On arrival they find a bed of tradition with theological legs, organizational frame and cultural mattress on which they are forced to lie. Unacceptable experiences labeled "enthusiastic" are cut off. Unfamiliar teachings are branded "heretical" and stretched to fit the dominant doctrine. The price of lodging is adjustment to the status quo. Only if the bearers of renewal have enough strength to redesign the bed is there significant change.

Our study has shown how the charismatic renewal, like others in church history, has encountered this pattern of reaction as well as openness to a new understanding of spiritual gifts. Now it is time to pull together several major threads that have woven their way through this study. What salient features have made the charismatic renewal different from earlier revivals? Amid the diversity of ecclesiastical fireplaces, what is the essence of the fire? How are we to evaluate the strengths and weakness of the renewal in this fourth decade? And what can we see as we peer down the road?

A Unique Renewal

The Pentecostal/charismatic renewal has been unique in several major respects that point not only to the past but also to the future.[1]

Unplanned and unexpected. The Pentecostal movement cannot be traced to one influential leader in the usual sense of the word. Although this movement is commonly thought to have begun at Charles Parham's Bible school in Topeka, Kansas, as we have seen, it was Azusa Street in Los Angeles that gave birth to a movement of explosive power that soon spread to all continents. Yet Pentecostalism was never dependent on William Seymour's preaching, of which there was little. He presided over the meetings and avoided any kind of organization. Visitors were mostly struck by the spirit of the meetings, by what they heard and saw in testimonies of those baptized by the Spirit. Azusa Street was an event, an outbreak, a corporate experience similar to Pentecost in Jerusalem.[2]

Leaders of the charismatic renewal as it emerged in the 1960s and 1970s were not so much founders as pioneers, thrust into positions they had not sought and for which they felt ill prepared. Most of the men and women suddenly blessed in this way were taken by surprise. Although many had prior longing for a more satisfying spiritual life, they did not expect that it would come through a baptizing/filling of the Spirit and spiritual gifts. People were faced not by an organized movement but by personal witness to healings, prophecies, reconciliations, changed lives. At first there were no programs, committees or seminars for renewal—only acts of God that called for a response.

Across all the churches. Just as the charismatic renewal had no one founder, it has not been tied to a single church. It belongs equally to every Christian tradition. There are not separate Protestant and Catholic movements. Rather, as a renewal of the Holy Spirit, there is only one movement with expressions among Baptists, Catholics, Episcopalians, Lutherans, Mennonites, Methodists, Presbyterians and many others. This underlying unity is evident in the many interdenominational prayer and praise meetings, conferences and communities.

The unprecedented range of the charismatic renewal became evident with its appearance in the Roman Catholic Church in 1967. Not since before the sixteenth-century Reformation had Protestants and Catholics come together in the same revival. Now both were being equally touched by the same Spirit. This spiritual ecumenicity became publicly evident in the 1977 Kansas City Conference with an attendance of fifty thousand from across the entire spectrum of Christian churches.

No single pattern. No one path has led to the Spirit's filling, nor have all experiences been the same. Initially some heard about it from the Pentecostals, others by reading David Wilkerson's *The Cross and the Switchblade.* Some were led into new charismatic experience through prayerful study of Acts. Many who had never sought such an experience have found themselves unexpectedly praising God in other tongues. The varied ways in which the Holy Spirit has continued to work in different circumstances reveals no prevailing pattern. The style of charismatic prayer and praise meetings often reflects the local church and cultural scene to which they are indigenous.

Common Elements
Nevertheless, the diverse forms of charismatic renewal have in common several main elements.

New dimensions of worship. Like earlier major renewals such as the Reformation in Germany and the Wesleyan movement in England, the charismatic renewal has produced an abundant fruit of new "psalms, hymns and spiritual songs." From the beginning, weekly gatherings have usually been labeled "prayer and praise." The new hymnody features biblical psalms set to music as well as modern spiritual songs, often accompanied by a guitar or combination of instruments. Visitors are impressed by the centrality and joy of praise and thanksgiving in song. Far from a warm-up while latecomers straggle in, or preparation for preaching, the singing is central; it provides the context of worship for meditation and reading of Scripture, personal witness and prophecy.

The Trinity a reality. The Holy Spirit, the long "forgotten person" of the Trinity, is recognized in his gracious gifts to the church. God becomes visible in Jesus, who becomes present through the Spirit. The charismatic renewal has rediscovered a distinct "third dimension" of the Spirit's activity that has long been misunderstood and neglected by theologians: in addition to regeneration (the new birth) and sanctification (Christlike character), there is empowerment (through spiritual gifts) for worship, service and witness. The full range of these charisms is expected, for the unbiblical dichotomy between natural and supernatural has been abandoned along with relegation of the "supernatural" gifts to the first century.

A deeper relationship with Jesus Christ. Participants witness to a new realization of what it means to confess the lordship of Jesus Christ. They have a deeper experience of his love and grace. Jesus is Lord not only of the Christian's life but also of the nations, as all authority in heaven and on earth has been given to him (Mt 28:18). He makes possible all gifts through the Spirit whom he has sent to empower the worship, service and witness of his church.

A love of Scripture. Prominent in the charismatic witness is a strong desire to read the Word of God. The Holy Spirit who inspired the writings also illuminates them. Bible study and meditation foster an experience like that of Jesus' disciples on the road to Emmaus after his resurrection: "Were not our hearts burning within us while he talked with us on the road and opened the Scriptures to us?" (Lk 24:32). In testimonies people regularly tell how they have begun to hear the Lord speak through biblical truths applied to specific situations in daily life. At times a message of knowledge or wisdom illumines a decision or course of action.

Enthusiasm for evangelism. People who have never shared their faith in Jesus Christ with others now experience a desire and power to evangelize.

Witnessing is no longer an obligation; it is a joy. There is not only a clearer understanding of the gospel but also an anointing by the Spirit that reaches the heart of hearers. Many are also awakening, in their prayers and financial support, to the worldwide mission of the church.[3]

Spiritual gifts for the body. Not only is the charismatic renewal open to the full range of spiritual gifts as the Holy Spirit directs, but it has also given them a new focus and context. Whereas classical Pentecostalism continued to reflect a preoccupation with the individual believer, the charismatic renewal views spiritual gifts as a central function of the Christian community. The focus is on the manifestation of these gifts in and through the body of Christ.

The Christian should not concentrate on discovering his or her individual gift and then wonder where to use it. Rather, the member participates with others in the body of Christ and trusts the sovereign Spirit to manifest gifts according to the needs of the community. In the apostle Paul's model, charisms are neither the prerogative of a few leaders nor the private possession of individual members.

In theological terms, spiritual gifts are no longer to be considered a category of individual sanctification but an essential dimension of *ecclesiology,* the doctrine of the church. This shift in focus challenges the prevalent institutional model of the church. Early in the renewal, pastor Harold Snyder noted, "The contemporary church in its institutional form makes little room for spontaneous spiritual gifts. Worse yet, too often it does not need spiritual gifts in order to function more or less successfully. When the local church is structured after an institutional rather than a charismatic model, spiritual gifts are replaced by aptitude, education and technique, and thus become superfluous."[4]

Much hostility toward charismatic renewal is deeper than objection to the fire of a few controversial gifts; it is perceived by the custodians to be a threat to their leadership in the institutional model of the fireplace. This is perhaps the most significant issue facing the Christian church today.

Lowered denominational barriers. While denominational structures and theological systems stand in the way of organizational unity from the top down, charismatic renewal has brought a grassroots ecumenical experience.

In local prayer and praise meetings, area conferences and national conventions, thousands of Christians for the first time have worshiped with those of other denominations. They experience their essential unity in Christ, as members of the same body in which "there is neither Jew nor Greek, slave nor free, male nor female, for you are all one in Christ Jesus" (Gal 3:28).

Baptized in the Spirit

In chapter three we considered how this phrase appears in two distinct contexts. In 1 Corinthians 12:13 Paul declares to the Corinthian Christians, "For we were all baptized [in] one Spirit into one body." In conversion and new birth they had become members of the body of Christ, his church. The context is their unity in one body undergirding a diversity of spiritual gifts. In Acts 2, however, the context is the first public proclamation of the gospel. All the disciples are baptized in the Spirit (clothed with power, filled with the Spirit) and are able to "speak in other tongues . . . declaring the wonders of God" (vv. 4, 11).

The Acts 2 baptism in the Spirit also has a connotation of initiation in the sense that for the disciples, the Pentecost experience is their initial reception of Jesus' promised power for witness, first in Jerusalem and then all nations. Spirit baptism also has a prophetic dimension in demonstrating the arrival of the long-expected messianic age, which was to be characterized by an outpouring of the Holy Spirit.

After evaluating the strengths and weaknesses of the various models of Spirit baptism, Henry I. Lederle offers an alternative, a reinterpretation of baptism in the Spirit that he calls the "charismatic dimension of normal Christian life."[5] It provides a new theological framework for understanding the function of spiritual gifts.

First, what is meant by the "charismatic dimension" of the Christian life? It is an *experiential faith* dimension of all forms of vital Christianity that expresses itself in worship, prayer, meditation on Scripture, fellowship, witness, acts of compassion and so forth. It includes an experience of the whole spectrum of charisms mentioned in the New Testament; it also encompasses other gifts and ministries energized by the power of the Spirit such as intercession, promoting justice, defeating evil spirits, practicing a profession, rearing children and promoting ecological balance. "In this sense every Christian is, and should be increasingly, charismatic. . . . The church should strive towards expressing the fullness of life in the Spirit and exercising all its charisms."[6]

We should resist two common errors based on the unbiblical natural-supernatural dichotomy: reducing the charismatic dimension to the "natural"; limiting it to the "supernatural" or extraordinary. German theologian Arnold Bittlinger's definition avoids this dilemma: "A charism is a gratuitous manifestation of the Holy Spirit, working in and through, but going beyond, the believer's natural ability for the common good of the people of God."[7]

In this light it is possible to use the term *charismatic* in the more restricted sense of spiritual gifts without limiting it to stereotypes of "supernaturalism" and emotionalism. In its openness to the full range of New Testament gifts, the charismatic renewal has rendered a great service in recovering several long-neglected charisms. But no matter how many or how few charisms, their manifestation in the body of Christ underscores our mutual interdependence.

Within this charismatic dimension there is also room for a wide range of spiritual experiences, often influenced by factors of culture and individual personality. There are two dominant models of spiritual growth: the "breakthrough" and the "gradual." The crisis experience is a sudden action of the Holy Spirit, a moment of decision. The step-by-step advance marks a gentler, continuing work of the Spirit.

Spirit baptism is by no means something "extra" or "more than" the work of Christ. "Living the life of Christ" and "walking in the Spirit" are two biblical ways of viewing the same thing. In Romans 8 Paul uses the phrases "in Christ" and "in the Spirit" to denote the same concepts. In verse 9 the "Spirit of God" is also called the "Spirit of Christ." According to Peter's sermon at Pentecost, Jesus is the baptizer (Acts 2:32-33). In this respect the New Testament has a remarkable parallel between christological and pneumatological categories: the doctrines of Christ and the Holy Spirit.

Lederle concludes that "baptism in the Spirit" refers primarily to the communal initiation of the early church at Pentecost, when the Spirit was poured out, and secondarily to the Christian baptism referred to by Paul in 1 Corinthians 12:13. Spirit baptism in this model is essentially "the dimension of the Spirit, the charismatic element of normal Christian life—in Christ, walking by the Spirit."[8]

This view is broadly based on New Testament teaching and practice without stretching or truncating it to fit the Procrustean bed of a theological system. Thus it provides the possibility of integration into the various non-Pentecostal branches of the church.

A Question of Labels

The church often faces a problem of the medicine bottle and its label. Good medicine may be incorrectly labeled, while an accurate label can adorn an empty bottle. Likewise it is possible for our experience of God to be better than our explanation of it. Unfortunately, the reverse can also be true. Orthodox theology is often affirmed with little evidence of Christian character and commitment.

Charismatic renewal has produced good biblical medicine. The common elements in its diverse forms are dimensions of Christian experience taught and practiced in the New Testament. Except for the exercise of certain extraordinary charisms, these elements have also characterized great revivals of the past. We have seen how generic charismatic medicine has been labeled with a variety of brand names, some of which may be modified by further theological reflection. Meanwhile, the medicine is improving the health of the church around the world on an unprecedented scale.

The charismatic renewal has often been criticized for being long on experience and short on doctrine—mostly subjective emotion with little, if any, rational biblical basis. This critique mistakenly equates "experience" with "subjectivity" or feelings—simply what goes on in a person's consciousness. Actually, in daily life most of our "experience" involves an encounter with objective reality—a red traffic light, a helpful friend, an angry boss, a delicious dinner.

Genuine Christian experience involves a conscious encounter with an action of God, having observable results in the lives of individuals and communities. Charismatic experience stems from the Word of God, which is also its final norm. It may affect a person's inner life, or the environment, or both. A witness may say, "The Lord gave me peace . . . guided me . . . provided a job . . . healed me." *Charismatic experience is tested within the objective framework of the Scripture and the Christian community.* Subjectivity, on the other hand, is like a boomerang that misses its target and circles around to return to where it started. It is fantasy or illusion generated from within, unconnected with reality.

The powerful, observable working of the Holy Spirit spans a wide range of experiences. For some it is a life-changing commitment to the lordship of Christ—for the first time or in rededication. For others it is a new openness to spiritual gifts in worship, service or witness. Still others find a new dimension of prayer in praise and intercession.

Charismatic renewal has become grounded in biblical exposition of the first order. Over three decades it has produced an extensive literature that ranks with the best current theological scholarship. Ironically, it is anticharismatic writing that is largely based on experience—a litany of bizarre behavior in the renewal—rather than on biblical exegesis. Rare is the opposing book that interacts with the best charismatic scholarship as it interprets the relevant Scripture passages.

Weaknesses and Dangers

Like other major movements in the church's history, the charismatic renewal has its peculiar weaknesses. The rushing stream not only waters the countryside but also throws debris onto the riverbank.

Early in the renewal, Catholic theologian Edward O'Connor recognized that it was a "complex melange of human energies that in part correspond to the Spirit's plan, but in part deviate from it, conflict with it and counterfeit it."[9] Any good gift of God can be used for the wrong motives or in mistaken ways, O'Connor noted as he described two major errors in what he called "charismania."

First is a mentality that views the charismatic as the principal, if not the sole, criterion of spiritual excellence. It identifies spiritual growth with abundant exercise of charisms, especially the most spectacular. It forgets that love, a fruit of the Spirit, is the major measure of Christian spirituality. To counteract this kind of charismania, we need to stress that spiritual gifts are not goals in themselves but a means of building up the body of Christ in love. While miraculous charisms have long been minimized or rejected, they should not now be overemphasized.

A second error expects spiritual gifts to take the place of the ordinary exercise of human abilities and normal activities of church life. While some Christians program the Spirit *out* of certain charisms, others try to program him *into* a predictable pattern of gifts. Some seem to want their entire life to be guided by heavenly messages and all sickness to be miraculously healed. Others want theological study and sermon preparation to be replaced by prophetic utterance, church governance to be superseded by charismatic leadership.

Our Lord is not building his church of charisms but of people, with all their faculties of mind and will and emotions. The Holy Spirit works *through* as well as *beyond* our planning and programs. It is in a well-built fireplace that we should expect the fire of his sometimes unpredictable activity and strive to keep it burning.

A third danger in the renewal can be the demand for immediate results. Our fast-food, quick-fix technological culture expects instant solutions to problems. It has little patience for gradual healing of complex illness, ingrained habit patterns, fractured relationships.

The biblical cure for charismania is not to deny or disparage certain misused charisms. Paul's prescription for the Corinthians was an understanding of their nature and purpose. He did not advocate surgery, the amputation of errant members, but the therapy of providing for their proper use. No spiritual gift can be depreciated without slighting the Giver.

There is a danger of omission as well as commission, of failure to act as well as acting in the wrong way. Inaction is often due to fear of abuse or misuse. Charisms such as prophecy, healing and tongues *are* sometimes abused. But so are the more familiar gifts of evangelism and teaching, for example, which are not ruled out for that reason. An anticipated danger can become an opportunity to move carefully in the right way. By now many examples of success and failure indicate pitfalls to avoid along a well-traveled path of renewal.

Gripping many is a deeper fear of the unknown, of what we cannot predict and control. A technological age, abounding in prepackaged programs for guaranteed results, makes it difficult even in church activities to trust God himself to work in unexpected ways. Since we are secure with familiar forms, remodeling the fireplace often seems too risky. Yet at times that is the only way to experience more of the Spirit's power—or even a continuation of existing fire.

Unity and Division

The charismatic renewal, like others before it, has often been charged with divisiveness. This criticism raises questions about the nature of biblical truth, revivals and the cause of division.

We first note that according to the Scriptures, truth involves more than the mind; it is a revelation from God that calls for a response of the heart and will. Since biblical truth requires decision, its proclamation inevitably results in a division between those who respond positively and others who react negatively. At the temple in Jerusalem, Simeon declared that Jesus would cause the "falling and rising of many" (Lk 2:34). Jesus himself said that he had come to bring not peace but a sword; his teaching would result in division even within families (Mt 10:34-36).

Ultimately it is not truth but people who divide. Any truth can become an occasion for division if the people concerned consider it worth dividing over. The important issue is not that we disagree, but what we disagree about and how we handle our differences. Every church has essential doctrines that must be accepted by all members and other teachings about which they agree to disagree. Unfortunately, churches sometimes split over minor disagreements that are more a matter of personality than of biblical principle.

By its nature, every revival becomes an occasion for division. Reflecting judgment on current ways of thinking and acting, it calls for change. Some welcome the call, while others oppose it. Sometimes the disagreement is a result of faulty communication. For that reason it is essential to define crucial terms as they appear in a potential controversy.

Unlike Pentecostalism at the start of the century, the charismatic renewal has not brought a large-scale exodus from the mainline Protestant denominations. Leaders such as Dennis Bennett and Larry Christenson have worked primarily for renewal in their own churches, even though their concerns were also ecumenical. From the beginning the Roman Catholic renewal leaders and the hierarchy viewed it as a work of the Holy Spirit in their church.

Nevertheless, across the country many participants have encountered in their local churches indifference or opposition that led them to go elsewhere. Enough fire left the fireplace that new hearths have been built on a charismatic model. The progress of the renewal within the mainline denominations has been uneven, depending on the effectiveness of their leadership. The independent and nondenominational charismatic groups are still growing the most rapidly. (See appendix G.)

David Barrett's table of participation in all types of "charismatic" groups shows that the overall annual growth of the renewal is six percent. This average figure does not reflect specific areas of saturation, decline and explosive growth. Mainline Protestant and Catholic participants, however, are involved in regular group activities for only two or three years on the average. After this period of active weekly attendance at prayer meetings, many become irregular or nonattending. Calling them "postcharismatics" in his tables, Barrett notes, "This 'revolving door syndrome' results in an enormous annual turnover, a serious problem that has not yet begun to be adequately recognized or investigated."[10] (See appendix H.)

The charismatic renewal is not a panacea; it does not deal with historic theological differences about the nature and organization of the church, nor does it need to. God works through the uniqueness of each denomination. Nor does it call for a standard design of fireplace—only for sufficient changes, if necessary, for the Holy Spirit to work creatively. The renewal recognizes that he is sovereign and free to blow when, where and how he wills in the life of the community. Each church faces the challenge to recognize and receive this creativity according to its own situation.

This renewal was not initiated by human planning, and it does not provide a blueprint for the future. Nevertheless, it offers a challenge to discover new directions for assisting the church to carry out its worldwide mission.

15 The Road Ahead

*O*n the English Channel, an hour south of London, lies the popular resort and conference center of Brighton. Among many fascinating buildings in Brighton is the famous Royal Pavilion, built in 1822 as an exotic seaside home for the Prince Regent (later King George IV). A center for sightseeing in southeast England, this city attracts thousands of tourists each year.

In the history of Christian missions, Brighton is best known for the experience of Hudson Taylor on Sunday, June 25, 1865. Taylor later wrote of that day, "Unable to bear the sight of so many Christians rejoicing in their own security while millions were perishing for lack of knowledge, I wandered out on the sands at Brighton alone in great spiritual agony; and there the Lord conquered my unbelief and I surrendered myself to God for this service." Taylor then pioneered the China Inland Mission, through which thousands of young men and women carried the good news of Jesus Christ to China, and eventually many other lands.

Brighton was chosen for the International Charismatic Consultation on

World Evangelism (ICCOWE), convened July 9-14, 1991. Two years earlier, one hundred charismatic leaders from all over the world had met for a week-long prayer vigil in Jerusalem. In their discussion of such a conference two words predominated: *unity* and *evangelization.* Unlike the very large charismatic conventions of Kansas City in 1977 (fifty thousand) and New Orleans in 1987 (twenty thousand), Brighton 91 was designed as a working conference of leaders present by invitation only. The significance would lie not in its size but in its agenda.

Despite the great travel expense, a limited budget and repercussions of the Gulf War, thirty-one hundred leaders in charismatic renewal from one hundred nations and major denominations attended the conference. They gathered to affirm their unity in Christ and commitment to worldwide evangelization. The first such ecumenical and charismatic world conference, Brighton 91 had the widest ever representation of Christian churches. Only 25 percent of participants came from the United Kingdom, and 30 percent from the rest of Europe. An evidence of the conference's international character was the seventy-nine-page program, including more than sixty hymns and songs, in English, French, German and Spanish.

Groups with the largest representation were Roman Catholic (26 percent), Anglican (23 percent), nondenominational (16 percent), Lutheran (12 percent) and Pentecostal (7 percent). Morning sessions were offered in three major "streams": Anglican/Protestant, Roman Catholic and Pentecostal/nondenominational. Each had topics of special interest to that group. On three afternoons a dozen concurrent workshops covering a wide range of topics were available to all the participants.

On the first evening George Carey, the new archbishop of Canterbury, welcomed the delegates. He declared, "I have every reason to be personally grateful for the impact of the charismatic renewal in my life and for enriching my theology and experience of the Holy Spirit." He stated that "true evangelism is never imposed, it is lived, then believed. . . . Proselytism is the imposition of my faith on you, not taking into account your culture, your needs and your history." This decade will be a "make or break" time to put our house in order, he continued, to "ask the living God to renew us in a new unity of love 'that the world may believe.' "

Each evening in the plenary session, several brief testimonies were given before the main speaker addressed the theme of the day. Here also there was representation of the major church groups and continents. From China and Eastern Europe came reports of how the church had grown and become holy through persecution and martyrdom. They showed that a message that cannot speak to the depths of human suffering is a distorted version of the gospel. Leaders from Christian minorities in Lebanon and Iran challenged the "softness" of much Western Christianity as they reported the strength of witness in the fire of Beirut's civil war and of small islands of Christianity in a sea of Islamic fundamentalism.

The conference also featured a "theological stream," which ran concurrently with the main program during the day in a nearby hotel. About 120 theologians were invited to participate in this first international symposium of its kind. The planners, Harold Hunter (Pentecostal) and Peter Hocken (Roman Catholic), made prodigious efforts to identify, recruit and schedule fifty-seven biblical scholars from around the world to give papers and serve as respondents.

At the outset Archbishop Carey spoke to us on "The Importance of Theology for the Charismatic Renewal," highlighting the need to mediate the biblical message to our own culture through a partnership of theology and experience, each informing the other. German theologian Jürgen Moltmann's theme was "The Spirit of Life: Spirituality and New Vitality" as he explained the nature and use of spiritual gifts within the Christian community. He emphasized healing of the sick as an essential element in the life and message of the church, an important witness to the kingdom of God. Scripture's pouring and filling metaphors convey the dynamic nature of the Spirit's action as he empowers our worship and witness.

Differing points of view, at times spirited, were shared in a professional, loving manner. Informal conversations afforded opportunities for following up particular interests. An immediate fruit was the formation of the Association of African Church Planters, representing a dozen countries and several major denominations. The AACP planned to meet next in Zimbabwe in 1993.

As a longer-range benefit, the theological deliberations at ICCOWE stimulated further reflection on the nature of the charismatic renewal, its role in worldwide evangelization and possible future directions.

In October 1992, ICCOWE sponsored a consultation on Short-Term Mission. Thirty-two denominational and other Christian leaders met in Virginia to evaluate STM, which now accounts for sixty percent of all mission activity. The participants were Anglicans, Lutherans, Methodists, Pentecostals, Presbyterians, Reformed, Roman Catholics and independents from twelve countries. They experienced a remarkable unity in their plenary sessions and working groups which dealt with future STM opportunities and problems.

Alternative Paths

The conclusions of a forecaster—economic, political or religious—are at best precarious. Even an accurate grasp of present realities in the light of the past does not ensure a clear picture of the future. Although there seems to be nothing new under the sun, as King Solomon observed three thousand years ago, history—especially the sovereign actions of God—has a way of *not* repeating itself in predictable patterns. Even the person who takes a careful look down the road may not spot a distant turn or an unexpected fork. Nevertheless, as we assess the current situation we can at least identify possible directions for the charismatic renewal and make some estimate of their consequences.

Although Pentecostalism recovered for the church an openness to the full range of spiritual gifts, it perpetuated the American Protestant emphasis on the experience of the *individual.* The charismatic renewal has gone a step further in its understanding of spiritual gifts primarily in and for the Christian *community.* Peter Hocken looks ahead to a wider recognition of the *ecumenical* significance of the renewal—its meaning for the entire church, worldwide, in its many denominational divisions.[1]

As this renewal of the Spirit touches Christians of every tradition, it raises two basic questions.

☐ *For the existing churches:* How do we as churches respond to this ecumenical movement of God's Holy Spirit?

☐ *For participants:* How do we as Christians filled with the Spirit and part of an ecumenical work of God relate to this grace in our own church?

The churches face a work of the Lord who is pouring his Spirit on Christians in all traditions and backgrounds. This activity is wider than organized forms of what we call the charismatic renewal. Church authorities need to relate to both the leaders of charismatic organizations and the people in their own congregations. The renewal consists not primarily of organizations but of men and women touched and united by God.

The participants, however, face a fork in the road, two different paths. One group is drawn to the way of "nondenominationalism." They feel their new life in the Spirit is inhibited by traditional programs and attitudes. They encounter so much misunderstanding or rebuff that bringing renewal to their own church seems to be a lost cause. At the same time they enjoy fellowship and encouragement with Christians of other denominations. So they decide to leave their own church hearth and seek another for spiritual light and warmth.

Members of a different group realize that their church has been a spiritual home that nourished them in the faith. Instinctively they want to live their new spiritual life in that home. Its traditions are so dear to them that they can't even consider leaving. This group wants to integrate the new "charismatic" elements into their own tradition. Furthermore, they want to have their church's blessing on this new experience and share it with others in the congregation. Many of these people live in a country or region where their church is dominant and the ecumenical dimension of the charismatic renewal is not evident. In this situation it is easy to see one's own church tradition as the structure within which new experiences must be integrated.

Both groups have limitations to which they can be blind. Yet each sees its own position as authentic and misses the truth expressed in the other. The nondenominational Christians reject traditions of the past as they seek to build directly from the New Testament. The denominational members keep their own church tradition at the center as they seek to bring renewal to it.

A Third Way

Peter Hocken sees the Lord pointing to a "third way" that transcends this impasse. It "builds upon the ecumenical character of the renewal as a work of God. It will do justice to both truths." God's present grace cannot be subordinated to the life of any one church, but he does not forsake his work in the past. "This third way is itself a new thing because the renewal is new. The churches do not know how to receive a fully ecumenical work of the Spirit. But the Spirit will teach those who humbly seek to know."[2]

In John 16 Jesus teaches that the Holy Spirit, whom he would send, has a twofold mission of convicting of sin and revealing the truth. That revelation is centered in Christ and his purposes for the church. Through the Spirit we no longer look at life from a human point of view, but from the perspective of our Lord (2 Cor 5:16).

This activity of the Holy Spirit can be seen in the way he both challenges and confirms the church through the charismatic renewal. His conviction of sin exposes and challenges every tradition and activity that is not centered on Jesus. The Spirit's ministry challenges every aspect of individual and corporate life, including how we think, make decisions, deal with conflict, do theology, worship, form fellowship and serve. Every Christian tradition is challenged by the ecumenical outpouring of the Spirit of God.

The Spirit not only disturbs but also encourages, since he is called the Paraclete (encourager, strengthener, consoler). In the midst of its specific weaknesses, each church is confirmed in its particular light on the person and work of the Lord Jesus. *A rediscovered center in Jesus Christ, deeper than our differences, is the point of our newfound unity in the Spirit.*

The third way of avoiding denominationalism and nondenominationalism involves holding in balance the challenging and confirming activities of the Spirit. It is not a matter of compromise, a negotiated tradeoff by organizational leaders. Rather, it is a grace in the hearts of the people, experienced in charismatic fellowships around the world.

260 FIRE IN THE FIREPLACE

Although the challenge to each church comes first through its members who are involved in charismatic renewal, it is strengthened by the reality that this grace of God has been poured out on all the churches, transcending their divisions. The third way involves two principles:

☐ All church traditions need this renewal of the Spirit.

☐ The renewal needs all the churches.

This requires a mutual submission of individual churches and the renewal in ways that still need to be worked out under the guidance of the Holy Spirit.

We have seen how the charismatic renewal began as an "event" rather than as an "idea." It did not start as a concept with a coherent plan, but in persons with changed lives who faced questions about what the renewal meant and what should be done with it. The first question must be answered in light of the ecumenical scope. Otherwise each church is likely to "domesticate" this new spiritual power, fitting it into its old ways of thinking and acting. The renewal needs to become "embodied," not as a church in itself but in the life of all the churches, receiving their input and correction. Cross-pollination can keep it from becoming domesticated and culturebound, so that it can break down racial and ethnic barriers.

In the charismatic renewal the Lord of the church has created a new ecumenical situation. In all the centuries of Christian division there has not been such an example of one grace poured out on believers of all theological traditions around the world. But the renewal does not bring with it an automatic understanding of its meaning or program for maturity. It must be guided by the Holy Spirit step by step.

Hocken concludes, "An ecumenical grace calls for an ecumenical theology. Anything less will distort the gift of God, and thwart the fulfillment of God's purpose. . . . The initial out-pouring of the charismatic renewal is an act of creation that has later to be shaped and built upon. The renewal is not just an unprecedented gift. It is also an unprecedented task."[3]

Pentecost and Parousia
The coming of the Holy Spirit at Pentecost to empower the church for its

mission was only a partial fulfillment of Old Testament prophecy. The disciples' Spirit baptism also looked forward to the *parousia* ("coming") of Christ—his "Messianic Advent in glory to judge the world at the end of the age."[4]

Most Old Testament prophecies of salvation find their fulfillment in two stages, the first and second advents of the Messiah. Peter's address at Pentecost explicitly states that the Spirit's outpouring is a fulfillment of prophecy. To his quotation of Joel he adds his own words "in the last days," linking this event with prophecies of Jeremiah and Ezekiel about the messianic age. The crucial point in Peter's sermon is his declaration, "Exalted to the right hand of God, he [Jesus] has received from the Father the promised Holy Spirit and has poured out what you now see and hear" (Acts 2:33).

Peter's quotation from Joel also looks to a future event, the return of Christ to reign over the earth.

I will show wonders in the heaven above
    and signs on the earth below,
    blood and fire and billows of smoke.
The sun will be turned to darkness
    and the moon become as blood
    before the coming of the great and glorious day of the Lord.
    (Acts 2:19-20)

The disciples' experience of Spirit baptism at Pentecost was not a particular stage of individual Christian life different from other stages. It was essentially a corporate experience of participation in the new covenant of the messianic age. Pentecost was a pledge of the final outpouring that will be the climax of all history. The complete fulfillment of salvation will take place in the parousia—the visible glorification of the risen Christ.

The seventh angel sounded his trumpet, and there were loud voices in heaven, which said:
    "The kingdom of the world has become the
        kingdom of our Lord and of his Christ,
    and he will reign for ever and ever." (Rev 11:15)

In 1 Corinthians 15:57-58 the apostle Paul concludes his great discourse on the resurrection with an exclamation of triumph and a call to commitment. "Thanks be to God! He gives us the victory through our Lord Jesus Christ. . . . Let nothing move you. Always give yourselves fully to the work of the Lord, because you know that your labor in the Lord is not in vain."

The charismatic renewal is both the sign and empowerment for Christians to fulfill this responsibility. We do so with the last prayer of the Bible in Revelation 22:20: "Come, Lord Jesus."

Appendix A
The Spirit
in Luke-Acts

Luke's writing covers seventy crucial years, bridging the Old Covenant and the New, Israel and the church, the synagogue and the Christian community. The two eras witness both continuity and discontinuity in God's redemptive activity. In the Old Testament the Spirit came upon individuals and groups at special times for specific tasks. In the New Testament the same "Spirit of the Lord" who spoke through the prophets now appears in a new role.

For Luke, the presence and action of the Spirit occupy a central place in the drama of redemptive history. The Spirit is prominent at each stage of the coming of the messianic age, including the revelation of Jesus' mission and the empowerment of his ministry in the Gospel and of the church in Acts.

In the Gospel, Luke unfolds his message in a carefully designed sequence. The first act of this drama features three visions and three prophecies. The angel Gabriel appears to the priest Zechariah in the temple, promising a son, John, who will be "filled with the Holy Spirit even from birth" (1:15). Gabriel appears to the virgin Mary in Nazareth and promises a son, Jesus, to be conceived by the Holy Spirit and called the Son of God (1:35). An angel of the Lord also appears to shepherds in the fields, announcing the birth of the Messiah in Bethlehem (2:11). Prophecies are given by three persons empowered by the Holy Spirit: Elizabeth (1:41), Zechariah (1:67) and Simeon (2:25).

In recent years there has been growing concern over a neglect of the Holy Spirit in several areas of theology, especially the ministry of Jesus.[1] This neglect has been due in part to the nature of the Spirit's work as the agent of God—he represents another and not himself. By the very nature of his mission the Spirit points to the Father and the Son.

Furthermore, in our century the denial of Jesus' deity has required so much rebuttal that his true humanity has been neglected. Therefore, it is important to recognize Luke's teaching about Jesus' genuine growth in strength, wisdom and favor with both God and others (2:40, 52). Fully human, he was anointed, filled, led and empowered by the Holy Spirit for his messianic ministry.[2]

In the Acts of the Apostles, Luke features the activity of the Holy Spirit—sent by the risen Lord—in the ever-widening expansion of the church. At each crucial stage the Spirit's guidance and empowerment are evident as he works in a variety of ways through individuals and groups.

No event in Acts provides one basic model for the sequence of the individual's repentance and faith, water baptism and initial reception of the Spirit. Nor does Luke prescribe a standard pattern for subsequent manifestations of the Spirit. If there is a pattern, it is one of diversity, the sovereign action of the Spirit who blows when and where he wills.

In Luke-Acts we see Luke as an excellent historian and theologian. Like other his torians, he has his own perspective on events and a particular purpose for reporting them. That purpose guides his selection of the facts, they way they are related and the meaning they communicate. The narratives of the two books are no more purely descriptive than are the personal testimonies of Paul. Both are designed to teach. Each event Luke records serves his theological purpose. "Because he was a theologian he had to be a historian. His view of theology led him to write history."[3]

Appendix B
Interpretations of Spirit Baptism

In recent decades the doctrine of Spirit baptism, at the heart of charismatic renewal, has continued to generate discussion and controversy. To many it has served as a source of light on the Christian life; to others it has been a lightning rod for charges of heresy. Current theological debate raises crucial questions: How is the phrase *baptized in the Spirit* used in the New Testament? How can we evaluate this experience, attested by so many people? Does the Christian life have a two-stage pattern? If so, are there two groups of Christians, those who have received Spirit baptism and those who have not? How is it related to conversion, water baptism and confirmation? Does it enrich the church, or is it on the lunatic fringe of the faith?

The issues surrounding this subject are more complex than they initially appear. They involve questions of biblical interpretation as well as perceptions of the Holy Spirit's activity. In the following pages we first focus on several pre-Pentecostal views of Spirit baptism in Acts. We will then review the standard twentieth-century evangelical and classical Pentecostal interpretations. Finally we will consider several alternative views proposed in recent scholarly literature as theologians work through the meaning of Spirit baptism within their own ecclesial (denominational) structures.

Pre-Pentecostal Interpretations
The contrasting evangelical and Pentecostal views of Spirit baptism in Acts focus on

the crucial question of whether the Christian life is characterized by one or two "definitive stages." This complex issue has long been debated. Over the centuries a one-stage model of Christian experience has dominated, envisioned in two main forms: standard evangelicals identify Spirit baptism with regeneration or conversion, while sacramentalists link it with either baptism or confirmation. On the other hand, a wide variety of groups have accepted a basic pattern of two stages: new life in Christ followed by a "second blessing" of some kind.

The charismatic renewal has put this vital question on the front burner as theological reflection struggles to keep pace with worldwide growth. A diversity of experience and biblical insight has prompted disagreement and controversy; it is also producing bridges between long-opposing views. In 1988, Reformed theologian Henry I. Lederle published *Treasures Old and New: Interpretations of "Spirit-Baptism" in the Charismatic Renewal Movement*.[1] This definitive work is based on his doctoral dissertation at the University of South Africa, which was inspired by unexpected charismatic experience for which he was not theologically prepared. Here I briefly draw on Lederle's study to put the question of Spirit baptism in historical perspective, then sketch several approaches to integrating it with diverse ecclesial structures.

Three groups that advocated a two-stage pattern not only prepared the ground for the current charismatic renewal but also continue to find support to one degree or another. They advocate a second experience of the Holy Spirit called a baptizing, sealing or filling.

1. Reformed Sealers. These seventeenth-century Puritans, who included John Owen, focused on the "sealing" work of the Holy Spirit. This experience, subsequent to conversion, enables a communion with God that assures believers of belonging as the Spirit testifies they are God's children (Rom 8:16). Thomas Goodwin sees the Spirit's sealing in Ephesians 1:13 as intensely experiential, "a light that overpowereth a man's soul, and assureth him that God is his and he is God's."[2]

Two additional facets of the Spirit's sealing are a ratifying of the validity of the gospel and the eschatological implications of the gift of the Spirit. In contrast to later developments, the Sealers do not see a necessary connection between this experience and the fruit or gifts of the Spirit. The only prominent modern teacher of this view is the late Martyn Lloyd-Jones, minister of Westminster Chapel in London.[3]

2. Wesleyan sanctification. This doctrine of a "second blessing," a distinct work of grace subsequent to conversion, is also called "entire sanctification" or "Christian perfection." There has been considerable debate over the meaning of John Wesley's innovative teaching in this regard. In a tract he defines Christian perfection as "the loving [of] God with all our heart, mind, soul, and strength. This implies that no wrong temper, none contrary to love, remains in the soul; and that all the thoughts, words, and actions are governed by pure love.["4] Yet Wesley does not affirm that it excludes all "infirmities, ignorance, and mistake." This work of perfection later became known as a "baptism with the Holy Spirit." In the last decades of the nineteenth century this teaching, now scarcely found at all in the larger Methodist churches, became the hallmark of the Wesleyan-Holiness movement.

Although Wesley himself did not explain this concept within a two-stage framework, it evolved into such a pattern. As a result, there are two groups within the church—those who have only received the new birth and others who are both saved and sanctified. For our study, the importance of this view lies not in the validity of Wesley's view of sin and salvation but in the fact that this two-stage pattern provided the foundation on which the Pentecostal movement was later built.

3. *Keswick teaching.* The Keswick message, which originated in England, developed more on the level of sermons and piety than on the level of reflection. Its popular appeal comes from its promise of the victorious life, the deeper or higher Christian walk. It retains the Wesleyan two-stage pattern but rejects the belief that believers' hearts become perfect in love. Instead, the second work of grace produces a victorious life with a perfection of *deeds.* The key is "resting," looking to Christ for perfection of performance. The crisis in the Keswick form of Spirit baptism is followed by a process through which the individual maintains this commitment and faith. The focus is on a life of practical holiness and service.[5]

In North America, Keswick teaching shifted toward enduement of power for ministry, as prominent evangelical leaders such as D. L. Moody, R. A. Torrey, A. B. Simpson and A. J. Gordon propagated the message. Unlike the Wesleyan-Holiness movement, those influenced by Keswick thinking did not form new denominations. It has been supported mainly by evangelicals in mainline denominations and some Free churches. There are still annual Keswick conventions, but they are not marked by the original doctrinal emphases of its founders.

The Pentecostal Interpretation

While early Pentecostalism shared with Holiness and some evangelical groups the doctrine of a crisis experience subsequent to conversion, it was unique in its insistence that speaking in tongues is *the* initial physical evidence of this experience. This doctrine became the central point of controversy, a "great divide" between Pentecostals and other Christians. (To distinguish it from the more recent "neo-Pentecostal" renewal of the 1960s, the original movement is often designated as "classical Pentecostalism"—a term coined by Catholic scholar Kilian McDonnell.)

Two midwives assisted the birth of classical Pentecostalism. The Wesleyan-Holiness movement provided the basic two-stage pattern, while the more Reformed evangelical revivalism emphasized baptism in the Spirit as enduement of power for Christian life and witness. Here two main doctrinal groupings are of interest: Wesleyan-Holiness and Baptistic Pentecostals.[6]

Wesleyan-Holiness Pentecostals outlined a three-stage pattern for the Christian life. They kept the Wesleyan model of conversion and then sanctification as a subsequent blessing at a specific time to remove the carnal nature so that the heart becomes totally pure in love. To this was added a third stage, baptism in the Spirit, with speaking in tongues. Since purification had already occurred in stage two, the third stage echoed the Keswick focus on enduement of power for service, but with the innovative distinguishing element of glossolalia.

Baptistic Pentecostals include the largest Pentecostal denomination, the Assemblies of God. They have three main characteristics that can be termed "Baptistic": their doctrine of sanctification is basically Reformed, their system of church government is congregational, and they practice believer's baptism. This group views sanctification not as a second work of grace but as a process. The second stage is not a component of salvation but an equipping with power for spreading the gospel.

As Pentecostalism came on the scene, its message of external physical evidence appealed to many Christians who doubted their Spirit baptism because they seemed to have lost their "purity" or "power." In that atmosphere the message of a physical evidence of Spirit baptism spread like wildfire.

Pentecostals see two definitive events in the life of Jesus' disciples. In regeneration each believer receives the Holy Spirit; later baptism in the Spirit involves receiving him fully. Donald Gee, a widely respected teacher-leader, declares that Spirit baptism is the central issue in Pentecostalism. "The designation 'Pentecostal' arises from its emphasis upon a baptism in the Holy Spirit such as that recorded in Acts 2. . . . as a separate individual experience possible for all Christians . . . subsequent to, and distinct from, regeneration."[7] Gee is very clear on speaking in tongues as the initial physical evidence of this experience.

Pentecostals note the disciples' initial reception of the Holy Spirit reported in the Gospel of John. Soon after his resurrection, Jesus appeared as they gathered behind locked doors, fearful of the Jewish authorities. He showed them his hands and side, then declared, "Peace be with you! As the Father has sent me, I am sending you." And with that he breathed on them and said, "Receive the Holy Spirit" (20:21-22). This initial reception fulfills the Lord's earlier promise to send another Counselor; now in words and actions he graciously communicates this reality in the context of the disciples' mission, which would begin at Pentecost (see appendix C).

Pentecostals recognize Luke's theology of empowerment for prophetic ministry foretold by Joel, promised by Jesus and explained by Peter. But they go a step further in making baptism in the Spirit a definitive second experience, "distinct from and subsequent to" conversion, for all believers. While in their model the Holy Spirit baptizes a person into Christ at conversion, Christ later baptizes the believer into the Spirit (1 Cor 12:13). Pentecostals see this pattern not only in Acts 2 but also with the new Christians in Samaria (Acts 8), the Roman centurion Cornelius and his household (Acts 10), and the disciples of John the Baptist (Acts 19).

The Holy Spirit is not expected to fill Christians automatically or imperceptibly; rather, they should actively seek this experience, for which they must meet certain conditions. The nature and number of these conditions vary with the particular Pentecostal teacher. Many agree, however, on three requirements they believe the disciples met prior to Pentecost: conversion, obedience and faith. "If we live a yielded, pure and holy life, in close fellowship with Him, the experimental side of this mighty baptism must come."[8]

Pentecostals generally recognize that the letters of Paul and other apostles do not explicitly teach this doctrine. But they believe that such teaching was unnecessary since these letters were written to established churches in which the majority of the members had already received this experience. Like the first disciples, they were baptized in the Spirit soon after their conversion. Pentecostals not only teach this doctrine, they experience it.

The Pentecostal view of baptism with the Spirit in Acts 2 correctly interprets Luke's teaching. Here the baptizing is a pouring out, a filling, a clothing with power from on high, through which the Holy Spirit equips the disciples for their mission. But there is no ground for interpreting this as a unique inner experience, a second stage in the disciples' spiritual pilgrimage. We have seen that this is not Luke's concern; he is not writing spiritual biographies of early Christian leaders. On this point both Pentecostals and standard evangelicals import into Acts an issue foreign to the intent of the author.

Furthermore, the coming of the Spirit in Acts 2 was related not to the disciples' "tarrying" in Jerusalem to satisfy certain conditions, but to the arrival of Pentecost with its thousands of pilgrims from all over the Roman Empire. The Spirit's timetable was not personal but historical—the full arrival of the messianic age, whose dawn appears at the beginning of Luke's Gospel. Speaking in tongues was not evidence of the disciples' individual spiritual maturity but a means of communicating in the pilgrims' own languages the good news of Jesus Christ. This speaking was also a powerful symbol in relation to unity and a reversal of the diverse languages at Babel (Gen 11:1-9).

The Standard Evangelical View

This interpretation, represented by British theologian Donald Guthrie among others, holds that the outpouring of the Spirit at Pentecost marks the origin of the Christian church, the beginning of a new age of the Spirit. Guthrie views the disciples' experience (like that of the three thousand) as the beginning of their Christian life. The whole company of believers were "in one act sealed by the same Spirit." Or, in the apostle Paul's words, they were "baptized [in] one Spirit into one body [of Christ]" (1 Cor 12:13).

This view does not recognize what we have seen to be the different experiences and meanings of Pentecost for the disciples and the new converts. Guthrie states categorically, "There is no suggestion in Acts 2 that the outpouring of the Holy Spirit was primarily to give power to existing believers as some have maintained. On the contrary, it relates to the experience of conversion."[9]

Guthrie rejects a "double coming of the Spirit." Therefore he considers Jesus' breathing of the Spirit on the disciples in John 20:22 as *proleptic* ('anticipatory'), a foreshadowing of Pentecost."[10] In other words, the Spirit didn't actually come at that time, even though the verb *receive* is in the present (not future) tense, the same as "Peace be with you. . . . I am sending you."

As we have noted, the didactic-descriptive dichotomy for applying Scripture to our lives ignores the fact that biblical literature largely takes the form of history—stories of individuals, families, tribes and nations, battles and sieges, friendships and love affairs, betrayals and murders. All are intended to teach. Jesus' most effective teaching makes use of parables. His description of the good Samaritan's action was more effective than a lecture on the Ten Commandments. The story itself teaches, penetrating defenses against explicit commands and judgments, as suddenly we identify with one of the characters. In much of biblical revelation "the medium is the message."

In recent decades some scholars have developed a narrative theology that emphasizes the teaching power of the story itself, whether historical event or parable, to convey God's word to us and invite us to relate our own "story" with this greater narrative.[11] Nevertheless, just as every command does not apply today, neither is every scriptural example to be followed. The application of biblical teaching, whatever form it takes, requires diligent study.[12]

We have seen that all the terms Luke uses to explain the disciples' experience at Pentecost, including the promised "baptism in the Spirit," contribute to his theology of the Holy Spirit's empowering the church for its worldwide mission. Peter's sermon explaining the disciples' experience quotes Joel's vision of widespread prophecy in the messianic age. It is significant that the apostle does *not* proclaim Pentecost as a fulfillment of Ezekiel 36:26-27: "I will give you a new heart . . . and I will put my Spirit in you and move you to follow my decrees and be careful to keep my laws." That experience of regeneration (new birth) and sanctification (holy living) is explained in Paul's theology of the Holy Spirit in the Christian life.

Charismatic Views of Spirit Baptism

During the decade of the 1960s the charismatic renewal permeated a wide spectrum of Protestant mainline, Roman Catholic and independent churches. Attempts to construct a theology of Spirit baptism at first generalized on reflections about personal experience. Even those denominational leaders who welcomed the renewal were not prepared to help their members interpret it within their own church traditions. In recent years, however, a number of competent theologians have made progress in providing a comprehensive theology of this central renewal experience.

Attempts to classify different emphases within the charismatic renewal according to denominational or standard doctrinal categories have not succeeded. They fail to cope with a more fluid situation in which specific views of Spirit baptism cross over traditional boundaries. In some ways this concept is as difficult to define as *water baptism* or *church*. Lederle deals with this problem in terms of three major categories which provide a useful framework for both initial understanding and further study.[13]

1. Neo-Pentecostal model. This view is essentially like the classical Pentecostal doctrine of Spirit baptism. When charismatic renewal unexpectedly surfaced among mainline Protestants in the early 1960s, they were encouraged by Pentecostals in the Full Gospel Business Men's Fellowship International who also provided their interpretation of baptism in the Spirit. With minor modifications, this became the predominant view in the early years of the charismatic renewal, which flowed in two main Protestant streams: mainline and independent churches.

Neo-Pentecostals faced the dilemma of whether to stay in the denominational structures or leave them. Pentecostal leader David Du Plessis encouraged Christians who received the baptism in the Spirit to remain in their own churches, but others strongly disagreed. Dennis Bennett's decision to stay in the Episcopal Church was a significant step. Here is how he and his wife, Rita, define Spirit baptism in their influential book *The Holy Spirit and You:* "The second experience is the receiving, or making welcome, of the Holy Spirit, so that Jesus can cause Him to pour out this new life from our spirits."[14] Other influential neo-Pentecostals have been Roman Catholic Steve Clark,[15] Presbyterian Rodman Williams[16] and (in the early years) Lutheran Larry Christenson.[17]

Don Basham, a leader in nondenominational neo-Pentecostalism, explains baptism in the Holy Spirit as "a second encounter with God in which the Christian begins to receive the supernatural power of the Holy Spirit into his life . . . given for the purpose of equipping the Christian with God's power for service."[18] Basham stays close to the classic Pentecostal doctrine of initial evidence, but he is not dogmatic about its being tongues. Other spiritual manifestations may accompany the experience, but "speaking in tongues remains the primary initial evidence." (It should be noted that neo-Pentecostals do not accept the concept of conditions—other than faith in Christ—for receiving Spirit baptism.)

Early in the charismatic renewal, many participants had difficulty accepting the neo-Pentecostal model, which generalizes the legitimate experience of *some* Christians into rules for all. Implicit in its teaching is the concept of Spirit baptism as *the* gateway to exercising spiritual gifts. Yet in the New Testament they found no prescribed pattern of specific events or experiences for growth in the Christian life, no second-stage reception of the Spirit with one particular charism as an essential manifestation. Speaking in tongues, a valuable gift, might be used by God more frequently than others for breaking through Western rationalism and resistance to spiritual reality. But it is still one among many charisms—to be neither despised nor overrated.

However unintentionally, neo-Pentecostalism fosters an elitism of two classes of Christians: those who have received Spirit baptism and those who have not. Concerns over this view of charismatic experience led some theologians in the mainline churches to explore another way of understanding baptism in the Spirit.

2. Sacramental model. As the charismatic renewal flowed into mainline churches, there arose a need to interpret the "Pentecostal experience" within the theological framework of other ecclesiastical traditions. Although the renewal had started in the Episcopal, Lutheran and Presbyterian churches, it was the Roman Catholic Church that pioneered in-depth theological interpretation of Pentecostal categories. Soon it became apparent that different models were being developed.

Catholic theologian Kilian McDonnell played a major role in formulating a "sacramental" interpretation of Spirit baptism. He also sounded the call to several Protestant denominations that a similar task lay ahead of them; he even outlined how a Lutheran charismatic theology might be developed. As early as 1974 McDonnell showed that a "theological ecclesial culture"—a shared heritage of belief, worship and piety—is essential to the life of the church.[19] The task of "charismatic" theologians is to integrate that dimension into their own theological ecclesial culture—Catholic, Lutheran, Presbyterian and others. It also became apparent that within any one such theological framework various views of Spirit baptism are possible.

The original Catholic interpretation of Spirit baptism views it as a "release" of the Spirit—a flowering of the sacramental grace received in Christian initiation. Although later voices declared that there are also other ways to interpret Spirit baptism within the Catholic framework, this view comes close to being the official position. It has also received support within Anglican, Lutheran and Presbyterian circles.

This view is associated with Kilian McDonnell and Leon Joseph Cardinal Suenens, the primate of Belgium until 1979. The latter brought together an international team of Catholic theologians and lay leaders in Malines during May 1974. McDonnell, who wrote the final document, states by way of introduction to the text, "Baptism in the Spirit was seen to be related to the celebration of initiation (baptism, confirmation, Eucharist) in that it brings to conscious awareness the graces received during that introduction to the Christian life."[20] A more recent study, *Christian Initiation and Baptism in the Holy Spirit,* by Kilian McDonnell and George T. Montague, provides evidence from the first eight centuries that throws light on the sacramental model of Spirit baptism.[21]

Other Catholic theologians, however, are concerned that this view does not recognize Spirit baptism as something new that God is doing in people's lives at the time they experience it. They point out that the charismatic experience doesn't fit the sacramental categories themselves. Simon Tugwell rejects the neo-Pentecostal doctrine of Spirit baptism but is highly critical of attempts to reinterpret it within traditional categories. He believes that we should acknowledge a variety of experiences of the Spirit and not generalize from one particular kind.[22]

The sacramental position is also found in some Protestant churches, especially in the Lutheran tradition. In the summer of 1981 an International Lutheran Charismatic Theological Consultation was convened in Finland to study the nature and role of charismatic renewal in the Lutheran Church. The one hundred participants from twelve countries represented a broad range of experience with the renewal. After five years of further discussion, conclusions were published in *Welcome, Holy Spirit: A Study of Charismatic Renewal in the Church,* a 412-page volume of historical, biblical and practical theology.[23]

Editor Larry Christenson, an early leader in the charismatic renewal, was initially neo-Pentecostal but later moved toward the sacramental view. In his 1976 book *The Charismatic Renewal Among Lutherans* he notes that the two-stage view of classical Pentecostalism was widely used as a theological model during the early 1960s. "By the end of the decade, however, another view, more akin to the historic view, was emerging. This could be characterized as an 'organic view' of the Spirit's work." Although some aspects of Christenson's view are not clear, it is largely sacramental, for he speaks of Spirit baptism as "a flowering or actualization of baptismal grace."[24]

3. Integrative models. This category covers a variety of views that attempt to relate

Spirit baptism and ongoing charismatic experience to other elements of the Christian life. Lederle classifies the many miscellaneous positions in four major subcategories.[25] One sees Spirit baptism as the final stage of an otherwise incomplete Christian initiation. A series of overlapping concepts are involved in becoming a Christian: conversion, repentance, justification, new birth and baptism in the Spirit. Although this view has the advantage of considering the charismatic dimension an essential in the Christian life, it can erroneously imply that those who miss this experience are incomplete Christians.

A second position identifies *Spirit baptism* with *filling with the Spirit*. Both terms are used to describe the Acts 2 experience. In both Luke's and Paul's use of the latter term, it refers to a repeated empowerment of the Holy Spirit, the manifestation of a spiritual gift. Yet *Spirit baptism* has a unique initiatory and prophetic dimension that needs to be recognized.

In a third view, Spirit baptism, as a part of Christian initiation, is a renewal in the Spirit that is "an openness to the Spirit and his charisms." This position rejects the view that one needs a particular experience to start exercising spiritual gifts.

A fourth position is similar to the above but without the need for a sacramental renewal. "Breakthrough" experiences are seen as "comings" of the Spirit, but not in one prescribed fashion. After such an experience charisms may flow more freely, but they are not dependent on a specific kind of experience. Following his presentation of the above interpretations of Spirit baptism, Lederle offers his own view, that it is "the charismatic dimension of normal Christian life," which we have noted in chapter three.

My evaluation of widely diverse theologies of Spirit baptism here should not obscure the fact that these theologies have been a means of providing good spiritual medicine to countless thousands of believers. Aided by these teachings, many have experienced the essentials of Christian faith: repentance toward God and faith in Jesus Christ, new birth and holy life, fruit and gifts of the Spirit, effective witness and selfless service to the sick and the poor at home and in foreign lands.

In our pursuit of a biblical theology of Spirit baptism let us beware of the illusion that we *have* everything that we state in our doctrines. *Welcome, Holy Spirit* reminds us that embracing such an illusion is like "claiming a victory on the battlefield because you have a textbook on military strategy. The strategy of the Spirit is calling the church to experience more of what the doctrines talk about . . . a demonstration of the Spirit and his power (1 Cor 2:4) to extend our expectation of the Spirit's working to the horizons of Scripture."[26]

Appendix C
The Impartation of the Spirit in the Gospel of John

Although John's theological perspective is different from Luke's, both writers closely link the Spirit to Jesus. In one sentence John conveys a wealth of meaning as he reports the words of the Baptist: "The one who sent me to baptize with water told me, 'The man on whom you see the Spirit come down and remain is he who will baptize with the Holy Spirit' " (Jn 1:33). The phrase *come down and remain* parallels Luke's description of Jesus as the bearer of the Spirit, while the promise of baptism indicates that Jesus will also be the giver of the Spirit.[1]

John again links Jesus and the Spirit in Jesus' invitation at the Feast of Tabernacles: " 'If anyone is thirsty, let him come to me and drink. Whoever believes in me, as the Scripture has said, streams of living water will flow from within him.' By this he meant the Spirit, whom those who believed in him were later to receive. Up to that time the Spirit had not been given, since Jesus had not yet been glorified" (Jn 7:37). John uses the words *glory* and *glorify* forty-one times—more than the other three Gospels put together. Furthermore, unlike their focus on a future exaltation, John presents Jesus' glorification in his earthly life and death. After Judas had left the Upper Room, Jesus said, "Now is the Son of Man glorified" (Jn 13:31). G. M. Burge points out, "It is not just a transport to a realm of glory (as in the Synoptics). It is an unveiling, a fresh radiating of God showing himself once more at work."[2]

John also connects the Holy Spirit with mission. In chapter 16 Jesus promises the

Spirit to guide the disciples into all truth and to convict the world of sin, righteousness and judgment. In fact, the Upper Room Discourse, with its dominant theme of continuity between the ministries of Jesus and the Spirit, is in this respect John's preview of Acts.

The strongest link between Jesus, the Spirit and mission comes after the resurrection in words to the disciples gathered in fear behind locked doors: "Jesus came and stood among them and said, 'Peace be with you!' After he said this, he showed them his hands and side. The disciples were overjoyed when they saw the Lord. Again Jesus said, 'Peace be with you! As the Father has sent me, I am sending you.' And with that he breathed on them and said, 'Receive the Holy Spirit' " (Jn 20:19-22). A valid interpretation of this passage must fit within the framework of John's purpose, taking what he means to teach, no more and no less.

It has long been recognized that in purpose and style the Fourth Gospel differs from the first three. While securely anchored in history, John's narrative cannot be neatly dovetailed with Luke's as if they were moving along the same linear track.[3] John is not filling a gap in Luke's sequence; nor does he need events in Acts to complete his own story of the relationship between Jesus and the Spirit.

In his Gospel John emphasizes the *unity* of the final decisive events in Jesus' ministry: death, resurrection, ascension and gift of the Spirit. On the day of his resurrection Jesus says to Mary, "I am ascending to my Father" (Jn 20:17 NRSV). He does not say "I will ascend."[4] Likewise, in the Upper Room Jesus uses three verbs in the *present tense:* "Peace be with you [now]! . . I am sending you. . . . Receive the Holy Spirit [a present imperative]." Furthermore, John records that Jesus breathed on them; an impartation actually took place, reminiscent of the Creator's action in Genesis 2:7.[5]

Nevertheless, the standard evangelical interpretation changes John's meaning to fit the assumption that Jesus' "glorification" must have been his later visible ascension and exaltation recorded in Acts 1. Here (as with the importation of Paul's definition of baptism in the Spirit into Luke's account of Pentecost) John's teaching is adjusted to fit the Procrustean bed of a different theological concept.

The meaning for the disciples in the Upper Room that Sunday lies in the link between Jesus and the Spirit. The Lord demonstrates to them that the coming of the Spirit is something he does for them, just as he promised. Before his departure, he graciously gives them not only their commission but also an experience of the Spirit that they need as they await his full coming in power at Pentecost.

Appendix D
New Testament Lists of Spiritual Gifts

The New Testament has nine lists of gifts, eight of which appear in the writings of Paul. Of the latter, six consist of charisms (Rom 12:6-8; 1 Cor 12:8-10; 13:1-3; 13:8; 14:6; 14:26). One list comprises gifted individuals (Eph 4:11). And one has both categories (1 Cor 12:28). Peter's list consists of charisms (1 Pet 4:9-11).

It is commonly assumed that the biblical writers provide an order in rank, so that the relative value of a gift can be determined by its place on a list. For example, in the 1 Corinthians 12:8-10 list a message of wisdom is to be considered most important because it appears first, while speaking in tongues and its interpretation are the least of the charisms because they come last. This conclusion, however, is valid only if the context and usage show that the author *intends* to list the gifts in order of rank. Otherwise, this assumption reflects our own view rather than that of the biblical writer. The following brief analysis of the data examines the way spiritual gifts are listed and how their order should be understood.

Romans 12:6-8: **prophesying, serving, teaching, encouraging, contributing, leading, showing mercy**
Prophecy is prominent in most of Paul's lists, as it provides "strengthening, encouragement and comfort" to the church. The other gifts, apparently a random sample, give no indication of rank. And Paul hardly considers of least importance "showing mercy," that marvelous action of God toward those who repent of their sin.

1 Corinthians 12:8-10: **wisdom, knowledge, faith, healings, miracles, prophecy, discerning of spirits, speaking in tongues, interpretation of tongues**
The misuse of wisdom and knowledge in the Corinthian church is at the heart of the serious problems to which Paul devotes most of the first four chapters of his letter. The rest of the list also appears to be a random sample. If there is an order, it could follow the degree of misuse in the Corinthian church, since this is a problem-oriented letter. First and last places on a list or in a sentence can be positions of emphasis. Both wisdom (first) and tongues (last) were being misused at Corinth.

1 Corinthians 12:28: **first apostles, second prophets, third teachers, then miracles, then gifts of healings, helpful deeds, administrations, different kinds of tongues**
An explicit order, which may be chronological, is assigned only to the three gifted individuals in the list. The five charisms are not ranked; this part of the list appears to be another random sample.

Similar examples of unranked diversity of spiritual gifts appear in the four brief lists of 1 Corinthians 13 and 14:

13:1-3	13:8	14:6	14:26
tongues	prophecies	revelation	instruction
prophecy	tongues	knowledge	revelation
knowledge	knowledge	prophecy	tongues
faith		teaching	interpretation

Most of these charisms involve speech and knowledge. Since the context in chapter 14 is public worship, this focus on gifts of speech is understandable. The heterogeneous lists above clearly shows that the apostle does not intend to teach the relative value of spiritual gifts by the place they occupy on a list.

Ephesians 4:11: **apostles, prophets, evangelists, pastors, teachers**
In this letter Paul stresses the importance of the founding role played by the first

apostles and prophets in the church (Eph 2:20; 3:5). Evangelists then preach the gospel and bring others into the Christian community. Pastors and teachers provide ongoing nurture and guidance needed by the new converts and older believers as well. This list of "gifted individuals" (not charisms) seems to indicate a *chronological* order in the initial establishment of the church. There is no evidence that Paul considers teachers of least importance because he lists them last.

1 Peter 4:9-11: hospitality, prophecy, service

Hospitality without grumbling, speaking the very words of God and serving with the strength God provides are all spiritual gifts. The context and order of these charisms show no intent by Peter to assign value according to place. This sample illustrates his teaching that gifts should be used in love "to serve others, faithfully administering God's grace in its various forms" (4:10).

Conclusions

This overview shows that the lists of charisms are samples to illustrate their diversity, not to assign them value in a hierarchy according to rank. Paul's random pattern is consistent with his model of the body in which each member serves a meaningful function according to the needs of the community.

Every charism, as a manifestation of the Holy Spirit for the common good, is valuable as it strengthens the body in its own way. Attempts to rank a gift according to its place on the list usually show a subjective bias. For example, scholars who assign the least value to speaking in tongues because it appears last in 1 Corinthians 12 do not draw a similar conclusion about their own profession of teaching, which appears last in Ephesians 4.

Equally important is the recognition that these lists of spiritual gifts provide no basis for the frequently used categories of natural and supernatural, permanent and temporary, normal and abnormal. These unbiblical distinctions, derived largely from experience, should not be imposed on the text. For example, the normal-abnormal dichotomy involves a quantitative conclusion based on a statistical analysis of what *is,* not a qualitative biblical doctrine of what *ought to be.*

The charismatic renewal marks a widespread return to the New Testament model of the church, in which members of the body of Christ manifest the full range of charisms to empower its worship, service and witness.

Appendix E
Natural-Supernatural Distinctions

In our scientific age, how can we accept the biblical concept of miracle? Influential philosopher David Hume rejected the possibility of miracles, which he defined as supernatural activity that violates or interferes with the laws of nature. On the other hand, the Bible reports many miracles.

Most controversy over miracles and scientific laws arises from misunderstanding due to a failure to define terms. What is a biblical miracle? What is a scientific law? What do we mean by "supernatural" and "natural"?

The Biblical Worldview
The Bible reveals God as both Creator and Sustainer of the universe. "He has spoken to us by his Son . . . through whom he made the universe . . . sustaining all things by his powerful word" (Heb 1:2-3). "By him all things were created. . . . [I]n him all things hold together" (Col 1:16-17). According to the Bible, our universe depends for its entire existence—past, present and future—on the creative power of God.[1]

The biblical view of God as Creator includes what theologians call "providence," his continuing sustenance and renewal of the world. The prophet declares, "He who created the heavens and stretched them out, who spread out the earth, . . . gives breath to its people" (Is 42:5). The psalmist attributes to God's activity what we call "natural" events:

He makes grass grow for the cattle,
  and plants for man to cultivate. . . .
The lions roar for their prey
  and seek their food from God. . . .
When you take away their breath,
  they die and return to the dust.
When you send your Spirit,
  they are created,
  and you renew the face of the earth. (Ps 104:14, 21, 29-30)

The biblical writers do not portray an independent "nature," ticking away on its own like a giant clock. They see God active in all events—whether rain or resurrection or invading armies—as he constantly works in nature and history.

How, then, does God relate to the world of nature? Thomas Aquinas made a distinction between reason and faith, between "natural" and "supernatural." We start with reason, he said, to explain as much as possible about the physical world; then through faith we accept revealed doctrines of Scripture such as creation, the Trinity and the Incarnation. Aquinas believed that the regular order of nature has been instituted by God, who from time to time overrules it in a supernatural way.

Unfortunately, this distinction paved the way for a "God of the gaps" who is less and less needed as science explains more and more about the way the physical world works. In the popular mind, this model has demoted God from his initial position of founder and director of the organization to part-time employee and finally to occasional trouble-shooter when all else fails.

In Scripture, however, we see God acting through both recurring, predictable events and unique, unexpected events called "miracles," "signs" and "wonders." The contrast is not between "natural" and "supernatural" as defined by Hume, but between *recurring* and *miraculous*. A miracle is an extraordinary event produced by God at a specific time as a sign of his activity and purpose in human history.

Scientific Laws and Miracles

Strictly speaking, scientists do not discover "laws of nature." Rather, they observe patterns of forces which they attempt to explain in "scientific" laws or theories. Such fallible explanations—just one way of looking at nature—are subject to change or replacement. Our scientific laws and theories do not prescribe (legislate) what must happen; they simply describe (explain in mathematical terms) patterns of natural forces that *are* happening. At best they predict what probably will happen in similar circumstances. They certainly have no validity to pronounce what can or cannot happen under quite different circumstances through unknown forces.

According to the Bible, God does not break or suspend natural laws, "intervening" in a semi-independent order of nature; nor is he a "God of the gaps," working only in the cracks and crevices of the universe. In what we call "miracles" he is simply choosing to work in an unprecedented rather than in a customary way. If there is an almighty God, "Maker of heaven and earth," couldn't he have at his disposal forces as yet unknown, even to a scientific age? It is unreasonable to complain that a miracle breaks scientific laws, as if, like criminal and civil laws, scientific laws prohibit certain activities.

In the last analysis, the question of miracles is an issue for philosophy and history. As a unique, nonrecurring event, a miracle lies beyond the purview of science, which looks for patterns of *repeated* observable events.

Technically, a miracle can be called *"supra*natural," that is, *beyond* or *above* ordinary events of daily life. But it should not be called *super*natural, "occurring outside normal human experience or knowledge."

And dividing spiritual gifts into natural and supernatural categories is both unbiblical and counterproductive. For example, an unexpected, unexplainable healing through prayer—serving as a special sign of God's presence and power—is no more an act of God than his healing through medicine or surgery. Every spiritual gift, regardless of our assessment on this score, is a gracious empowerment by the Holy Spirit for the common good to be received with thanksgiving.

Signs and Wonders

The Gospel of Mark reports the promise of Jesus to his followers that they would perform signs such as driving out demons, speaking in tongues and healing the sick (16:17-18). The last half of this chapter (vv. 9-20) presents a major textual problem. It does not appear in several early texts but has been included in others. The summary style of these verses is different from the vividness of detail so characteristic of Mark. Although they were probably added to the abrupt ending of verse 8 by another writer, the content of these verses is in harmony with the teaching of the other Gospels and the New Testament letters.

Appendix F
Weapons of Spiritual Warfare

In Ephesians 6:10-18 Paul describes the nature of spiritual warfare: the Christians' formidable enemies and effective armor. We fight against rulers and authorities, "powers of this dark world and . . . spiritual forces of evil in the heavenly realms" (v. 12). For that conflict we are to "put on the full armor of God" (vv. 11, 13); twice mentioned, the armor is both complete and divine.

Spiritual warfare is described as defensive; four times Paul uses the word *stand,* calling us to take a posture that resists attack (vv. 11-14). This warfare is also offensive, through proclamation of the gospel and the word of God (vv. 15, 17). Following are comments on each part of the armor of God.[1]

Stand firm then, with the belt of truth buckled around your waist (v. 14). Roman soldiers wore leather belts to secure their tunics while marching and to carry their lethal short swords. A part of their underwear, the buckled belt gave a sense of support and confidence. Likewise for the Christian, who fights against the devil, the "father of lies" (Jn 8:44), truth is foundational. We must have both complete confidence in the reliability of Scripture and full personal integrity.

With the breastplate of righteousness in place (v. 14). This corset of leather or metal provided the major protection for a soldier's vital organs. For the Christian this second item is also one of character. It is the righteousness of Christ put to our account so that we can be justified by faith. And it is a matter of moral conduct, righteous living, as

Paul spells out in his second letter to Corinth: "in purity, understanding, patience and kindness; in the Holy Spirit and in sincere love; in truthful speech and in the power of God; with weapons of righteousness in the right hand and in the left" (2 Cor 6:6-7). *And with your feet fitted with the gospel of peace as a firm footing (v. 15, my translation).* Roman infantry wore a "half-boot" *(caliga)* of leather that left the toes free, had a heavy studded sole and was tied to the shin or ankle with a strap. This footwear equipped the soldier for a long march and a solid stance in battle. Paul may have had in mind another statement of Isaiah, "How beautiful on the mountains are the feet of those who bring good news, who proclaim peace, who bring good tidings, who proclaim salvation" (Is 52:7). The gospel of peace provides a firm footing for the Christian in God's forgiveness and promises. It is also good news of salvation to those who are still under Satan's power.

Take up the shield of faith, with which you can extinguish all the flaming arrows of the evil one (v. 16). The shield here is not the small round kind for hand-to-hand combat, but the long oblong one (2.5 by 4.5 feet) which covered the whole body. It was made of laminated wood, covered with leather and soaked in water to put out incendiary arrows that had been dipped in pitch. Faith in God's protection and guidance shields us from Satan's arrows of fear, anxiety, doubt, guilt and temptations of all kinds.

Take the helmet of salvation (v. 17). The Roman helmet was made of bronze or iron and lined with felt or sponge to make it bearable. Nothing short of a battle-ax could pierce such a helmet. In some cases a hinged visor was attached for frontal protection. *Salvation* is an umbrella word that covers all God's blessings for us in Christ—past, present and future. The helmet of salvation especially protects our minds, for which a battle is raging. Paul writes, "The weapons we fight with are not the weapons of the world. On the contrary, they have divine power to demolish strongholds. . . . And we take captive every thought to make it obedient to Christ" (2 Cor 10:4-5). Earlier in 2 Corinthians Paul declared, "So from now on we regard no one from a worldly point of view" (5:16).

And the sword of the Spirit, which is the word of God (v. 17). While most of the Romans' enemies fought with large, heavy swords that required room to swing, the Romans used a "short sword" (12-14 inches long). With a pinpoint tip that could cut in any direction, this sword was deadly in close quarters. Of the six pieces of armor, this is the only one designed for attack (cf. Heb 4:12). "The word of God" refers not only to all Scripture but also to a special word from God given by the Holy Spirit for a specific target.

Paul's instruction concludes in verse 18 with the importance of prayer, which he emphasizes by the use of the word *all* four times: "all occasions," "all times," "always" and "all the saints." The apostle then asks prayer for himself as he proclaims the gospel (vv. 19-20).

This passage shows that spiritual warfare is more proactive than reactive. It involves preparation before the storm, resistance to attack and taking the good news into enemy territory.

Appendix G
Renewal Organizations

General

North American Renewal Service
  Committee
Vinson Synan, Chairman
5601 NW 72nd Street, Suite 242
Oklahoma City, OK 73132

Denominational Groups
Assemblies of God

  Office of Information
  1445 Boonville Avenue
  Springfield, MO 65802

  Karl Strader
  Carpenter's Home Church
  P.O. Box 95020
  Lakeland, FL 33804

Baptist

American Baptist Charismatic
  Fellowship
Gary K. Clark
1386 N. Sierra Bonita
Pasadena, CA 91104

Southern Baptist Charismatic Renewal
Bishop Paul Morton
Full Gospel Baptist Church
5600 Read Blvd.
New Orleans, LA 70127

Brethren/Mennonite

Doug Fike
53395 Fox Chase Court
Bristol, IN 46507

Catholic

Canadian Catholic Charismatic
Fellowship
Fr. Eugene Raimbault
852 St. Mary's Road
St. Vital, Manitoba R2M 3P7
Canada

Evangelization 2000
Tom Curran
3045 North Street NE
Washington, DC 20017

Hispanic National Service Committee
Fr. Joseph Malagreca
218-26 106th Avenue
Queens Village, NY 11429

National Service Committee
Sr. Nancy Kellar
194 Gaylor Road
Scarsdale, NY 10583

Jim Murphy
P.O. Box 628
Locust Grove, VA 22508

Church of Christ (Restoration)

Don Finto
Belmont Church
P.O. Box 40325
Nashville, TN 37204

Church of God (Cleveland)

Office of Public Relations
Keith and 25th Streets
Cleveland, TN 37311

Church of God in Christ

Bishop Ithiel Clemmons
1001 E. Washington Street
Greensboro, NC 27401

Episcopal

Episcopal Renewal Ministries
Charles B. Fulton Jr.
1341 Terrell Mill Road
Marietta, GA 30060

Foursquare

Harold Helms
International Church of the
Foursquare Gospel
1100 Glendale Blvd.
Los Angeles, CA 90026

Lutheran

International Lutheran Renewal
Larry Christenson
South Route Box 58-A
Northome, MN 56661

Renewal In Missouri
Delbert Rossin
1727 Kaneville Road
Geneva, IL 60134

Pentecostal Church of God

James D. Gee
P.O. Box 850
Joplin, MO 64802

Pentecostal Holiness

Pentecostal Renewal Service
Committee
Bishop B. E. Underwood
P.O. Box 12607
Oklahoma City, OK 73157

Presbyterian and Reformed

Bradford Long
P.O. Box 429
Black Mountain, NC 28711

United Church of Christ

Focus Renewal Ministries
Vernon Stoop
P.O. Box 12
Sassamansville, PA 19472

United Methodist

United Methodist Renewal Services
Gary Moore
P.O. Box 120157
Nashville, TN 37214

Wesleyan Holiness

Wesleyan-Holiness Charismatic
Fellowship
Wilbur Jackson
P.O. Box 24008
Cincinnati, OH 45224

Nondenominational Groups

AIMS
Howard Foltz
P.O. Box 74534
Virginia Beach, VA 23464

Chaplaincy, Full Gospel Churches
E. H. Jim Ammerman
2721 Whitewood Drive
Dallas, TX 75233

Charisma Ministries
Stephen Strang
600 Rinehart Road
Lake Mary, FL 33804

Christian Believers United
Jim Jackson
P.O. Box 1000A
Montreat, NC 28757

Full Gospel Business Men's Fellowship
Jerry Jensen
3150 Bear Street
Costa Mesa, CA 92626

International Missions Services
Wick Nease
P.O. Box 4600
Tyler, TX 75712

Jews for Jesus
Bob Mendelsohn
P.O. Box 5594
Washington, DC 20016

Women's Aglow
Jane Hansen
P.O. Box 1
Lynnwood, WA 98046

Youth With A Mission
Leland Paris
P.O. Box 4600
Tyler, TX 75712

Appendix H
Major Religion Statistics

Major Religions in 1992[1]

World Religions

	(millions)
Christian	1,830
Muslim	990
Hindu	740
Buddhist	330
Jewish	20

Christians

	(millions)
Roman Catholic	990
Pentecostal/Charismatic	410
Evangelical	320
Orthodox	180
Anglican/Episcopalian	60

Protestants

Denominational Pentecostal	205
Baptist	55
Anglican/Episcopalian	55
Lutheran	50
Presbyterian	45
Methodist	30

Pentecostals/Charismatics

Pre-Pentecostal (Holiness)..10

Denominational Pentecostal...205

Chinese Pentecostal..60

Protestant Charismatic (mainline and independent).....................................60

    Active...24

    Postcharismatic[a]...36

Catholic Charismatic...80

    Active...13

    Postcharismatic[a]...67

Mainline Third-Wavers[b]...40

    World Total...410

Pentecostal/Charismatic Percent of Christians Worldwide..........................24

---

[a]This category includes those who no longer attend a regular charismatic activity such as a weekly prayer and praise service. Many of them, however, remain committed to charismatic renewal within other areas of church activity.
[b]Members of this group avoid the "Pentecostal" and "charismatic" labels but are committed to the teaching and practice of the full range of spiritual gifts.

Notes

Chapter 1: The Fireplace and the Fire

[1]John Randall, *In God's Providence: The Birth of a Catholic Charismatic Parish* (Locust Valley, N.Y.: Living Flame, 1973).

[2]Charles H. Troutman, "Speaking in Tongues," memorandum 22 to members of IVCF staff, April 2, 1963: "Over the years our policy has been deliberately to set aside as the non-essentials to our task such matters as the mode of baptism, the essential nature of the Lord's supper, and speaking in tongues. . . . If this is a movement of God for all His children—even though it may be abused—then we want to be part of it. If this is not a movement of God, we want to help those of our brethren who have become enmeshed. If there is a misplaced emphasis, we want to bring a balance. We must in no way hinder the Spirit of God from working in individuals as He wills" (pp. 1, 3).

[3]David B. Barrett, *World Christian Encyclopedia* (Oxford: Oxford University Press, 1982). Updated in a special survey, "Global Statistics of the Pentecostal/Charismatic Renewal," Tables for 1988, *Ministries Today* Annual Supplement, 1991, pp. 6-25. The worldwide figures here come from the annual update for 1992.

[4]John F. MacArthur Jr., *Charismatic Chaos* (Grand Rapids, Mich.: Zondervan, 1992).

Chapter 2: A Surprising Renewal

[1]Peter Hocken, *The Glory and the Shame* (Guilford, U.K.: Eagle, 1994).

[2]David B. Barrett, "Global Statistics of the Pentecostal/Charismatic Renewal," *Ministries Today* Annual Supplement, 1991, pp. 12-13 (table 2), updated to 1992.

[3]Edith Blumhofer, *The Assemblies of God: A Chapter in the Story of American Pentecostalism* (Springfield, Mo.: Gospel Publishing House, 1989); Edith Blumhofer, "Assemblies of God," in *Dictionary of Pentecostal and Charismatic Movements,* ed. Stanley M. Burgess and Gary B. McGee (Grand Rapids, Mich.: Zondervan, 1988), pp. 23-28.

[4]Donald W. Dayton, *Theological Roots of Pentecostalism* (Peabody, Mass.: Hendrick-

son, 1987). Walter J. Hollenweger, *The Pentecostals* (Minneapolis: Augsburg, 1972), pp. 63-65. Vinson Synan, *The Holiness-Pentecostal Movement in the United States* (Grand Rapids, Mich.: Eerdmans, 1971).

[5]C. M. Robeck Jr., "Azusa Street Revival," in *Dictionary of Pentecostal and Charismatic Movements,* ed. Stanley M. Burgess and Gary B. McGee (Grand Rapids, Mich.: Zondervan, 1988), pp. 31-36.

[6]C. M. Robeck Jr., "Pentecostal World Conference," in *Dictionary of Pentecostal and Charismatic Movements,* ed. Stanley M. Burgess and Gary B. McGee (Grand Rapids, Mich.: Zondervan, 1988), pp. 707-10.

[7]Dennis J. Bennett, *Nine O'Clock in the Morning* (Plainfield, N.J.: Logos International, 1970), pp. 66ff. Bennett also wrote the widely read and influential book *The Holy Spirit and You* (Plainfield, N.J.: Logos International, 1971).

[8]Barrett, "Global Statistics," pp. 12-13.

[9]Kevin and Dorothy Ranaghan, *Catholic Pentecostals* (New York: Paulist, 1969), pp. 21-23. In 1971 the Ranaghans edited *As the Spirit Leads Us* (New York: Paulist), in which the term *charismatic renewal* was used to describe this movement.

[10]Edward D. O'Connor, *The Pentecostal Movement in the Catholic Church* (Notre Dame, Ind.: Ave Maria Press, 1971), pp. 61ff.

[11]Barrett, "Global Statistics," pp. 12-13. Worldwide figure updated to 1992.

[12]Hocken, *The Glory and the Shame,* chap. 2, "The Surprises of the Holy Spirit." Barrett, however, has a different classification of this century's "charismatic" renewal in its broadest sense. He calls classic Pentecostalism the First Wave. The charismatic renewal in major denominations is the Second Wave, in which he includes Orthodox and Messianic Jewish participants and the growing number of independent churches. He also identifies a Third Wave, which he calls "mainstream"—evangelicals and others not identified with the first two waves but remaining in their non-Pentecostal denominations. I examine Barrett's terminology in chapter twelve, "The Vineyard Fellowship."

[13]Vinson Synan, *The Twentieth-Century Pentecostal Explosion* (Altamonte Springs, Fla.: Creation House, 1987), chap. 12, "The Orthodox Renewal."

[14]Hocken, *The Glory and the Shame,* chap. 2.

Chapter 3: The Promise of Pentecost

[1]See appendix A, "The Spirit in Luke/Acts." See also Charles E. Hummel, *Fire in the Fireplace: Contemporary Charismatic Renewal* (Downers Grove, Ill.: InterVarsity Press, 1978), chap. 6, "Christ and the Spirit."

[2]The Greek preposition *en* can be translated either "in" or "with." Most modern versions translate the *en pneumati* of John's promise as "with the Spirit." In the charismatic renewal the phrase *baptism in the Spirit* is common and will be used in following chapters dealing with current issues.

[3]James D. G. Dunn, *Baptism in the Holy Spirit* (London: SCM Press, 1970). At each stage Jesus enters a new relationship with the Spirit: "First, when his human life was the creation of the Spirit (Lk 1:35); second, when he was anointed with the Spirit and thus became the Anointed One, the unique Man of the Spirit (Lk 3:22; 4:18); third,

when he received the promise of the Spirit at his exaltation and poured the Spirit forth on his disciples, thus becoming Lord of the Spirit" (p. 41).

[4]J. B. Job, "Pentecost, Feast of," in *The New Bible Dictionary,* ed. J. D. Douglas (Grand Rapids, Mich.: Eerdmans, 1979), p. 964. This holy convocation, a day of joy, was also called the "feast of weeks" (Ex 34:22; Deut 16:10), the "feast of harvest" (Ex 23:16) and the "day of firstfruits" (Num 28:26). It was also a reminder of Israel's deliverance from Egypt.

[5]William F. Arndt and F. Wilbur Gingrich, *A Greek-English Lexicon of the New Testament* (Chicago: University of Chicago Press, 1959), p. 31: "Acts 2:4 may mean either *speak with different* (even other than their own) *tongues* or *speak in foreign languages.*"

[6]The apostle Paul would be among the first to recognize that a word can have more than one meaning. In a single letter to the Romans he uses the word *sarx* ("flesh") to mean four different things: "human nature" (1:3); "body" (2:28); "person" (3:20); "sinful nature" (7:5). And in 2 Corinthians 5:16 *flesh* has a fifth meaning of "worldly point of view." Paul would hardly have appreciated another author's redefining his key terms for meanings contrary to his intent. This error is often made in cross-reference studies that lift a word or phrase out of its varied contexts and assigns the same meaning to all occurrences.

[7]Roger Stronstad, *The Charismatic Theology of St. Luke* (Peabody, Mass.: Hendrickson, 1984), p. 37: "Luke's use of the aorist indicative for seven of the nine references confirms the potentially repetitive character of being filled with the Spirit. . . . This contrasts with the ingressive aorist which would give the meaning '*became* filled with the Holy Spirit.'"

[8]The didactic-descriptive distinction is designed to guard against the practice of making every example in Scripture a model for Christian conduct today. However, the complex problem of applying the Bible to modern life is not solved by this simplistic either/or. For example, most of the "didactic teaching" (explicit commands) for Israel in the Pentateuch—dozens of pages of regulations—do not apply to the church.

[9]Gary B. McGee, ed., *Initial Evidence* (Peabody, Mass.: Hendrickson, 1991). The most complete and scholarly treatment to date of glossolalia as "initial evidence" of baptism in the Holy Spirit. A diverse collection of articles on the central issue of Pentecostalism.

[10]Clark Pinnock, "The New Pentecostalism: Reflections of an Observer," in *Perspectives on the New Pentecostalism,* ed. Russell Spittler (Grand Rapids, Mich.: Baker Book House, 1976), p. 186: "This later experience, or experiences, should not be tied in with the tight 'second blessing' schema."

[11]Henry Lederle, *Treasures Old and New: Interpretations of "Spirit-Baptism" in the Charismatic Renewal Movement* (Peabody, Mass.: Hendrickson, 1988), p. 227. See appendix B.

Chapter 4: Gifts of the Spirit
[1]David Prior, *The Message of 1 Corinthians,* The Bible Speaks Today Series (Downers Grove, Ill.: InterVarsity Press, 1985), p. 211.

[2]The phrase *we were all given the one Spirit to drink* is simply another way of saying that the Corinthians were united with the Spirit in the body of Christ. Making it refer to a subsequent experience imports a meaning foreign to the context of Paul's teaching about the beginning of their Christian life.

[3]The contrast between "natural" and "supernatural" is an unbiblical dichotomy. It assumes an autonomous universe, running on its own according to "natural laws," in which God occasionally "intervenes" with his miracles. The Bible reveals a Creator who not only brought the universe into existence but also continually upholds it (Gen 1; Ps 104; Heb 1). The biblical contrast is between recurring events, which are predictable, and miracles, which are unpredictable—all the work of God. See appendix E, "Natural-Supernatural Distinctions."

[4]James D. G. Dunn, *Jesus and the Spirit* (London: SCM Press, 1975), p. 221.

[5]I. Howard Marshall, "Apostle," in *New Dictionary of Theology,* ed. Sinclair B. Ferguson, David F. Wright and J. I. Packer (Downers Grove, Ill.: InterVarsity Press, 1988), p. 40.

[6]Arnold Bittlinger, *Gifts and Ministries* (Grand Rapids, Mich.: Eerdmans, 1973), pp. 18, 24.

[7]F. F. Bruce, *The Epistle to the Romans* (London: Pickering & Inglis, 1961), p. 111.

Chapter 5: Where Have All the Charisms Gone?

[1]Merrill F. Unger, *The Baptism and Gifts of the Holy Spirit* (Chicago: Moody Press, 1974), p. 143.

[2]Justin Martyr, quoted in Ronald A. N. Kydd, *Charismatic Gifts in the Early Church* (Peabody, Mass.: Hendrickson, 1984), p. 26. In *Christian Initiation and Baptism in the Holy Spirit: Evidence from the First Eight Centuries* (Collegeville, Minn.: Liturgical Press, 1991), pp. 83-315, Kilian McDonnell and George T. Montague provide evidence in the postapostolic age of an expectation that charisms will be manifested, and of actual manifestations.

[3]Irenaeus, quoted in Kydd, *Charismatic Gifts,* p. 44.

[4]Kydd, *Charismatic Gifts,* p. 4.

[5]Tertullian, *Martyrdom of St. Perpetuae,* quoted in Kydd, *Charismatic Gifts,* p. 68.

[6]Novatian, *Concerning the Trinity,* quoted in Kydd, *Charismatic Gifts,* p. 61.

[7]Hilary of Poitiers *On the Trinity* 2. 34. NPF 2nd series 9. 61.

[8]Augustine of Hippo *The City of God* 12. 8.

[9]Athanasios F. S. Emmert, "Charismatic Developments in the Eastern Orthodox Church," in *Perspectives on the New Pentecostalism,* ed. Russell P. Spittler (Grand Rapids, Mich.: Baker Book House, 1976), p. 40.

[10]John Calvin, *The Institutes of the Christian Religion,* trans. F. L. Battles (Philadelphia: Westminster Press, 1960), p. 1467.

[11]John Wesley, quoted in Michael Harper, *As at the Beginning* (Plainfield, N.J.: Logos International, 1971), pp. 17-18.

[12]Charles Hodge, *Commentary on the First Epistle to the Corinthians* (Grand Rapids, Mich.: Eerdmans, 1950), pp. 262ff.

[13]Charles E. Hummel, *The Galileo Connection: Resolving Conflicts Between Science*

and the Bible (Downers Grove, Ill.: InterVarsity Press, 1986), pp. 192-94.
[14]Hendrikus Berkhof, *The Doctrine of the Holy Spirit* (Richmond, Va.: John Knox, 1967), p. 89.
[15]David B. Guralnik, ed., *Webster's New World Dictionary* (New York: World Publishing, 1978), p. 316.
[16]Arnold Bittlinger, *Gifts and Ministries* (Grand Rapids, Mich.: Eerdmans, 1973), p. 18. Bittlinger explores the relationship between charisms and the ministries of Ephesians 4:11.
[17]*Spiritual Gifts and Church Growth* (Pasadena, Calif.: Fuller Evangelistic Association, Department of Church Growth, 1978).

Chapter 6: "They Will Prophesy"
[1]Lee Grady, "Resolving the Kansas City Prophecy Controversy," *Ministries Today,* September-October 1990.
[2]Paul Boyer, *When Time Shall Be No More: Prophecy Belief in Modern American Culture* (Cambridge, Mass.: Harvard University Press, 1992). Boyer gives a historical perspective of prophetic writings and an analysis of current scenerios, showing which scenarios are updated versions of ancient ones.
[3]Graham Houston, *Prophecy: A Gift for Today* (Downers Grove, Ill.: InterVarsity Press, 1989), p. 35.
[4]Wayne Grudem, *The Gift of Prophecy in the New Testament and Today* (Westchester, Ill.: Crossway Books, 1988).
[5]Mark 3:14. The phrase *designating them apostles* is omitted in some MSS.
[6]Grudem, *Gift of Prophecy,* pp. 63-64.
[7]Ibid., pp. 57-63. *Hendiadys* is a figure of speech in which two words are connected by *and* to express a single concept. For example, in everyday language we use the phrase *wife and mother* for a wife who is also a mother (Houston, *Prophecy,* p. 79).
[8]Donald Bridge, *Signs and Wonders Today* (Downers Grove, Ill.: InterVarsity Press, 1985), p. 204.
[9]David Prior, *The Message of 1 Corinthians,* The Bible Speaks Today Series (Downers Grove, Ill.: InterVarsity Press, 1985), p. 251.
[10]George Mallone, *Those Controversial Gifts* (Downers Grove, Ill.: InterVarsity Press, 1983), pp. 39-40.
[11]Grady, "Resolving," p. 50.
[12]Grudem, *Gift of Prophecy,* pp. 116-17, 135-48.
[13]Lindsey's *The Late Great Planet Earth* is reported to have sold thirty million copies in about thirty languages. In *The 1980s Countdown to Armageddon* (New York: Doubleday/Bantam, 1983), Lindsey selects passages of Scripture to form a pattern similar to current events in order to predict an end-times schedule. His interpretation is based on faulty exegesis and misuse of biblical prophecy.
[14]John F. MacArthur Jr., introduction to *Charismatic Chaos* (Grand Rapids, Mich.: Zondervan, 1992). MacArthur quotes admittedly grotesque illustrations from his earlier work *The Charismatics: A Doctrinal Perspective* (Grand Rapids, Mich.: Zondervan, 1978). "On television I saw a lady tell about how her flat tire was healed. . . .

a wonderful testimony by a woman who had her dog praise the Lord in an unknown bark." With tabloid tactics he reports these and many other bizarre events, charging that "in the Charismatic ranks no experience has to stand the test of Scripture" (*Charismatic Chaos,* p. 15).

[15]Wayne Grudem, "Why Christians Can Still Prophesy," *Christianity Today,* September 16, 1988, p. 35.

Chapter 7: Speaking in Tongues

[1]In 1 Corinthians 14:21 Paul has a condensed quotation of Isaiah 28:11-12. This difficult passage has given rise to several different interpretations, depending on an understanding of two key words: *sign* and *tongues* (see Charles E. Hummel, *Fire in the Fireplace: Contemporary Charismatic Renewal* [Downers Grove, Ill.: InterVarsity Press, 1978], pp. 152-53). When Israel was disobedient to the prophets who spoke in their own language, God sent invading Assyrians whose language they could not understand. The lesson is that unbelievers will be given unintelligible teachers as a sign of God's active presence.

[2]William F. Arndt and F. Wilbur Gingrich, *A Greek-English Lexicon of the New Testament* (Chicago: University of Chicago Press, 1959), p. 161.

[3]David B. Guralnik, ed., *Webster's New World Dictionary* (New York: World Publishing, 1978), p. 237.

[4]This translation is more accurate than the NIV. H. E. Dana and Julius Mantey, *A Manual Grammar of the Greek New Testament* (New York: Macmillan, 1955). "A prohibition in the present imperative demands that action then in process be stopped" (p. 301). The common subjective assertion that here Paul gives grudging assent to the use of tongues is unsupported by the text.

[5]Arndt and Gingrich, *A Greek-English Lexicon,* p. 29.

[6]Morton T. Kelsey, *Tongue Speaking* (Garden City, N.Y.: Doubleday, 1964), pp. 34ff.

[7]Irenaeus *Against Heresies* 5. 6. 1.

[8]Tertullian, quoted in Kelsey, *Tongue Speaking,* pp. 37-38.

[9]Cyril of Jerusalem *Catechetical Lectures* 16. 12, 17. 37, quoted in Michael Green, *I Believe in the Holy Spirit* (Grand Rapids, Mich.: Eerdmans, 1975), p. 172.

[10]Philip Weller, trans. and ed., *The Roman Ritual* (Milwaukee: Bruce, 1952), 2:169.

[11]Ronald A. Knox, *Enthusiasm: A Chapter in the History of Religion* (Oxford, U.K.: Clarendon, 1950), p. 551. Nevertheless, the Roman Catholic Church honored tongue-speaking as an evidence of piety in canonizing several illustrious people. See Stanley M. Burgess, "Medieval Examples of Charismatic Piety in the Roman Catholic Church," in *Perspectives on the New Pentecostalism,* ed. Russell P. Spittler (Grand Rapids, Mich.: Baker Book House, 1976), pp. 15-26.

[12]Bruce Yokum, *Prophecy* (Ann Arbor, Mich.: Word of Life, 1976), pp. 22ff.

[13]*The Interpreter's Bible* (New York: Abingdon, 1953), 10:155.

[14]Ibid., p. 155.

[15]Eddie Ensley, *Sounds of Wonder* (New York: Paulist, 1977). Ensley describes the different types of jubilation in church history. "The tradition of jubilation and other forms of expressive prayer gives a new conceptual framework for understanding glos-

298 FIRE IN THE FIREPLACE

solalia. . . . A profound identity between New Testament, traditional and present day
glossolalia emerges. All three are wordless vocalized entrance into the mystery of
God's love" (pp. 125, 119). See Paul Hinnebusch, *Praise: A Way of Life* (Ann Arbor,
Mich.: Word of Life, 1976).
[16]Russell P. Spittler, "Glossolalia," in *Dictionary of Pentecostal and Charismatic Movements,* ed. Stanley M. Burgess and Gary B. McGee (Grand Rapids, Mich.: Zondervan,
1988), pp. 33-41, gives an account of non-Christian varieties, biblical data, historical
survey and varied explanations.

Chapter 8: Biblical Health and Wholeness
[1]Douglas R. Groothuis, *Unmasking the New Age* (Downers Grove, Ill.: InterVarsity
Press, 1986), chap. 3, "Holistic Health."
[2]James F. Jekel, "A Biblical Basis for Whole-Person Care: Theoretical and Practical
Models in Health and Healing," in *Whole-Person Medicine: An International
Symposium,* ed. David E. Allen, Lewis P. Bird and Robert Herrmann (Downers
Grove, Ill.: InterVarsity Press, 1980), pp. 121-51. The term *whole-person care* in a
Christian context should not be confused with secular and New Age "holistic health"
concepts.
[3]William F. Arndt and F. Wilbur Gingrich, *A Greek-English Lexicon of the New
Testament* (Chicago: University of Chicago Press, 1959), pp. 805-6.
[4]Morton T. Kelsey, *Healing and Christianity* (New York: Harper & Row, 1973), chap.
5, "What, How and Why Did Jesus Heal?"
[5]Evelyn Frost, *Christian Healing* (London: A. R. Mowbray, 1949), pp. 64-70. Frost
gathered writings from the period A.D. 100-250 which show a continuation of the
healing practices described in the New Testament.
[6]Kelsey, *Healing and Christianity,* pp. 150-51, 184ff. This comprehensive history traces
the record from biblical times until the present.
[7]Origen *Against Celsus* 1. 46, 67, quoted in Kelsey, *Healing and Christianity,* p. 136.
[8]Cyprian *Epistle* 6. 1, 4.
[9]Gregory of Nyssa *On the Making of Man* 25. 6ff., quoted in Kelsey, *Healing and
Christianity,* p. 174.
[10]Augustine of Hippo *The City of God* 12. 8.
[11]A. J. Gordon, *The Ministry of Healing,* 2nd ed. (Harrisburg, Penn.: Christian Publications, 1961), p. 206.
[12]A. B. Simpson, *The Gospel of Healing* (Harrisburg, Penn.: Christian Publications,
1915).
[13]Andrew Murray, *Divine Healing* (Plainfield, N.J.: Logos International, 1974), p. 2.
[14]Donald W. Dayton, *Theological Roots of Pentecostalism* (Peabody, Mass.: Hendrickson, 1987), chap. 5, "The Rise of the Divine Healing Movement."
[15]David Edwin Harrell Jr., *All Things Are Possible: The Healing & Charismatic Revivals in Modern America* (Bloomington: Indiana University Press, 1975). Section 2,
"The Healing Revival, 1947-1958," offers a scholarly analysis of the rise and decline
of the independent healing movement.
[16]P. G. Chappell, "Healing Movements," in *Dictionary of Pentecostal and Charismatic*

Movements, ed. Stanley M. Burgess and Gary B. McGee (Grand Rapids, Mich.: Zondervan, 1988), pp. 353-72.

Chapter 9: Healing of Persons
[1]Emily Gardiner Neal, *The Healing Power of Christ* (New York: Hawthorne, 1972), p. 24. This is an excellent autobiographical account of a pioneer healing ministry within the context of the local church. Note chap. 17, "The Body of Christ."
[2]Francis MacNutt, *The Power to Heal* (Notre Dame, Inc.: Ave Maria Press, 1977), pp. 27-33. In the chapter "Degrees of Improvement" MacNutt observes several levels of improvement short of complete healing: cessation of pain, removal of side effects of treatment, stabilization of sickness, return of physical function without healing of the illness, degrees of bodily healing (pp. 57-62). Since writing this book Father MacNutt has left the Roman Catholic Church but continues his ministry through the Institute of Christian Healing.
[3]Neal, *Healing Power,* chap. 5, "Delayed Healings." She recounts a brief two-stage healing of blindness similar to the event in Mark 8:22-25. She also describes the gradual healing of her back during several years of sharp pain that often abated just enough for her to lead a healing service.
[4]Francis MacNutt, *Healing* (Notre Dame, Ind.: Ave Maria Press, 1974), pp. 161-68. MacNutt identifies the type of prayer for (a) spiritual sickness due to sin—prayer for repentance; (b) emotional sickness from past hurts—prayer for inner healing; (c) physical illness from disease or accident—prayer for physical healing; (d) problems caused by demonic oppression—prayer for deliverance (exorcism).
[5]Don H. Gross, *The Case for Spiritual Healing* (New York: Thomas Nelson & Sons, 1958), pp. 208-9.
[6]This verse states that the servant of the Lord would be "pierced for our transgressions . . . crushed for our iniquities" and that "by his wounds we are healed." For a discussion of this prophecy see chapter thirteen.
[7]Roy Lawrence, *Christian Healing Rediscovered* (Downers Grove, Ill.: InterVarsity Press, 1980), p. 122.
[8]Peter May, "Focusing on the Eternal," in *Signs, Wonders and Healing,* ed. John Goldingay (Leicester, U.K.: Inter-Varsity Press, 1989), pp. 27-45. This book comprises an informative set of papers and responses dealing with issues involving health, healing, suffering, miracles and church life.
[9]Some liberal theologians argue that since the apostle Paul did not refer to the virgin birth of Jesus, he did not believe in it. But his silence could have been due to other reasons: like Mark and John, Paul does not comment on Jesus' infancy; also, the virgin birth was so widely accepted that there was no need to mention it. An argument from silence can be made to support almost any idea that an interpreter desires to get from a passage.
[10]Robert Young, *Analytical Concordance to the Bible* (Grand Rapids, Mich.: Eerdmans, 1951), p. 945. See my chapter twelve for further comment on suffering in the New Testament.
[11]Henri Nouwen, *The Wounded Healer* (San Francisco: Harper & Row, 1985), p. 27.

[12]Mark A. Pearson, *Christian Healing* (Old Tappan, N.J.: Chosen Books, 1990), chap. 11, "How to Introduce a Healing Ministry into Your Church." Canon Pearson covers major aspects of healing in this helpful manual based on years of healing ministry within the Episcopal Church. Also see Ken Blue, *Authority to Heal* (Downers Grove, Ill.: InterVarsity Press, 1987). In part 3, "Beginning a Healing Ministry," Blue presents principles and practice of healing in the context of kingdom conflict on the basis of his experience as a pastor of a large Vineyard fellowship.

Chapter 10: Inner Healing

[1]David A. Seamands, *Healing for Damaged Emotions* (Wheaton, Ill.: Victor Books, 1983), chap. 1, "Damaged Emotions."

[2]Each dimension of the person—mind, will and emotion—has its own kind of "roadblock to faith" which obstructs effective reception of the Christian message. Many today have an *intellectual* problem of doubting the historical reliability of the biblical records. They first need the kind of assurance given by classics scholar F. F. Bruce in *The New Testament Documents: Are They Reliable?* 5th rev. ed. (Downers Grove, Ill.: InterVarsity Press, 1960). Others have a *volitional* block to understanding the message—an unwillingness to obey the Lord. They need to hear the word of Christ: "If anyone chooses to do God's will, he will find out whether my teaching comes from God" (Jn 7:17). Some have an *emotional* block—a distorted view of the heavenly Father sometimes based on unhealed hurts of an abusive earthly father. They need a repair of those damaged feelings. Some have all three. In each case the most articulate and persuasive presentation of the biblical message does not achieve effective reception until the critical roadblock is removed.

[3]Mark A. Pearson, *Why Can't I Be Me?* (Tarrytown, N.Y.: Chosen Books, 1992). Pearson defines and illustrates the wounded personality and its healing. He draws on Myers-Briggs categories to enhance the appreciation and use of the rich diversity of personality in the body of Christ. Pearson founded the Institute For Christian Renewal to strengthen churches in this dimension of their activities.

[4]Agnes Sanford, *Behold Your God* (Saint Paul, Minn.: Macalester Park, 1958). Her first book, *The Healing Light,* became a bestseller in 1947. Subsequent books were *The Healing Gifts of the Spirit* (1966), *The Healing Power of the Bible* (1969) and her autobiography, *Sealed Orders* (1972).

[5]David A. Seamands, *Healing of Memories* (Wheaton, Ill.: Victor Books, 1985), chap. 6, "Indications for the Healing of Memories." This is a comprehensive manual, based on many years of healing ministry, that presents biblical principles, practice and problems. It includes a selected bibliography of a dozen useful books, pp. 126-27.

[6]Pearson, *Christian Healing,* chap. 10, "Ministering Healing Using Spiritual Gifts." This book covers the biblical basis and practice of healing and how to train a healing team and introduce this ministry into a church; it includes a list of healings recorded in Scripture.

[7]Seamands, *Healing of Damaged Emotions,* p. 68.

[8]Douglas R. Groothuis, *Unmasking the New Age* (Downers Grove, Ill.: InterVarsity

Press, 1986), chap. 1, "The One for All."

9David E. Allen, Lewis P. Bird and Robert Herrmann, eds., *Whole-Person Medicine: An International Symposium* (Downers Grove, Ill.: InterVarsity Press, 1980).

10Dave Hunt and T. A. McMahon, *The Seduction of Christianity* (Eugene, Ore.: Harvest House, 1985), chap. 7, "Sorcery, Scientism and Christianity." Hunt is a widely known writer and lecturer on cults, the New Age movement and prophecy.

11Ibid., p. 23.

12Ibid., p. 9.

13Ibid., pp. 127-28. Most of the 450 footnoted quotations are selected phrases or brief paragraphs quoted without their original contexts. The sheer number of references is not a sure sign of good scholarship. The book's style, with its purple prose of alarm and denunciation, is more tabloid than treatise.

14Although some of Agnes Sanford's early speculations about how inner healing takes place and her terminology which was later adopted by the New Age are questionable, her ministry was biblical. Like the early Pentecostals, she was not a theologian but a practitioner whose writings were not designed to contribute to or withstand scholarly debate.

15Hunt and McMahon, *Seduction of Christianity,* pp. 183-84.

Chapter 11: Spiritual Warfare

1George Eldon Ladd, *A Theology of the New Testament* (Grand Rapids, Mich.: Eerdmans, 1974), p. 51.

2William F. Arndt and F. Wilbur Gingrich, *A Greek-English Lexicon of the New Testament* (Chicago: University of Chicago Press, 1959), pp. 113, 277-78.

3Ibid., pp. 206-7.

4Clinton E. Arnold, *Powers of Darkness: Principalities and Powers in Paul's Letters* (Downers Grove, Ill.: InterVarsity Press, 1992), p. 91.

5John Wimber with Kevin Springer, *Power Healing* (San Francisco: Harper & Row, 1987), p. 109. See also Fred Dickason, *Demon Possession and the Christian* (Chicago: Moody Press, 1987), p. 130.

6Arnold, *Powers of Darkness,* p. 128.

7Thomas B. White, *The Believer's Guide to Spiritual Warfare* (Ann Arbor, Mich.: Servant, 1990), pp. 42-43.

8Russ Parker, *Battling the Occult* (Downers Grove, Ill.: InterVarsity Press, 1990), pp. 71-72.

9George Mallone, *Arming for Spiritual Warfare* (Downers Grove, Ill.: InterVarsity Press, 1991), p. 37.

10Arndt and Gingrich, *Greek-English Lexicon,* p. 184.

11David Prior, *The Message of 1 Corinthians,* The Bible Speaks Today Series (Downers Grove, Ill.: InterVarsity Press, 1985), p. 208.

12Michael Scanlon and Randall J. Cirner, *Deliverance from Evil Spirits* (Ann Arbor, Mich.: Servant, 1980), p. 65. See also Matthew Linn and Dennis Linn, *Deliverance Prayer* (New York: Paulist, 1981).

13Timothy M. Warner, *Spiritual Warfare: Victory over the Powers of this Dark World*

(Wheaton, Ill.: Crossway Books, 1991), p. 66.
[14]Ibid., p. 36.
[15]Ibid., p. 125.
[16]Neil T. Anderson, *The Bondage Breaker* (Eugene, Ore.: Harvest House, 1990), p. 25.
[17]Ibid., pp. 22-23.
[18]Ibid., p. 209.
[19]C. Peter Wagner, preface to *Engaging the Enemy: How to Fight and Defeat Territorial Spirits* (Ventura, Calif.: Regal Books, 1991), p. viii.
[20]Vernon J. Sterk, "Territorial Spirits and Evangelization in Hostile Environments," in *Engaging the Enemy: How to Fight and Defeat Territorial Spirits,* ed. C. Peter Wagner (Ventura, Calif.: Regal Books, 1991), pp. 151-54. In the same volume see also Jacob Loewen, "Which God Do Missionaries Preach?" pp. 171-74.
[21]Clinton E. Arnold, *Ephesians: Power and Magic* (Cambridge, U.K.: Cambridge University Press, 1987), p. 27: "Few NT scholars have referred to the Artemis cult as relevant to the background of Ephesians, much less as relevant to the teaching on the hostile 'powers.' "
[22]C. Peter Wagner, *Warfare Prayer* (Ventura, Calif.: Regal Books, 1992). A biblical basis for this warfare is presented in chap. 5, "Territoriality Then and Now."
[23]Warner, *Spiritual Warfare,* p. 137.
[24]John Wimber and Kevin Springer, *Power Points* (San Francisco, Calif.: Harper, 1991), pp. 182-87. These authors outline four steps in fighting the battle against evil spirits (pp. 181-82). See also *Equipping the Saints* 7 (Winter 1993).

Chapter 12: The Vineyard Fellowship

[1]John Wimber with Kevin Springer, introduction to *Power Evangelism* (San Francisco: Harper & Row, 1986).
[2]C. Peter Wagner, "A Third Wave?" *Pastoral Renewal* 8 (July-August 1983).
[3]C. Peter Wagner, "The Third Wave," *Christian Life,* September 1984.
[4]C. Peter Wagner, *Look Out! The Pentecostals Are Coming* (Carol Stream, Ill.: Creation House, 1973).
[5]Donald Gee, *Concerning Spiritual Gifts* (Springfield, Mo.: Gospel Publishing House, 1972). Morton Kelsey, *Healing and Christianity* (New York: Harper & Row, 1976).
[6]Wimber and Springer, *Power Evangelism,* pp. 46, 51.
[7]John Wimber with Kevin Springer, *Power Evangelism,* rev. ed. with study guide (San Francisco: Harper & Row, 1993).
[8]George Eldon Ladd, *Jesus and the Kingdom* (New York: Harper & Row, 1964). Wimber's summary appears in *Power Evangelism.*
[9]John Wimber with Kevin Springer, *Power Healing* (San Francisco: Harper & Row, 1987).
[10]Ibid., pp. 101-2.
[11]Ibid., pp. 154-55.
[12]Ibid., appendixes C, D, E, pp. 244-47.
[13]John Wimber with Kevin Springer, *Power Points* (San Francisco: Harper & Row,

1991). This practical guide has sections on the dynamics of spiritual growth, hearing God's voice, believing God's word, seeking the Father, submitting to Christ, taking up the cross, depending on the Holy Spirit and fulfilling the Great Commission.

[14] *Christian Life* 44 (October 1982). C. Peter Wagner, *Signs and Wonders Today: Fuller Theological Seminary's Remarkable Course on Spiritual Power* (Altamonte Springs, Fla.: Creation House, 1987).

[15] Lewis B. Smedes, ed., *Ministry and the Miraculous,* foreword by David Allan Hubbard (Pasadena, Calif.: Fuller Theological Seminary, 1987).

[16] C. Peter Wagner, *The Third Wave of the Holy Spirit: Encountering the Power of Signs and Wonders* (Ann Arbor, Mich.: Servant, 1988).

[17] Smedes, *Ministry and the Miraculous,* p. 17.

[18] James W. Sire, *The Universe Next Door* (Downers Grove, Ill.: InterVarsity Press, 1976), p. 17. Charles H. Kraft, *Christianity with Power: Your Worldview and Your Experience of the Supernatural* (Ann Arbor, Mich.: Vine Books, 1989).

[19] Wimber and Springer, *Power Evangelism,* rev. ed. See chap. 18, "In the Eye of the Beholder," and chap. 20, "How Do We See the World?"

[20] Smedes, *Ministry and the Miraculous,* pp. 27-28.

[21] Kevin Springer, ed., *Power Encounters* (San Francisco: Harper & Row, 1988), pp. 43-56.

[22] John Wimber, "Introducing Prophetic Ministry," *Equipping the Saints,* Fall 1989, pp. 4-6, 30. (In 1992 Paul Cain, no longer in Kansas City, declared, "The charismatic renewal is now over, but God is going to move again and speak again, even to the very ones who rejected Him in the last movement. . . . Over a million Baptists are about to be endued with this power." See "The Post Charismatic Era," *The Morning Star: Prophetic Bulletin,* September 1, 1992, pp. 1-2.

[23] John Wimber, "Why I Respond to Criticism," Vineyard Position Paper 1, May 1992. Jack Deere, "The Vineyard's Response to 'The Briefing,' " Vineyard Position Paper 2, May 1992. Wayne Grudem, "The Vineyard's Response to 'The Standard,' " Vineyard Position Paper 3, June 1992. Michael Scott Horton, ed., *Power Religion* (Chicago: Moody Press, 1992). Many factual errors and misrepresentations in several chapters are corrected by Wayne Grudem, "Power and Truth: A Response to the Critiques of Vineyard Teaching and Practice by D. A. Carson, James Montgomery Boice, and John H. Armstrong," Vineyard Position Paper 4, March 1993.

[24] Ralph W. Neighbour Jr., *Where Do We Go from Here?* (Houston: Touch, 1990).

[25] Wimber and Springer, *Power Evangelism,* p. 122.

[26] Peter Hocken, *EPTA Bulletin* 7, no. 3 (1988): 104-7.

[27] David B. Barrett, "Global Statistics of the Pentecostal/Charismatic Renewal," *Ministries Today* Annual Supplement, 1991, p. 23.

[28] Ibid., p. 21.

[29] Ibid., p. 6.

[30] Thomas D. Pratt, "The Need to Dialogue: A Review of the Debate on the Controversy of Signs, Wonders, Miracles and Spiritual Warfare Raised in the Literature of the Third Wave Movement," *Pneuma: The Journal of the Society for Pentecostal Studies* 13 (Spring 1991): 7-32.

Chapter 13: The Prosperity Gospel

[1]Bruce Barron, *The Health and Wealth Gospel* (Downers Grove, Ill.: InterVarsity Press, 1987), pp. 5-6. Chap. 3, "The Roots of the Health and Wealth Gospel," sketches key antecedents of the Faith Movement.

[2]Brief but useful biographies of these men can be found in Daniel G. Reid et al., eds., *Dictionary of Christianity in America* (Downers Grove, Ill.: InterVarsity Press, 1990), pp. 487, 1087, 365.

[3]See ibid., pp. 865, 1078.

[4]Ibid., p. 611.

[5]D. R. McConnell, *A Different Gospel* (Peabody, Mass.: Hendrickson, 1988), pp. 39-41.

[6]Ibid., under the chapter titled "The Role of Kenneth Hagin in the Faith Movement."

[7]Ibid., pp. 6-12. From eight of Hagin's books McConnell has discovered five pages of material taken from Kenyon's writings.

[8]E. W. Kenyon, *The Two Kinds of Knowledge* (Seattle: Kenyon's Gospel Publishing Society, 1942), p. 34. McConnell presents many quotations of Kenyon's views documented in forty-two of Hagin's publications.

[9]Kenneth Hagin, *Right and Wrong Thinking* (Tulsa, Okla.: Faith Library, 1966), p. 27.

[10]E. W. Kenyon, *The Hidden Man: An Unveiling of the Subconscious Mind* (Seattle: Kenyon's Gospel Publishing Society, 1970), p. 158.

[11]Kenneth Hagin, "The Resurrection," *Word of Faith,* April 1977, p. 6.

[12]Robert Tilton, *God's Laws of Success* (Dallas: Word of Faith, 1983), pp. 170-72.

[13]E. W. Kenyon, *The Two Kinds of Faith: Faith's Secrets Revealed* (Seattle: Kenyon's Gospel Publishing Society, 1942), p. 20.

[14]Kenneth Hagin, *How to Write Your Own Ticket with God* (Tulsa, Okla.: Faith Library, 1979), pp. 5, 20-21, 32.

[15]E. W. Kenyon, *What Happened from the Cross to the Throne* (Seattle: Kenyon's Gospel Publishing Society, 1945), p. 47.

[16]Frederick K. C. Price, *Ever Increasing Faith Messenger Newsletter* (Crenshaw Christian Center, Inglewood, California), June 1980, p. 7.

[17]E. W. Kenyon, *Jesus the Healer* (Seattle: Kenyon's Gospel Publishing Society, 1943), p. 26.

[18]Frederick K. C. Price, *How Faith Works* (Tulsa, Okla.: Harrison House, 1976), pp. 92-93.

[19]E. W. Kenyon, *Advanced Bible Course: Studies in the Deeper Life* (Seattle: Kenyon's Gospel Publishing Society, 1970), p. 59.

[20]Kenneth Hagin, *Redeemed* (Tulsa, Okla.: Faith Library, 1966), p. 5.

[21]Gloria Copeland, *God's Will Is Prosperity* (Tulsa, Okla.: Harrison House, 1978), p. 54.

[22]Edwin M. Yamauchi, "Gnosticism," in *New Dictionary of Theology,* ed. Sinclair B. Ferguson and David F. Wright (Downers Grove, Ill.: InterVarsity Press, 1988), pp. 272-74.

[23]This appeal to so-called natural laws shows a misunderstanding of modern science,

which studies the forces of nature (such as electricity and gravity). It discovers regular patterns called "scientific laws"; these are mathematical explanations which are always subject to change. See Charles E. Hummel, *The Galileo Connection: Resolving Conflicts Between Science and the Bible* (Downers Grove, Ill.: InterVarsity Press, 1986), chap. 7, "Modern Science: A New Perspective."

[24]Barron, *Health and Wealth Gospel,* pp. 93-98.

[25]Robert Bellah et al., *Habits of the Heart: Individualism and Commitment in American Life* (Berkeley: University of California Press, 1985), pp. 124-27.

[26]Susanne Heine, quoted by Donald Bloesch in a review of *Matriarchs, Goddesses and the Image of God,* in *Christianity Today,* October 8, 1990, p. 76.

Chapter 14: Charismatic Renewal Today

[1]Peter D. Hocken, "Baptism in the Spirit as Prophetic Statement: A Reflection on the New Testament and on Pentecostal Origins," *Conference Papers from the Society of Pentecostal Studies* (Springfield, Mo.) 1 (November 1992): 1-22.

[2]Peter D. Hocken, *One Lord, One Spirit, One Body* (Gaithersburg, Md.: The Word Among Us, 1987), chap. 4, "A New Thing."

[3]Vinson Synan, *The Spirit Said "Grow"* (Monrovia, Calif.: MARC Publications, 1993).

[4]Howard A. Snyder, *The Problem of Wineskins* (Downers Grove, Ill.: InterVarsity Press, 1975), p. 130.

[5]Henry Lederle, *Treasures Old and New: Interpretations of "Spirit-Baptism" in the Charismatic Renewal Movement* (Peabody, Mass.: Hendrickson, 1988), p. 227.

[6]Ibid., p. 228.

[7]Arnold Bittlinger, *Gifts and Ministries* (Grand Rapids, Mich.: Eerdmans, 1973), p. 20.

[8]Lederle, *Treasures Old and New,* p. 40.

[9]Edward D. O'Connor, *The Pentecostal Movement in the Catholic Church* (Notre Dame, Ind.: Ave Maria Press, 1971), pp. 221ff.

[10]David B. Barrett, "Global Statistics of the Pentecostal/Charismatic Renewal," *Ministries Today* Annual Supplement, 1991, p. 22. A possible "Fourth Wave" comprises groups such as the Salvation Army which eschew labels of the first three waves but affirm that they have long appreciated the full range of spiritual gifts.

Chapter 15: The Road Ahead

[1]Peter D. Hocken, *One Lord, One Spirit, One Body* (Gaithersburg, Md.: The Word Among Us, 1987), p. 70.

[2]Ibid., p. 70.

[3]Ibid., pp. 46. Chap. 8, "The Essential Work of the Holy Spirit," gives criteria for how the third way will work.

[4]William F. Arndt and F. Wilbur Gingrich, *A Greek-English Lexicon of the New Testament* (Chicago: University of Chicago Press, 1959), p. 635.

Appendix A: The Spirit in Luke-Acts

[1]In 1890 Dutch theologian Abraham Kuyper wrote, "The Church has never sufficiently confessed the influence of the Holy Spirit exerted upon the work of Christ. The

FIRE IN THE FIREPLACE

general impression is that the work of the Holy Spirit begins when the work of the Mediator on earth is finished, as tho until that time the Holy Spirit celebrated His divine day of rest" (*The Work of the Holy Spirit* [Grand Rapids, Mich.: Eerdmans, 1956], p. 97). A century later that attitude is still prevalent.

[2]Ibid., p. 100: "He was guided, impelled, animated, and supported by the Holy Spirit at every step of His Messianic ministry." See also John Owen, *The Holy Spirit* (Grand Rapids, Mich.: Kregel, 1960), p. 99.

[3]I. Howard Marshall, *Luke: Historian and Theologian* (Grand Rapids, Mich.: Zondervan, 1970), p. 45.

Appendix B: Interpretations of Spirit Baptism

[1]Henry Lederle, *Treasures Old and New: Interpretations of "Spirit-Baptism" in the Charismatic Renewal Movement* (Peabody, Mass.: Hendrickson, 1988).

[2]Ibid., p. 6.

[3]Ibid., p. 8.

[4]Ibid., p. 10.

[5]Ibid., pp. 11-15.

[6]Ibid., pp. 15-19.

[7]Donald Gee, "To Our New Pentecostal Friends," *New Covenant*, September 1974, pp. 21-22.

[8]Lewi Pethrus, *The Wind Bloweth Where It Listeth* (Chicago: Philadelphia Book Concern, 1945) p. 51.

[9]Donald Guthrie, *New Testament Theology* (Downers Grove, Ill.: InterVarsity Press, 1981), pp. 539-40.

[10]Ibid., p. 534. The metaphor of Pentecost as the birthday of the church is apt since on that day it "went public" and became visible and audible. Following that analogy, its conception was earlier, in the Upper Room of John 20:21, when the disciples inwardly and quietly received the Spirit. Whatever the merits of the birthday metaphor, it hardly implies a conception on the same day of Pentecost.

[11]Stanley J. Grenz and Roger E. Olson, *20th-Century Theology: God & the World in a Transitional Age* (Downers Grove, Ill.: InterVarsity Press, 1992). Chap. 9, "Transcendence Within the Story: Narrative Theology," describes the theological background, contributions and current status of this relatively new approach to the biblical narratives.

[12]Gordon D. Fee and Douglas Stuart, *How to Read the Bible for All Its Worth* (Grand Rapids, Mich.: Zondervan, 1982). This excellent guide to interpreting the various kinds of biblical literature has a good treatment of the nature, interpretive principles and application of narratives, the literary genre that is most prevalent in the Bible.

[13]Lederle, *Treasures Old and New*, pp. 37-44.

[14]Dennis Bennett and Rita Bennett, *The Holy Spirit and You: A Study Guide to the Spirit-Filled Life* (Plainfield, N.J.: Logos International, 1971), p. 20.

[15]Stephen Clark, *Baptized in the Spirit and Spiritual Gifts* (Ann Arbor, Mich.: Servant, 1976).

[16]J. Rodman Williams, *The Gift of the Spirit Today: The Greatest Reality of the*

Twentieth Century (Plainfield, N.J.: Logos International, 1980). For many years this short book was the most extensive published monograph on Spirit baptism. In *Renewal Theology: Salvation, the Holy Spirit and Christian Living* (Grand Rapids, Mich.: Zondervan, 1990), Williams deals with Spirit baptism on pp. 177-79 and 198-200.

[17]Larry Christenson, *Speaking in Tongues and Its Significance for the Church* (Minneapolis, Minn.: Bethany House, 1968). Lederle, *Treasures Old and New,* pp. 85-90, shows Peter Hocken to be close to the neo-Pentecostal model but with certain reservations; he does not fall prey to the elitism inherent in its doctrine of subsequence. Lederle presents the views of many other leaders in chap. 2, "Neo-Pentecostal Interpretations of Spirit-Baptism" (pp. 37-103).

[18]Donald Basham, *A Handbook on Holy Spirit Baptism* (Springdale, Penn.: Whitaker, 1969), p. 21.

[19]Kilian McDonnell, "Introduction: Parameters, Patterns and the Atypical," in *International Documents,* vol. 3 of *Presence, Power, Praise: Documents on the Charismatic Renewal* (Collegeville, Minn.: Liturgical, 1980), p. 13.

[20]Leon Joseph Cardinal Suenens, *A New Pentecost?* (Glasgow: Collins, 1974), p. 81.

[21]Kilian McDonnell and George T. Montague, *Christian Initiation and Baptism in the Holy Spirit: Evidence from the First Eight Centuries* (Collegeville, Minn.: Liturgical, 1991). Part 1 offers eighty pages of New Testament evidence. McDonnell and Montague have edited a short companion booklet, *Fanning the Flame: What Does Baptism in the Holy Spirit Have to Do with Christian Initiation?* (Collegeville, Minn.: Liturgical, 1991).

[22]Simon Tugwell, *Did You Receive the Spirit?* (New York: Paulist, 1972). Lederle, *Treausures Old and New,* chap. 3, "Sacramental Interpretations of Spirit-Baptism" (pp. 104-43), presents other variations of this view.

[23]Larry Christenson, ed., *Welcome, Holy Spirit: A Study of Charismatic Renewal in the Church* (Minneapolis: Augsburg, 1987).

[24]Larry Christenson, *The Charismatic Renewal Among Lutherans: A Pastoral and Theological Perspective* (Minneapolis: Lutheran Charismatic Renewal Services, 1976), p. 37.

[25]Lederle, *Treaures Old and New,* chap. 4, "Integrative Interpretations of Spirit-Baptism," pp. 144-212.

[26]Christenson, *Welcome, Holy Spirit,* p. 84.

Appendix C: The Impartation of the Spirit in the Gospel of John

[1]John also declares in this passage the twofold role of suffering Servant and messianic Son: "Look, the Lamb of God, who takes away the sin of the world! . . . I have seen and I testify that this is the Son of God" (Jn 1:29, 34).

[2]G. M. Burge, "Glory," in *Dictionary of Jesus and the Gospels,* ed. Joel B. Green, Scot McKnight and I. Howard Marshall (Downers Grove, Ill.: InterVarsity Press, 1992), p. 270.

[3]James Dunn, *Baptism in the Holy Spirit* (London: SCM Press, 1970), p. 175. Systematic theology attepts to harmonize disparate biblical passages to make a unified doc-

trine—for example, of Christ or the Holy Spirit of the church. A danger in this process, however, is to treat the passages like pieces of a jigsaw puzzle that fit together to form a single picture. Pieces that don't seem to fit this two-dimensional model are then reshaped to conform. In reality, the biblical passages are facets of the same gem that must be appreciated in their own light.

[4]B. F. Westcott, *The Gospel According to St. John* (London: John Murray, 1903), p. 293.

[5]F. F. Bruce, *Commentary on the Book of Acts* (Grand Rapids, Mich.: Eerdmans, 1955). The author notes that Jesus' action should be translated "he breathed into them" and comments on the allusion to Genesis 2:7, where the Septuagint uses the same verb to describe the Creator's "breathing into" Adam's nostrils the breath of life (p. 32). Westcott says, "To regard the words and acts as a promise and symbol of the future gift is wholly arbitrary and unnatural" (p. 295).

Appendix E: Natural-Supernatural Distinctions
[1]Charles E. Hummel, *The Galileo Connection: Resolving Conflicts Between Science and the Bible* (Downers Grove, Ill.: InterVarsity Press, 1986), chap. 9, "Miracles and Scientific Laws," pp. 179-97.

[2]C. E. Graham Swift, "The Gospel According to Mark: The Consummation," in *The New Bible Commentary,* rev. ed., ed. D. Guthrie and J. A. Motyer (Downers Grove, Ill.: InterVarsity Press, 1970), pp. 885-86.

Appendix F: Weapons of Spiritual Warfare
[1]John R. W. Stott, *The Message of Ephesians,* The Bible Speaks Today Series (Downers Grove, Ill.: InterVarsity Press, 1979), pp. 275-83.

Appendix G: Major Religion Statistics
[1]Figures come from David B. Barrett, *World Christian Encyclopedia,* Annual Update 1992 (Lausanne: Statistical Task Force).

Author Index

Scripture Index

Subject Index